A–Z of Teaching

A–Z of Teaching

Jonathan Savage and Martin Fautley

Mc Graw Hill Education Open University Press

Open University Press
McGraw-Hill Education
McGraw-Hill House
Shoppenhangers Road
Maidenhead
Berkshire
England
SL6 2QL

email: enquiries@openup.co.uk
world wide web: www.openup.co.uk

and

Two Penn Plaza, New York, NY 10121-2289, USA

First published 2013

A catalogue record of this book is available from the British Library

ISBN-13: 978-0-33-524700-4 (pb)
ISBN-10: 0-335-24700-8
e-ISBN: 978-0-33-524701-1

Library of Congress Cataloging-in-Publication Data
CIP data applied for

Typeset by Aptara, Inc.

Fictitious names of companies, products, people, characters and/or data that may be used herein (in case studies or in examples) are not intended to represent any real individual, company, product or event.

Praise for this book

"Every so often, a new idea unfolds that seems so deceptively simple that one wonders why it hasn't appeared before now: this is the case with A–Z of Teaching. Serving as a high-definition map of classroom teaching, it provides mentorship for survival and thriving in the profession. Comprehensive without being laboured, rich in concepts without succumbing to clutter, ingeniously economic in the identification of key themes without being trifling, Savage and Fautley manage to distil the important and inspiring from vast amounts of theory, research and practical experience of teaching, and present the essential elements in a most accessible manner for early career teachers. More experienced educators will also find many gems to renew and inspire their practice. The approach is pragmatic whilst never seeking to trivialise the challenges of teaching or the vast amounts of extant theories. Most importantly, the reflective questions at the end of each section serve to provoke further thinking, research and action, thus contributing meaningfully to the development of effective and reflective teachers for contemporary schools."

Regina Murphy, PhD, Senior Lecturer, St Patrick's College,
Dublin City University, Ireland

"The construction of this book is very satisfying; it is so straightforward to access and simultaneously works at so many levels.

Using the tried and tested structure of an A to Z listing, Jonathan Savage and Martin Fautley consider a number of highly significant aspects of education, pedagogy, and professional issues for teachers at all stages of their professional development. In their consideration of some 103 topics, they skilfully blend key theoretical underpinning with current practice in the classroom, making this book extremely useable by teachers in all sectors and age-phases. The range of topics makes this especially useful because it covers some big issues but also explores some less frequently covered things such as audience and elicitation.

What I have found particularly helpful is the fact that, in this book, I readily recognise aspects of my own classroom practice in the overview of each topic, but I am encouraged and inspired to reflect more deeply on my professional development in the light of the collected wisdom and challenging questions.

This book will be an invaluable tool for training and beginning teachers as well as for those with years of experience. The inclusion of key questions and further reading means that it can serve as a very accessible reference book, an aide memoir or as a stimulus for more detailed debate, discussion or professional development. Consequently it will support the work of individuals, department or phase teams or even larger groups.

The potential to individualise training and coaching by referring trainees to relevant entries is great. I will certainly want to use it when working with trainee teachers and also with teachers undertaking CPD and Masters qualifications. I look forward to Volume 2 appearing in the future."

Simon Spencer, Birmingham City University, UK

"I am delighted to welcome this brief but important compendium of the 'A–Z of Teaching' written by Jonathan Savage and Martin Fautley, authors with extensive experience of teaching. This book provides eloquent insights and distilled definitions of key terms and concepts in an introductory way that will inform, inspire, engage and help navigate through the maze of key terms which busy students in initial teacher education and practising teachers simply must read."

Pamela Burnard, Faculty of Education, University of Cambridge, UK

"This is a very entertaining and well-structured resource, written in easy and accessible language. It contains a serious, carefully referenced introduction to a number of major issues encountered in the early stages of learning to teach. It will be equally useful for beginners or experienced teachers and mentors, as it gives practical guidance about some of the areas for discussion, coaching and assistance which commonly arise when learning to teach."

Professor Janet Hoskyns, Head of School: Education,
Birmingham City University, UK

Contents

Introduction

Welcome to our *A–Z of Teaching*! Thanks for buying this book – we trust that you will find it a really helpful introduction to the art and craft of teaching. But before we start the book's main content, we want to say a few introductory words about ourselves and the rationale that has underpinned our writing here.

First, we have both been school teachers. Our teaching experience spans from primary school to high school, undergraduate and postgraduate students, and also includes working regularly with groups of qualified teachers in a range of settings. But we are not perfect teachers! We regularly get things wrong and are constantly thinking about how to improve our teaching. This is important. In our view, teaching is an art, not a science. Although there is a 'craft' to teaching, for instance in terms of technical elements such as vocal projection, or structuring a good explanation, there are large elements of teaching that are difficult to pin down in words. How do you describe the flow in students' learning that a good teacher is able to inspire? Or how do you describe the subtle and skilful use of humour at a particular moment of a lesson that lightens the mood and enhances students' motivation? The art of teaching is something that takes a lifetime to explore.

But having said that, we are both experienced in helping novice teachers develop their craft of teaching and, hopefully, move them towards the development of their own art of teaching. We have both led and managed postgraduate courses for students wanting to become qualified teachers. We have observed hundreds, if not thousands, of lessons taught by beginner teachers and given feedback and constructive criticism following these lessons. In doing so, we have, ourselves, learnt so much about how to teach effectively. We know that many of these experiences have informed our writing here.

In addition, we are both engaged in various educational research projects. You might wonder why that it is important here. Well, in our view teaching and research are complementary and co-related activities. In other words, it is hard for us to do one without the other. We recognize that there are discrete and specific sets of skills needed for each activity. But following the example of Stenhouse, Somekh and others you will find mentioned throughout this book, we believe that the process of becoming a teacher researcher is something that can be very beneficial for your role as a teacher in any setting.

For this reason, we have made a conscious effort throughout this book to introduce you to some of the key ideas from the educational research literature as they relate to the topics we have chosen. We have tried to do this in a light-hearted way (although some of the topics are very serious). We have provided links to Further Reading for each topic in the hope that you will find time to pursue those that are of particular interest to you.

Working towards compiling a list for this *A–Z of Teaching* has been fun! Initially, we came up with a list of topics for each letter of the alphabet. We circulated these around a group of our colleagues who gave us a lot more ideas. In consultation with the Open University Press, these were whittled down to the selection of topics that you find in the book today.

We have worked with a common structure within each topic. This is made up of four key parts:

1   an introduction to the topic with a definition of the key term;
2   an exploration of key ideas within the topic, reference to the work of some of the key thinkers that have explored the topic in the educational literature and how these ideas apply to the day-to-day practices of teaching and learning;
3   a set of questions for you to consider as you seek to develop your pedagogy in a particular topic area;
4   further reading and references, including links to relevant writings in other publications or online sources.

We hope you will find this a useful format to work with.

Clearly, the overarching structure of the book is governed by the alphabet. For this reason, we are not expecting you to start at the beginning of the book and work your way through in a sequential manner. Pick and choose at will!

We trust that you will find the ideas contained within this book helpful and constructive as you seek to develop your own teaching skills. We wish you every success in this endeavour. At a time when the notion of teaching as a professional activity with a discrete set of skills and an associated understanding is under attack, we hope that this book demonstrates that teaching is a complex activity that requires dedication, practice and a sensitivity towards the complex processes that constitute learning in its various forms. We would welcome your feedback on our efforts.

Dr Jonathan Savage
j.savage@mmu.ac.uk

Professor Martin Fautley
martin.fautley@bcu.ac.uk

A

Ability

Ability is a problematic construct. In schools there can be a tendency to talk about ability as though it is a fixed determining factor in a pupil's success. This is not necessarily the case.

Notions of ability date back to IQ (intelligence quotient) testing, a procedure developed by the French psychologist Alfred Binet in the early years of the twentieth century. Binet devised tests which:

> consisted of a series of tasks of increasing difficulty, each task representing the typical performance of children at a particular chronological age level. The tasks were highly varied, but most of them relied in some way on the understanding of language and the ability to reason with either verbal or nonverbal (spatial, numerical) materials.
>
> (Carroll 1982: 33)

Many modern IQ tests continue to use this way of eliciting data about intelligence by testing. What results from these tests is an IQ score, which places a person's intelligence on a scale.

Unlike some of the later apologists for IQ testing, Binet did not believe that IQ was a fixed attribute; he thought it could be modified and developed. Many of the historical tests for IQ were based on theories of social superiority, and as Gordon Stobart argues:

> The history of intelligence testing reinforces the argument that assessment is a social activity, even though its advocates presented it as impartial scientific measurement. The leading figures were largely driven by their ideological beliefs, which themselves were based on hereditarian, racial and class assumptions.
>
> (Stobart 2008: 31)

One of the problems with the way IQ was viewed was as a fixed characteristic with which an individual was endowed at birth, and which remained constant:

> A major point of discussion is whether intelligence as measured by IQ tests is innate or learned, and to what extent. The initial theories largely stressed the innate nature of intelligence, seeing it as an inborn property. Subsequent research has, however, clearly shown that IQ can be raised through educational interventions, which means that it cannot be totally inborn.
>
> (Muijs 2007: 51)

Although we have now moved away to some extent from the notion of IQ as a fixed indicator of future success, IQ testing is still used, and something very similar to an IQ test forms the basis of the 11+ examination which many primary age children will take to determine whether or not they can go to grammar school.

Stobart argues that conceptions of ability have replaced IQ as fixed indicators of future performance: 'ability is seen as the cause of achievement, rather than a form of it' (Stobart 2008: 31). It is clear that many parents whose children will be taking these tests buy into the notion that they are not a fixed and impartial measure of raw intelligence, as otherwise the lucrative 11+ entry preparation business would have no foundations.

It was against this background that Howard Gardner produced his theory of multiple intelligences (see the entry on **thinking**), where he divided intelligences across a range of accomplishments, in stark contrast to the single score of the IQ test. Instead, Gardner says that ability is spread unequally across a number of domains. This has resonances for many teachers: the able athlete may not be good at maths, and the gifted musician may not be highly able in science.

This spread of ability becomes an issue when schools think about gifted and talented (G&T) pupils. Many schools have a register of such pupils, but there seems no fixed method of allocation. In normal parlance 'gifted' refers to pupils of high ability (whatever that is!) and 'talented' to pupils who demonstrate high levels of flair, in, say, the arts, or sports. Whatever these are, they are abilities, and they are not easily represented in a unitary score.

So how do setting and streaming based on ability work? For streaming, standard practice is to make a predictive assumption based on a variant of an IQ test, or on attainment scores in key dimensions, usually core subjects. For setting, subject-specific criteria are used, sometimes based on test scores, or a combination of test scores and teacher reports. This can mean that streamed classes, where the streaming factor is, say, maths/ English based, can present themselves as mixed ability in other areas, for example PE, and the arts. For further information on this see the entry on **streaming and setting**.

Ability, then, is not a simple and straightforward fixed attribute of an individual. In your dealings with classes you will encounter different abilities, and you may be surprised in the staffroom when you hear colleagues talk of pupils in a very different light to the way they seem in your lessons.

Key questions

1 What does ability look like in my subject area?
2 What does G&T mean in my school?
3 How do I cater for G&T pupils in my classroom?
4 How much use does my school make of ability testing?
5 Are there any issues with this?

References

Carroll, J. (1982) The measurement of intelligence, in R. Sternberg (ed.) *Handbook of Human Intelligence*, pp. 29–120. Cambridge: Cambridge University Press.

Muijs, D. (2007) Understanding how pupils learn: theories of learning and intelligence, in V. Brooks, I. Abbott and L. Bills (eds) *Preparing to Teach in Secondary Schools: A Student Teacher's Guide to Professional Issues in Secondary Education*. Maidenhead: Open University Press.

Stobart, G. (2008) *Testing Times: The Uses and Abuses of Assessment*. Abingdon: Routledge.

Further reading

Hodgen, J. (2011) Setting, streaming and mixed ability teaching, in J. Dillon and M. Maguire (eds) *Becoming a Teacher: Issues in Secondary Teaching*, 4th edn. Maidenhead: Open University Press.

Accountability

To be accountable means to be held to account for something, a phrase clearly deriving from finance. But how well does this transfer to education? After all, 'Pupil achievement is something very different from good or bad cash accounts' (Lawton et al. 2012: 254). We are moving into a time when schools and teachers are held accountable for many aspects of their students' learning. We have league tables published in national and local papers, which show the performances of students in individual schools. These are used as competitive features, and the drive to raise standards can in many cases be translated as trying to raise a school's performance in the league tables. Accountability in this sense is measured by examination results. Concomitantly, as a result of this public demonstration of what is meant by success teachers are:

> much more aware of the political push to raise standards. It is not surprising [given] the high stakes nature of this assessment agenda, with its published performance tables, its target setting based on national test results, its assumption that standards can be objectively measured . . .
>
> (Hall and Harding 2002: 12)

This links to the notion of *performativity*, which Stephen Ball describes in this fashion: 'Performativity . . . is a new mode of state regulation which makes it possible to govern in an "advanced liberal" way. It requires individual practitioners to organize themselves as a response to targets, indicators and evaluations' (Ball 2003: 215). There are all sorts of questions that you as a teacher need to ask which relate to this. Your students will be given a range of targets. These could be National Curriculum levels to reach by the end of the year, or exam grades to attain. You will need to find out how realistic these targets are, and upon what bases they have been compiled. For example, if targets are set based on statistical analysis of general trends, how likely are they to apply to the students in your school?

As a teacher you have responsibility for the learners in your care. You will be held accountable for their progress and attainment. These pressures are not coming from the school, they are pressure which the school is under:

> Teaching is framed and driven by the National Curriculum and a performance framework that is backed up by performance management, pay and target-setting. Evidence about performance

is based on pupil outcomes, classroom observation and personal statements. Students become objects and targets and the headteacher and senior management team are publicly accountable.

(Perryman et al. 2011: 182)

Everyone involved in your school will be subject to different layers of accountability, and it is important to realize that you are part of a system. What you do needs to mesh with other people. The aim of the whole school is to do the best it can for the learners in its care, and it is this which lies at the heart of accountability measures.

So what steps can and should you take with regard to accountability? One thing is to be aware of various audiences for accountability. You are responsible to a range of these in your daily work, including:

- students
- parents
- other teachers
- the school
- the community
- the area/region
- nationally
- and, importantly, yourself!

It is useful to bear all of these in mind when thinking about what you do. Talking to colleagues is important here, you need to find out not only *what* they are doing, but *how* they are doing it. Bear in mind, too, that your school will want you to be doing the best you can with the students you have, as the school is answerable via the league tables.

There is, of course, a whole separate discussion to be had about whether teacher and school effectiveness should only be measured by pupil attainment, but the reality of the situation is that that is how it is at present.

Key questions

1 Am I able to justify what I am doing in the classroom to different audiences?
2 What is expected of me and my students?
3 How can I ensure my students do as well as they possibly can?

References

Ball, S.J. (2003) The teacher's soul and the terrors of performativity. *Journal of Education Policy*, 18(2): 215–28.

Hall, K. and Harding, A. (2002) Level descriptions and teacher assessment in England: towards a community of assessment practice. *Educational Research Review*, 44(1): 1–16.

Lawton, D., Gordon, P., Ing, M. et al. (2012) *Theory and Practice of Curriculum Studies*. London: Routledge.

Perryman, J., Ball, S., Maguire, M. and Braun, A. (2011) Life in the pressure cooker – school league tables and English and mathematics teachers' responses to accountability in a results-driven era. *British Journal of Educational Studies*, 59(2): 179–95.

Further reading

Siskin, L., Carnoy, M. and Elmore, R. (2003) *The New Accountability: High Schools and High-stakes Testing*. London: Routledge.

Activities

The lessons that you teach should be full of activities! Regardless of the subject, curriculum focus or theme, these teaching and learning activities should have some core features, and then be varied in different ways. Every activity should be:

- purposeful: the main learning objective behind the activity should be communicated to students at some point during the activity (not always at the beginning!);
- dynamic: it should involve the students in doing something active (either physically or intellectually);
- differentiated: it should allow all students the chance to be challenged and, hopefully, successful at a level appropriate to their own abilities;
- time limited and sequenced: each activity should have a clear time limit and the links between activities should be carefully planned to ensure progression from one activity to the next.

That said, activities should also be varied in different ways. This is important. You do not want to become a 'one trick' teacher and surprising your students is a good way of challenging their thinking and motivating their learning.

So, when designing teaching activities for lessons think about varying the following:

The location of the activity

Are you always restricted to the immediate classroom environment? On the majority of occasions you probably will be, but there will be times when the activity could be delivered in a different space that might facilitate the type of dynamic interactions students can engage with through the activity. If you cannot easily move the class to an alternative space, what would happen if you rearrange the space in the classroom itself? How would this change the ways in which students interact within the activity? What would happen if you moved the activity outdoors?

The group structure for the activity

Are students going to be working individually, in pairs or small groups within the activity? What difference would it make if you adopted an alternative grouping? Whilst some activities might be suited to individual approaches, you can challenge students' ways of thinking by situating the activity in a different grouping. The construction of groups is also worth considering. There are numerous alternatives here, including grouping students by ability, gender, friendship or age. You can also scaffold the group work for a specific activity in different ways, e.g. by providing roles for particular students to play, or designating different ways of viewing the activity (de Bono's thinking hats is one example; see http://www.debonothinkingsystems.com/tools/6hats.htm for further details on this).

The resources needed to complete the activity

The tools that we provide for a particular activity will fundamentally alter the types of thinking and learning that our students are able to engage in. For example, working through long division in mathematics with a calculator facilitates a different type of mathematical thinking than working with a pencil and paper (see Wertsch 1998, especially Chapter 2, for a fantastic exploration of these ideas).

The time allocated for the activity

Recently, we have noticed, there seems to be a move towards including shorter, more targeted, teaching activities within lesson plans. This is fine. But do not forget that some things take time and are worthy of contemplation (by students and teachers). Long activities are still worthwhile and can help teach students the skills of independent learning when scaffolded appropriately.

The structure and sequence of activities

Generally, sequencing activities logically is a good strategy. But surprising students midway through an activity can be very productive too. So why not explore different ways of interrupting activities in order to channel students' thinking into new areas? This has implications for our final point.

The pedagogical approach within activities

In many schools we have observed learning objectives being displayed at the start of lessons. We understand the reasons behind this, but it could be seen as a very one-dimensional approach to the ordering of learning within a lesson. Done uncritically, it can destroy any sense of students being able to undertake a journey within a lesson and discovering new things. So, why not reconsider the pedagogy behind the activities that you build into your teaching. Do students need all the information up front, before the activity begins? Can you drip feed information, knowledge or skills into an activity at different points of the lesson? As we discussed above, why not interrupt and re-point an activity in a different direction, introduce a new challenge for a group, or reassign the roles of the group in order to challenge students' thinking at key moments? All of this, and more, can help make teaching activities within your lesson varied and exciting for your students.

Key questions

1   To what extent am I able to vary the activities that I include within my lessons?
2   How can I broaden my pedagogical approach in light of some of the suggestions above?

Reference

Wertsch, J.V. (1998) *Mind as Action*. New York and Oxford: Oxford University Press.

Further reading

Willis, D. and Willis, J. (2007) *Doing Task-based Teaching*. Oxford: Oxford University Press.

Aims

Right at the beginning of this *A–Z of Teaching*, it is probably a good time to reflect for a moment or two about what the aims behind your teaching are. Why are you a teacher? What are you hoping your teaching will achieve?

This kind of personal reflection is important. It can enable you to maintain a sense of purpose and helpful 'mission' in your work that can help pull you through difficult times or deal with shifting changes in the organization of schools or curricula that affect your day-to-day working life. It can also help you maintain a broader focus or perspective on the organization of your units of work across the year or Key Stage. Finally, it can provide a bedrock for those important, 'Why are we doing this, Miss?' type questions that students routinely ask!

Educational aims are normally expressed in eloquent language at the beginning of policy documents or curriculum frameworks. For example, the following extract appeared at the beginning of the most recent National Curriculum documentation in the United Kingdom:

> Education influences and reflects the values of society, and the kind of society we want to be. It is important, therefore, to recognize a broad set of common values, aims and purposes that underpin the school curriculum and the work of schools.
>
> Clear aims that focus on the qualities and skills learners need to succeed in school and beyond should be the starting point for the curriculum. These aims should inform all aspects of curriculum planning and teaching and learning at whole-school and subject levels.
>
> The curriculum should enable all young people to become:
>
> 1 successful learners who enjoy learning, make progress and achieve
> 2 confident individuals who are able to live safe, healthy and fulfilling lives
> 3 responsible citizens who make a positive contribution to society.
>
> (DSCF 2008: 3)

Aspirational language like this can also be found in many school brochures and websites. For example, one local school here in south Cheshire includes the following text on its website:

> The core values of Sandbach School are those embodied in the School's motto and crest displayed on all uniform badges and school documentation. Such values are known, understood and should be practised by all members of the Sandbach School Community.

The Latin motto 'Ut Severis Seges' broadly translates as 'As you sow, so shall you reap' or the more you put into school life, the more you will get out of it. The crest of the Cheshire wheatsheaf suggests that care, nurturing and commitment are needed to achieve a harvest of quality. Applying both concepts to an all-boys comprehensive school, the values which the motto and crest encapsulate are:

1   Commitment to excellence in all aspects of school life – working hard and playing hard;
2   Respect for self and others, combined with a responsibility and caring for all members of the school and its wider community;
3   Integrity, honesty and open-ness in how every member of the school community operates;
4   Encouragement of all to be creative, innovative and able to take initiative in order to develop every individual beyond their perceived potential.

(Sandbach School 2012)

These kinds of statements are important in framing our work as teachers. Although it is less common to find such statements about the aims and values of education from individual teachers, having a broader set of aims for our work with young people is important.

Finally, our identities as teachers are often bound up intricately with the various subjects that we teach or consider ourselves specialists within. Each subject has its own tradition and culture that impacts on our understanding of the world. Understanding the influence of our subject backgrounds, not just in terms of content but also in terms of the pedagogies that they value and represent, is an important strand in our generation of an individual set of aims for our teaching.

Key questions

1   How would you answer the questions posed in the opening paragraph of this section? Why not have a go at writing your own set of 'aims' for your work as a teacher and share it with a trusted friend.
2   Intergenerational knowledge should be valued more in education. Why not ask a teacher who is approaching the end of their career what they consider to be the most important aims for education that have spanned their career? How do they compare to the statements above and your own response to the above question?

References

DCSF (2008) *The National Curriculum for England*. London: DCSF.
Sandbach School (2012) http://sandbachschool.org/about-us/mission_values/ (accessed 24 June 2012).

Further reading

Moore, A. (2006) *Schools, Society and Curriculum*. London: Routledge.

Assessment

Assessment is a key issue in education today, and you will encounter a number of aspects of it thoughout your teaching career. There are many forms and types of assessment, but two you will encounter frequently are *summative assessment* and *formative assessment.*

Summative assessment is one which results in a grade, mark, or level being awarded. In essence the grade *sums up* the attainment of a pupil. This leads to a shorthand being used: pupils can be Level 4 English, Grade C GCSE, or Grade B at A level. These assessments are all examples of *high stakes* assessments, ones where the results really matter. Summative assessment can also take place in your classroom on a day-to-day basis; if you give the pupils a test, and the results are a mark out of 10, say, then this is a summative assessment.

Formative assessment refers to the judgements that a teacher makes whilst learning is taking place. It does not need to involve testing, grades or levels, but is about the teacher having conversations with the pupils to decide where they are in their learning, and what the next steps are that the teacher and learner need to take in order to move on to the next stage. Formative assessment is about making learning intentions clear, finding out what the pupils can actually do, providing appropriate feedback to the pupils that helps them take their learning forwards, and designing lessons to take account of this.

As you can see, the two are very different from each other. However, what has often happened in schools is that formative and summative assessments have become confused and conflated, so that in many schools formative assessment has come to mean doing summative assessment more often! The way these terms are used can differ from one school to the next, and so you will need to find out what exactly is meant by each term when you hear people talking about them.

Assessment results are in the news fairly frequently. Schools are judged by how well their pupils do in National Curriculum assessments, in GCSE,

BTec, A level, and other exams. Indeed, assessment for many has become a proxy for learning, it is the assessment grade which matters, not the learning gone through in order to attain that grade. As a teacher you will be judged by the assessment grades your pupils reach too. There are moves to evaluate teachers according to how their pupils do in examinations, so this is a topic that affects everyone. The use of assessment information in this fashion has been criticized, 'this system of surveillance carries Orwellian overtones' (Mansell 2007: 9), but seems set to be with us for a while.

One important aspect of assessment for the teacher is to do something useful and appropriate with the information which an assessment yields. There is an old country saying to the effect of 'the pig doesn't get fatter by weighing it', and the same is true here. In order for the pupils to improve at whatever it is that they are being assessed in, they do need to learn something in between assessments! This is why formative assessment takes the notion of *feedback* as being important.

Two more key assessment terminologies are *validity* and *reliability*. Validity refers to whether or not an assessment is assessing that which it sets out to. In terms of validity, if you as a teacher are designing tests for your pupils you need to be very clear that you are testing the concepts, skills, constructs and understandings that you want to be, and not simply the pupils' grasp of written English. This is a common error, and results in articulate and literate pupils doing much better in some forms of testing than others. After all, you would not test someone's ability to bowl a cricket ball or play the guitar by asking them to write about it!

Reliability in assessment was described by Black and Wiliam like this: 'We want variations in students' scores to be caused by differences that are relevant to the construct of interest, rather than to irrelevant factors, such as who did the scoring, the particular selection of items used for the test, and whether the student was having a "good" or a "bad" day' (Black and Wiliam 2012: 244). For individual purposes as a classroom teacher, you will want your assessments to be as reliable as you can make them, as all sorts of other decisions will be made on the basis of your assessment data.

Key questions

1 What am I assessing? Is what I am assessing in fact the thing I am trying to assess – is it reliable?
2 Is the assessment as valid as I can make it?
3 Is my formative assessment practice grounded in the classroom? Does my feedback help the students to make progress to the next stage?

References

Black, P. and Wiliam, D. (2012) The reliability of assessments, in J. Gardner (ed.) *Assessment and Learning*, 2nd edn, pp. 243–63. London: Sage.

Mansell, W. (2007) *Education by Numbers: The Tyranny of Testing*. London: Politico's Publishing.

Further reading

Black, P., Harrison, C., Lee, C., Marshall, B. and Wiliam, D. (2003) *Assessment for Learning: Putting it into Practise*. Maidenhead: Open University Press.

Fautley, M. and Savage, J. (2008) *Assessment for Learning and Teaching in Secondary Schools*. Exeter: Learning Matters.

Gardner, J. (ed.) (2012) *Assessment and Learning*, 2nd edn. London: Sage.

Attainment

Attainment has a very specific meaning, and refers to marks, grades or levels which a pupil has gained in terms of results from assessments. It is closely linked to two other terminologies, *achievement* and *progress*. Ofsted look at 'pupils' academic achievement over time, taking attainment and progress into account' (Ofsted 2012a: 8). Ofsted judgements about achievement are based on:

1   Pupils' attainment in relation to national standards and compared to all schools, based on data over the last three years, noting particularly any evidence of performance significantly above or below national averages, and inspection evidence of current pupils' attainment

2   Pupils' progress in the last three years as shown by value-added indices for the school overall and for different groups of pupils, together with expected rates of progress

3   The learning and progress of pupils currently in the school based on inspection evidence.

(Ofsted 2012b: 6)

Progress can be thought of as the speed at which pupils move up their attainments, bearing in mind the points from which they started.

Attainment, then, represents actual milestones the pupils have managed to reach. These are compared with the attainments of the wider cohort, and the country as a whole. This process is known as *benchmarking*. For the classroom teacher it is useful to distinguish between the three terms *attainment, achievement* and *progress*, as the words have very specific meanings.

Evidence for attainment can come from a variety of sources, but the important thing about it is that there is some degree of formalizing of the evidence process. This means that when discussing pupil attainment the teacher is able to produce evidence, not anecdote, and that this will stand up to scrutiny.

Achievement normally involves some evaluation of the progress involved. To use a sporting analogy, for some people running a mile would be a major accomplishment, whereas for athletes this could well be something they do on a daily basis. The differences matter because although the attainment is the same, in that a mile has been run, the differences in the effort put into it have been very significant. In educational terms this means that achievement needs to take progress into account. We hear of schools in some areas where doing very little with the pupils would result in high attainment, whereas for others in areas of significant deprivation, this is not the case. This is not to provide excuses, but it is important to be clear about what is being discussed.

Key questions

1 How do I know what level of attainment my pupils have? How does this compare with the rest of school . . . regionally . . . nationally?
2 What *evidence* do I have for the attainment levels of my pupils?
3 How does the achievement and progress of my pupils compare with the rest of school . . . regionally . . . nationally?

References

Ofsted (2012a) *The Framework for School Inspection from January 2012*. London: Ofsted.

Ofsted (2012b) *The Evaluation Schedule for Schools 2012*. London: Oftsed.

Further reading

Blanchard, J. (2009) *Teaching, Learning and Assessment*. Maidenhead: Open University Press/McGraw-Hill.

Freeman, R. and Lewis, R. (1998) *Planning and Implementing Assessment*. London: Kogan Page.

Gardner, J., Harlen, W., Hayward, L., Stobart, G. and Montgomery, M. (2010) *Developing Teacher Assessment*. Maidenhead: Open University Press.

Attitudes

Having a positive attitude to teaching and learning is essential. The most important step in creating a positive environment in your classroom is to start with yourself! Creating a positive teaching identity is contagious. It will rub off on your students.

Right now, determine in your mind that you are going to adopt a positive mental strategy towards your work. Try and be one of those teachers who is going to enjoy their work and be successful. You cannot underestimate the importance of having a positive mental attitude towards the events that every day will throw at you.

Having started out on the right foot, here are some tips about communicating that positive mental attitude through your teaching to your students:

- Welcome students into your lesson every day. Stand at your door and welcome students, individually, into your classroom.
- Welcome them with a smile, a personal greeting and use their name. Knowing your students' names is vitally important. If you are like us, you will need to make a conscious effort to learn these at the beginning of term. Learning names does not come naturally to many teachers, but it is time well spent. Use a photo register and, if possible, get someone to test you on the names.
- When the students are in your classroom, use a seating plan in the early stages of the term. This will allow you to enforce any behaviour management strategies effectively and, in particular, will allow you to continue using the students' names at every opportunity. Overdo this. It is one of the most important things a teacher can do to make a student feel valued and welcome and creates a positive attitude in their minds about you and the work you are asking them to engage with.
- Ensure that your lessons begin with an appropriate sense of expectation and a quick pace. Engage the students with something intriguing; create some curiosity in their minds about what they are going to discover today and be enthusiastic about the lesson even if you have taught it hundreds of times before. It will be the first time for them!
- Make your classroom a safe space where all students are valued and made to feel valued by yourself and by other students. This is really important. Your classroom needs to be a space where children can, to a large extent, be themselves, ask questions and express their worries and concerns, as well as celebrate their

successes and achievements. To this end, students enjoy a well-ordered and well-disciplined classroom and they really dislike classrooms where the teacher is not able to keep a good sense of control.

A positive attitude leads to positive and constructive thinking, an expectation of success, an optimistic outlook and a confident and appropriate belief in yourself and your abilities. Surely these are all things that we want for our young people?

Finally, a positive attitude is contagious. As teachers, we have a tremendous privilege in shaping the lives of the young people with whom we come into contact. Make a decision today to:

- choose to be a happy teacher who looks on the bright side of life within school;
- find reasons to smile more often with your colleagues and students;
- develop practical approaches to help communicate your positive attitude to your students in a natural way;
- determine not to let any negative attitudes or behaviour that other teachers or students may exhibit get you down personally.

If you can do these things, you will have a long and enjoyable teaching career. You will avoid many of the potential stresses of teaching, remain healthier in mind and body, and become someone whom students enjoy being around. Your colleagues will appreciate you and your company, your students will learn more effectively, and you will be remembered as a teacher who inspired them and helped them on their life's journey.

Key questions

1 What are the benefits of a positive attitude to teaching and learning?
2 How can I develop and sustain a positive approach regardless of the many stresses and strains that teachers have to cope with?

Further reading

Hadfield, S. (2012) *Brilliant Positive Thinking: Transform Your Outlook and Face the Future with Confidence and Optimism*. Harlow: Pearson Education Limited.

Audience

A performing arts teacher once observed that teaching was like doing five matinees a day! There is a degree of truth in this, and in this section we consider the notion of teaching as a performance, with the teacher as the performer, and the class as the audience. This, of course, begs the question as to who is doing the most work. We don't expect to go to the theatre and work harder than the actors, so there is a limit to this metaphor! But there are some truths in it, so let us consider some of the issues.

An actor needs to take the persona of the person they are playing. When we see the phrase 'Sean Connery is James Bond', we know what is meant. But when you step in front of a class, you too are playing a part; you are now Sir or Miss and you have responsibilities to the role, as well as to the students. One of the key aspects of this lies in the notion of developing your teaching persona. This is an important early stage in the development of a beginning teacher's journey, and one that can take some adaptation. One minute you are in the staffroom with Kevin, who is telling you the rudest joke you have ever heard and the next you are in the corridor with Kevin, who is now Mr Smith, a fearsome disciplinarian and guardian of the moral high ground. For new teachers in a school this instant switch seems strange. You will never call Mr Smith by the name 'Kevin' in the corridor, and he will never call you by your first name. The whole mood of your conversation changes too, you are now professional, and sensible. The audience has changed. The audience of the staffroom is not the audience of the corridor. You don't play Mr Bean in the court scene of *The Merchant of Venice*, and the same is true in the school!

Another feature of the audience watching a play is the suspension of disbelief: we know Kenneth Branagh is not really Henry V, but we watch him portray the emotions of the monarch. For you as a teacher, it is important that you create a teaching persona that is very slightly separated from you. This does not mean that you spend all your time acting; you do need to be yourself, but you do need to detach yourself slightly from situations. This is especially true of behaviour management. It is all too easy to get emotionally entangled in a confrontation, but this will not help. You need to retain your professional status and deal with situations dispassionately. This does not mean you do not care, but that your teaching persona is able to distance yourself somewhat from the issue.

Audience is key in behaviour management in other ways too. For some students, the game of 'wind the teacher up' is always worth playing, and all the better if the rest of the class can see them in action. This is a game you do not want! Do not play to the crowd, but adopt a neutral and unflappable stance, even if the comments are directly personal. The teacher persona needs to step in and deal with these professionally, not rise to the baiting.

In the entry on **humour** we warn against trying to be someone else whilst teaching; that is not the purpose of the teaching persona. What we are saying here is that you will need to develop the professional 'you', who is possibly a new creation, and this persona will need some work!

Key questions

1   What is my teaching persona and in what ways does it manifest itself?
2   How can I develop being professionally detached in difficult situations?
3   How can I practise keeping cool?

Further reading

Dillon, J. and Maguire, M. (eds) (2011) *Becoming a Teacher: Issues in Secondary Teaching*, 4th edn. Maidenhead: Open University Press.

B

Behaviour

One of the most common worries expressed by graduates coming into teaching relates to how they are going to control classes full of unruly children! Of course, in reality, and contrary to how the media commonly portrays the situation, the vast majority of schools are orderly and civil environments where teachers are able to get on with their jobs without mass student unrest.

However, this does not mean that teachers can expect their students to behave perfectly day in, day out. Teachers do not have that as a divine right! Managing student behaviour is an important aspect of a teacher's pedagogy and, like every aspect of teaching discussed in this book, needs to be considered carefully and practised.

The first and most important point about managing student behaviour is that you need to create a context for your teaching and learning that is exciting and engaging for your students. Getting this right will solve the vast majority of problems on the behavioural front. When students are bored they are more prone to misbehaviour. So make every effort to ensure that your lessons are planned well, contain a range of engaging activities and are presented in a lively manner. If you get this right, many of the common behavioural issues will look after themselves.

That said, there are, of course, occasions where you will need to be proactive in managing student behaviour. So, apart from teaching enthusiastically and with a focus on student engagement, what practical tips can we give you in a few words?

- Do not take bad behaviour personally. There are a whole range of complicated reasons why any one individual student may be misbehaving, and the vast majority of them will have nothing to do with you. So, please do not take things personally. This is really important for your own sense of self-esteem. As we considered in our entry on **audience**, you need to learn to detach yourself professionally at key points.
- Give students choices about their behaviour. Outline the consequences of continuing to misbehave and emphasize the positive benefits of choosing to behave appropriately. This is important

in shifting the perceived outcomes that spring from a student's misbehaviour and, hopefully, mitigating the effects of it in the future. You want your classroom to be characterized by a positive tone even when dealing with difficult behaviour.

- Have a range of informal sanctions ready in advance. Preparation is key here. You do not want to be making up sanctions on the spot. Work from a basis of least resistance. If students do not comply, then up the sanctions gradually.
- At some point, informal sanctions may not work so you will need to implement key features of the school's behaviour management policy. This is also important in enforcing your position as an individual teacher working within a broader educational framework. It depersonalizes the situation and will show the student that you are working within a set of ideas and sanctions that have been established and agreed by the school community.
- Finally, as we discussed in our entry on **attitude**, maintain a bright, enthusiastic and positive tone at all times. This is vitally important. Make sure your classroom is characterized by praise and encouragement more than anything else. Expect students to behave well, convey that expectation to them in your positive body language and verbal communications, teach at a good pace, do not allow students to become distracted or bored and nurture them on the pathway towards success in your subject. They will thank you for this and you will enjoy your teaching more.

Key questions

1 Is my classroom characterized by a sense of positive student engagement? Are my lesson plans and teaching activities designed to facilitate this?
2 When students do behave inappropriately, what practical steps can I take to give them choices about their behaviour?
3 What range of informal and formal sanctions can I adopt within my teaching when other positive reinforcement strategies have not had the desired effect?

Further reading

A Star Teachers (2012) Managing Behaviour in Your Classroom. http://www. astarteachers.co.uk/download_files/files/Useful_Info/Lessons/Managing_ behaviour_in_your_classroom.pdf (accessed 14 June 2012).
Rogers, B. (2011) *Classroom Behaviour: A Practical Guide to Effective Teaching, Behaviour Management and Colleague Support*. London: Sage.

Body language

Teaching is a tough physical and mental activity. Whilst other parts of this book have considered some of the cognitive dimensions of teaching, this entry reflects on the importance of a positive body language whilst teaching.

Some writers think about teaching as a performance, comparing it to the ways in which actors present themselves in a particular character or role. Within acting, it is important to think about how the whole body responds in representing a specific character; it is much more than just adopting the correct voice, or ensuring the script is delivered smoothly and accurately.

For teachers, whilst the planning may have been done, the key learning identified, the various activities resourced appropriately, and other preparations completed, the actual moment when the lesson begins can be compared to a physical performance. As we discussed in our entry on **audience**, you are on show and you need to be confident and assured. There are a whole host of things that can help you develop and maintain a confident teaching persona, including:

- dressing appropriately;
- being organized;
- maintaining your focus;
- using your voice effectively;
- not being distracted or inattentive.

But, perhaps equally importantly to all of these, positive body language can really help you present yourself as a confident teacher. So, practically, what does this entail?

First, teach standing up not sitting down. It might seem like a simple thing, but it is harder to maintain an appropriate degree of authority, as well as see what is going on around the room, when you are seated. When you are standing, do not jiggle around from side to side. Try to stand still unless you are consciously wanting to move to another area of the classroom.

Second, do not let furniture or other objects get in between you and your students. These create a physical barrier as well as pedagogical one. Don't hide behind a desk or computer screen! Do not talk directly to the whiteboard!

Third, use the classroom space confidently. Move around. Do not be tied to the front of the classroom. As you are teaching, move around the outside of the room. This can help sustain students' attention. But, as you do so, always keep the whole of the room within your vision. One way of doing this is always ensuring that your back is facing the wall.

Fourth, think about your proximity to the students in the room. Cultural and social conventions come into play here. You will not want to be too close to your students, invading their 'private' space, but nor will you want to be too far away. Touching students in any way is not advised.

Next, make eye contact with as many of your students as possible, as often as possible. Eye contact plays a key role in establishing rapport with students and can help provide a visual cue for others about their behaviour and identify opportunities to respond or listen further.

Along with your eyes, think about your facial expressions. In private, find a mirror and practise a range of expressions (e.g. varying degrees of 'sternness') and do not be afraid to use them in the classroom!

Finally, watch your hands. Do not put them in your pockets and do not wave them around incessantly. Use them to emphasize key points you are making. Many actors or storytellers use their hands very skilfully to help illustrate the points they are making or the story they are telling.

These things take time to develop. You also need to make a conscious decision to learn them. Watching other teachers can help to a point, but you are an individual and need to find your own teaching style. Practise, practise and practise! Refine your body language for the 'act' or 'performance' of teaching and you will find it more enjoyable and rewarding. And your students will enjoy your lessons too.

Key questions

1 What are the key elements of my body language that I need to improve? How will I know when I have improved them?
2 What feedback have I received from others about my body language (either in general or specifically as a teacher)? How can I build constructively on this advice?

Further reading

Alexander, B., Anderson, G. and Gallegos, B. (2005) *Performance Theories in Education: Power, Pedagogy, and the Politics of Identity*. Mahwah, NJ and London: Lawrence Erlbaum Associates.

Milne, F. (2010) Top Tips for Trainee Teachers: Use your body language to control the classroom. http://careers.guardian.co.uk/top-tips-for-trainee-teachers-use-your-body-language-to-control-the-classroom (accessed 26 June 2012).

Peachey, N. (2012) Listening to Body Language. http://www.teachingenglish.org.uk/articles/listening-body-language (accessed 26 June 2012).

Brain

It may seem obvious that the brain is a crucial part of any teaching and learning situation, but this fact can sometimes be overlooked! Indeed, there is a whole branch of educational endeavour which goes under the heading of 'brain based learning'. Sadly, this heading includes people whose sole aim is to peddle misleading products and courses for profit. Separating fact from fiction can be problematic here, and sometimes schools have been misled by following poor advice. Indeed, as Ben Goldacre observed, 'Banging your head repeatedly against the brick wall of teachers' stupidity helps increase blood flow to your frontal lobes' (Goldacre 2008)! Stories of left-brain and right-brain differences, for example, have been said to be 'often based on misconceptions and over-generalisations of what we know about the brain, and have little to offer to educators' (Bruer 1997: 4).

So what do we know about the brain, and what is there that you can do about it? We know that the brain develops at different rates during the early years and adolescence (Blakemore and Frith 2005a), and we know that *working memory*, our ability to hold a number of chunks of information at the same time, can vary. We know that the 'average upper limit of this type of memory is about seven chunks of information, but there are individual differences in this limit that are linked to differences in educational achievement' (TLRP no date: 17). One of the implications of this for teachers comes from:

> observations of the difficulties faced by many learners when engaging with new problems. In such situations, it can be particularly helpful for pupils to show their working since, apart from many other advantages, external representations can help offload some of these heavy initial demands upon working memory.
>
> (TLRP no date: 17)

Brain based research also tells us that:

> Learning from observation is usually easier than learning from verbal descriptions, however precise and detailed the descriptions may be. This might be because, by observing an action, your brain has already prepared to copy it. We are predisposed to imitate those around us. This echoes the belief of many educators that we should not just impart what to know, but also demonstrate how to know.
>
> (Blakemore and Frith 2005b: 463)

Links between neuroscience and education are still in their early stages, but already we know far more than we did.

Key questions

1 Is the brain based learning programme I am considering based on sound scientific principles?
2 What does brain based learning research have to offer my pedagogy?

References

Blakemore, S.-J. and Frith, U. (2005a) *The Learning Brain: Lessons for Education.* Oxford: Blackwell.

Blakemore, S.-J. and Frith, U. (2005b) The learning brain: lessons for education: a precis (target article with comments). *Developmental Science,* 8(6): 459–71.

Bruer, J.T. (1997) Education and the brain: a bridge too far. *Educational Researcher,* 26(8): 4–16.

Goldacre, B. (2008) www.badscience.net/2008/02/banging-your-head-repeatedly-against-the-brick-wall-of-teachers-stupidity-helps-to-co-ordinate-your-left-and-right-cerebral-hemispheres/ (accessed 1 June 2012).

TLRP (no date) *Neuroscience and Education: Issues and Opportunities. A Commentary by the Teaching and Learning Research Programme.* London: TLRP.

Further reading

Blakemore, S.-J. and Frith, U. (2005) *The Learning Brain: Lessons for Education.* Oxford: Blackwell.

Geake, J. (2008) Neuromythologies in education. *Educational Research,* 50(2): 123–33.

C

Career

If you are starting out in your career, perhaps by undertaking a course of postgraduate study leading to qualified teacher status, thinking beyond that course itself is going to be challenging! For those of you reading this who are working as teachers already, perhaps you feel that your career options are shaped by external forces and there is little that you can do to change them.

Whatever your immediate situation, developing your career as a teacher is something that requires careful thought. Traditionally, there have been two main options for teachers. First, develop your work within your curriculum area(s) and take on responsibilities for helping lead that subject within your school. For primary schools teachers, that may be through becoming the curriculum leader, writing units of work and working collaboratively with other teachers in the school; for secondary school teachers, there may be opportunities to become a 'head of department' and lead the curriculum developments in your subject area.

Second, there will be opportunities to develop your career in terms of the pastoral care of students within your school. This may be done through taking on a specific area of responsibility (e.g. coordination of the special educational needs provision) or more generally through becoming a 'head of year'. It is still the case that the vast majority of senior staff in our schools (headteachers and their deputies) all entered the profession as classroom teachers. The career development pathways to these positions are well understood and you can follow them if that is your passion. Whatever opportunities may interest you, it is important to plan for your own career development. Clearly, the most important elements that will shape your career are your own personal ambition and broader personal commitments (which we will not be attempting to explore here!)

Generally though, it is worth reflecting on how you might sustain a passion and interest in teaching over the long term. One of the key elements for us is challenge. Whilst the techniques of teaching effectively can be developed and honed over the years, it is easy for us to fall into familiar and unhelpful pedagogical habits. Challenging ourselves in different ways is important to keep our teaching fresh.

Challenge can come from different sources. Finding interesting people to work with is one of the most effective forms of challenge. There is an old saying that 'as iron sharpens iron, so one friend sharpens another'. Finding trusted colleagues to work with closely can really help you maintain a good understanding of the effectiveness of your work as a teacher and make conscious improvements. It will also help you stay engaged and motivated throughout your career. Isolation, professionally, is one of the key reasons that teachers become unmotivated and leave the profession. Please do not fall into that trap.

Second, an engagement with the 'literature' of teaching and education can provide you with challenge. By 'literature', we do not just mean academic literature such as books or journal articles (although both will be helpful too and we would encourage you to be a teacher who reads). We mean the broader discourse about teaching that you can find through online resources, teaching forums, publications developed through professional associations such as teaching unions or subject associations, and the like.

Finally, career development implies professional development. Challenge can come from formal and structured opportunities provided by universities and others that you can engage in at any point in your career. Courses like these should challenge you academically, but should also result in you becoming a stronger and more effective teacher.

Key questions

1 What are my aspirations in terms of my own teaching career?
2 What practical steps can I take to plan for my teaching career? What opportunities do I need to explore and engage with in the short, medium and longer term?

Further reading

Howson, J. (2007) *Taking Control of Your Teaching Career: A Guide for Teachers.* London: Routledge.

Classroom displays

Classroom displays are an integral part of creating a positive environment for teaching and learning within your classroom. In previous eras, teachers would have to invest a considerable amount of their time designing and producing classroom displays, making sure they looked attractive and presentable. We can both remember having to tidy up our displays prior to parent evenings and other school events! Today, you may have support in helping you produce such displays, but their role and function are still under your control.

Classroom displays can have a number of functions. They can be used to:

- celebrate students' achievements in your subject;
- provide key information about your subject, including subject knowledge or assessment processes;
- reinforce expectations for work within your subject or wider school environment;
- stimulate and create student interest in your subject;
- provide something extra for students to do;
- communicate what other classes, teachers or other groups from outside the school may be doing;

and probably a lot more besides!

For any display, there are some key features that ought to be considered:

- Make sure that each display has a teaching and/or learning focus. This might be linked to a particular unit of work that you are currently presenting or, alternatively, the previous unit of work so that you can remind students about what they have studied already.
- If displaying students' work, think carefully about whose work is being displayed, how it is displayed and why.
- Use high quality materials where possible, and keep the display well maintained (and protected if necessary). There is nothing worse that a shabby display.
- Make reference to your classroom displays as part of your regular teaching. Use them to highlight key teaching points, illustrate particular processes or exemplify a particular learning outcome.

There are a large number of companies producing classroom display materials. These are of variable quality. We would encourage you to display a broad range of material on the walls of your classroom. A mixture of published and home-made materials is probably common practice. However, we would urge you to create your own display materials whenever possible. This is going to create a more positive impact on your students and help you develop a more integrated pedagogy.

There are a range of other locations around the school and beyond where display materials are required. You may well be asked to provide materials and these can be a useful way to help promote your subject or class's work to the broader school or local community. Typical locations for these displays include corridors, staircases, reception areas, school library facilities, staffroom and even other public places in your local community such as the library, health centre, civic spaces, etc.

Although these wider displays are not going to be integrated within your teaching in the same way as classroom displays should be, we would encourage you to take the opportunity to build these displays when possible. Make sure that displays that are located in areas where there is significant movement are more highly protected. Accidental damage can ruin the overall effect of a display.

Finally, we would highly recommend the guide written by David Smawfield (see Further reading below). This free guide contains some excellent advice on how to produce high quality classroom and other displays. It covers many of the general points made here in more detail, and provides technical support for the alignment of display materials, the types of fonts to use, colour schemes, mounting and borders and outdoor displays.

Key questions

1 What are the key features of a successful classroom display?
2 How can the displays that I produce for my classroom help promote active learning?

Further reading

Smawfield, D. (2006) Classroom and School Display: A Guide for Teachers and for Teacher Training. Available from http://www.davidsmawfield.com/assets/img/classroom-display-handbook.pdf (accessed 7 July 2012).

Cognition

Cognition refers to conscious mental processes, appertaining to thinking. As White observes: 'Cognition concerns knowledge. It refers to both an act and a state. The act is the process by which the brain creates meanings from the impressions received by the senses, and the state is the knowledge that is the outcome of the act' (White 2000: 51). The cognitive tradition of developmental learning includes such figures as Piaget, Bruner and Vygotsky (see the entry on **ZPD**). Piaget's contributions to the field include the classification of stages of cognitive development, and in the ways in which an individual makes sense of the world, via the use of *adaptation, assimilation* and *accommodation*. Assimilation is where new information is taken in and related to things which are already known and understood, and accommodation occurs when things which are already known and understood need to be altered in some way so as to accommodate new information or experiences.

Piaget designated fours stages of cognitive development, and initially added guideline age ranges to them, although nowadays these tend not to be used:

1 Sensorimotor: where understating is based on sensory perception, feeling, taste, etc.;
2 Preoperational: where the child can express themselves through words and pictures;
3 Concrete operational: where the child can perform operations practically, arranging in order, and can perceive such ordering;
4 Formal operational: the final stage, where the individual can express themselves through symbols, and are able to think about abstract concepts.

The importance of Piaget's work for the teacher is wide ranging. One use is in knowing that there are certain points in an individual's development where they are not yet able to undertake certain types of processes, therefore learning needs to be structured and focussed with this in mind.

Bruner's work on *scaffolding* (see Wood et al. 1976) describes how the developing child's knowledge is supported by the teacher, focusing students on key points relating to the task in hand. As learning becomes more secure teacher interventions are required less frequently, and so scaffolding is gradually withdrawn.

Linked to the notion of cognition is that of *metacognition*. This is where students are encouraged to think about their own thinking, and ways in which they learn, in order to be able to most effectively take their own learning forwards. This can be seen in some school programmes with names like 'learning about learning'. (See also entries on **thinking skills, ZPD, reasoning.**)

Key questions

1 What do I want the students to learn, and how?
2 What is the most suitable method for this, given their stage of cognitive development?
3 What scaffolding strategies could I employ?

References

White, R. (2000) Cognition and teaching, in B. Moon, S. Brown and M. Ben-Peretz (eds) *Routledge International Companion to Education*, pp. 51–64. London: Routledge.
Wood, D., Bruner, J. and Ross, G. (1976) The role of tutoring in problem solving. *Journal of Child Psychology and Psychiatry*, 17: 89–100.

Further reading

Capel, S.A., Leask, M. and Turner, T. (2009) *Learning to Teach in the Secondary School: A Companion to School Experience*, 5th edn. London: Routledge.
Howe, M.J.A. (1999) *A Teacher's Guide to the Psychology of Learning*, 2nd edn. Oxford: Blackwell.
Piaget, J. (1952) *The Origin of Intelligence in the Child*. London: Routledge & Kegan Paul.

Collaboration

Whatever type of school you teach in, teaching is a collaborative activity. Perhaps you find this a strange statement to make. After all, for most of the time you spend teaching you are working on your own in your classroom with your classes. Whilst you could view your work as highly individual, our argument here is that teaching is essentially a collaboration at various levels.

First, and most importantly, it is a collaboration between you and the young people that you are teaching. It might not be considered much of a collaboration because, you might say, they have to be there. But your challenge is to try and make sure that through your teaching they want to be there!

Second, as we discussed in our entry on parents, it is a collaboration between you and your students' parents or carers. There are also plenty of things that you can do to ensure that your students' parents are actively involved in their child's learning and supporting you in your job too.

Third, unless you are the only teacher working in your school (unlikely!), your work is a collaborative one with the other members of staff within your institution. This is where most of our attention will focus in this short entry.

It is important to remember that every student receives their education in a variety of ways throughout their schooling. Specific lessons constitute a major part of this. Many of these will be delivered by you, working individually in your classroom or perhaps with the support of other adults such as teaching assistants or student teachers. However, there will be lessons where you can 'collaborate' in different ways with other curriculum areas or members of staff within the school. As we discuss in our entry on cross-curricular approaches to teaching and learning, the construction of links between curriculum subjects is something that all teachers can facilitate in a natural way throughout their pedagogy. Whilst the actual opportunities to collaborate physically with another member of staff within a particular lesson may be limited for all kinds of reasons, the chance to draw attention to the work being done in other teachers' classes can be very productive.

Although lessons constitute a major part of a student's education, there are plenty of other ways that you need to collaborate with your fellow members of staff. Not least, you need to collaborate in maintaining a consistent approach to the management of student behaviour outside of lessons. Teachers are often required to undertake various 'duties' around the school. These are important roles. School rules are normally discussed and agreed by the school community, including students, and need to be upheld. It is important that you do this in a consistent way.

It is also important to recognize the contributions of all the other adults working within the school. This will include people such as librarians, caretakers, kitchen staff, cleaners, visiting tutors and others. All these people have a vital role in ensuring that the school runs smoothly.

So, collaboration is important in maintaining the productive ethos and environment of the school at all levels. Work collegiately with your colleagues. Spend time talking to them and sharing your ideas in a constructive manner. Do not become so busy in your classroom, or with lunchtime or after-school clubs, that you lose the opportunity to bond with your colleagues and become part of that team. They will support you through rough times and you will support others in return. An isolated teacher is a weak teacher in all kinds of ways. Make sure you work collaboratively with others in all aspects of your work, whether inside or outside your classroom. It makes teaching that much more enjoyable.

Key questions

1 How can I plan to work collaboratively with other colleagues in terms of my curriculum provision and the opportunities therein? Are there simple steps I can take to organize my lessons and create links with what students are learning throughout the week?

2 In terms of my own professionalism and sense of well-being, how can I make sure that I organize my time effectively so that I can spend enough time in the staffroom to become an effective member of the staff 'team'?

Further reading

Bentham, S. and Hutchins, R. (2012) *Improving Pupil Motivation Together: Teachers and Teaching Assistants Working Collaboratively*. London: Routledge.

McDonald, E. (2012) Collaborating with Colleagues: Being a Team Player. Available from http://inspiringteachers.blogspot.co.uk/2009/10/collaborating-with-colleagues-being.html (accessed 16 July 2012).

Communication

To communicate is to exchange meanings with another person, to 'make common', according to its Latin roots. When we communicate, we send messages from one person to another. However, this process is not without problems:

> [A]n estimated 40–60 per cent loss in meaning is likely to occur during this fleeting process. The way that we receive a message depends on our perception (and interpretation) of it and this may not be quite the same as what the sender intended, as every one of us experiences the world differently. The actual words that are used, the way they are said, the type of body language

that accompanies the message, the ability and willingness of the receiver to listen to or otherwise 'read' the message, the presence of perceptual biases such as stereotyped assumptions, perceptions of power within the relationship, and individual or cultural differences can all distort intended messages and therefore create barriers to effective communication.

(Derrington and Goddard 2008: 131)

This matters to teachers. It matters that pupils are able to communicate effectively, and it matters that children who have communication problems are picked up on, and seen by specialists. Beitchman et al. observed that 'studies have shown that one-third of children seen in a psychiatric clinic for behavioural and learning problems have underlying language disorders. . . . Similarly, children presenting with a communication disorder are at risk of developing behavioral disturbances' (Beitchman et al. 1996: 173).

To say someone is a good communicator means that their messages are received clearly by the people with whom they are engaged. Central to this is the notion of *engagement*. As a teacher you need to be effective in communication, which involves more than simply speaking clearly:

Successful communicators need to be able to use language in a social context. These verbal and non-verbal communication skills begin to develop before spoken language and form the basis of our interactions. To be a successful communicator, you need to use eye contact and facial expression. You also need to be able to recognize the nuances of meaning that non-verbal communication provide, and let that influence your response.

(Cross and Cross 2011: 17)

Effective teachers will be doing all of these things, sometimes unconsciously. One of the problems with doing classroom observation is that an awful lot of the nuances that an experienced educator brings with them are lost on novice observers. It may seem that all the teacher is doing is talking, yet, rather like the effortless glide of the swimming swan, a great deal of rapid paddling is taking place under the surface! The effective teacher will be constantly monitoring the class, looking out for clues for students whose attention is wandering, scanning for behaviour management issues, and monitoring what they are saying in order to check that they think the students are understanding. All of these things require practice, and it is worth spending some time watching experienced teachers specifically for these tiny aspects of their communication skills. This is also a key area for you to get feedback on, both as a beginner and as a more experienced practitioner.

Communication, then, involves simultaneously giving *and* receiving. It involves thinking about what you will say, and monitoring what you are saying as you are doing so. It involves thinking about how the audience is reacting, and it involves engaging with learners.

Key questions

1 What do I need to do in order to maximize the learning opportunities for my pupils?
2 Am I always as clear as I might be?
3 Have I been observed with a focus on my classroom communication skills? Have I observed colleagues doing this?

References

Beitchman, J.H., Cohen, N., Konstantarea, M. and Tannock, R. (eds) (1996) *Language, Learning, and Behavior Disorders: Developmental, Biological, and Clinical Perspectives*. Cambridge: Cambridge University Press.

Cross, M. and Cross, M. (2011) *Children with Social, Emotional and Behavioural Difficulties and Communication Problems: There is Always a Reason*. London: Jessica Kingsley Publishers.

Derrington, C. and Goddard, H. (2008) *'Whole-brain' Behaviour Management in the Classroom: Every Piece of the Puzzle*. London: Routledge.

Further reading

White, J.N. and Gardner, J. (2012) *The Classroom X-factor: The Role of Body Language and Non-verbal Communication in Teaching*. New York: Routledge.

Concepts

The term *concept* is encountered frequently in education. Whole curricular frameworks have been built around notions of skills, concepts and understandings. Concepts themselves are building blocks of knowledge and understanding, as Margolis and Laurence observe: 'Concepts are the most fundamental constructs in theories of the mind' (1999: 3). Yet when we start to investigate in more depth we find that the very notion of what a concept might be is itself problematic: 'the notion of a concept cannot be explicated without at the same time sketching the background against which it is set, and the "correctness" of a particular notion of concept cannot be evaluated without at the same time evaluating the world-view in which it plays a role' (Jackendoff 1989: 68).

Education involves learning, learning involves knowing, and knowing is built upon concepts. One view of the nature of the concepts that learners hold involves some form of mental representation of a thing or an object. This representational theory of mind means that beliefs and understandings are held as a sort of internal language involving thoughts. The philosopher Kant believed that we hold a number of concepts that originate in the mind itself; these are termed *a priori* concepts, as they are not based on experience, but come before it. An *a posteriori* concept, on the other hand, is one which is known on the basis of direct and first-hand experience. Distinguishing between these two types is not only of philosophical interest, but has importance to the ways in which learning takes place in the classroom. What is also important is to not think of concepts solely as linguistic formulations, as White observes:

> Concepts are plainly not the same as words. The concept butterfly is expressed in the English language by the word 'butterfly', in German by 'Schmetterling', and in French by 'papillon'. Concepts, as it were, lie behind words. They are the ideas that words express. Does this mean, then, that concepts are separable phenomena from words?

> Beware the red light ahead. There is a danger we will find ourselves back inside the picture of the mind as a private space stocked with free-floating ideas. It is more reasonable to think of having a concept of, say, butterfly, as knowing how to use the word 'butterfly' in English (or 'Schmetterling' in German, etc.).
>
> (White 2002: 35)

This last factor is where knowledge of concepts is useful to the teacher. Holding a concept means that the students can do something with the information. Some concepts seem to be bound up with layers of meaning, so, for example, the concept of 'sheep' might be associated with the concept of 'white'. But when a black sheep is encountered, the individual needs to make some accommodation in order to categorize a black sheep as such. So, in teaching and learning, we need to be aware that if we do teach concepts that will need to be replaced or refined further along the learning pathway, we are clear in our own minds that we are doing this.

If a learner cannot categorize a black sheep as a sheep, because they have learned that sheep are unfailingly white, we have a conceptual problem that can become an issue for the future.

However, of far more immediate concern to the teacher in the classroom are the questions asked by Bruner et al.

> How do people achieve the information necessary for isolating and learning a concept? How do they retain the information gained from encounters with possibly relevant events so that it may be useful later? How is retained information transformed so that it may be useful for testing a hypothesis still unborn at the moment of first encountering new information?
>
> (Bruner et al. 1999: 101)

This takes us to the crux of what we want our learners to do. But it also has an impact upon us as teachers in planning the learning programmes for our students. We need to ask ourselves what it is that we want the students to learn, and we need to ask ourselves what ordering we need to sequence the learning. This means that teachers need to give thought to the ordering of concept acquisition, and how concepts can be employed. It means that in planning a learning programme we need to have thought about concept development in a sequential fashion, and need to have planned for learners to rehearse the application of this learning. If pupils need to learn how to read a map, we want them to have had some practice at navigating their way around a town before they try to climb a mountain. Although this seems entirely logical, it does require some planning preparation!

So, in preparing for a teaching and learning programme, a useful activity is to list the concepts required for a developed understanding of the topic. Then think about the sequencing of concepts, so that the pupils get a chance to put into action the things they have learned. Finally, think about the transferability of the concept, so that new examples can be dealt with appropriately.

See also **learning, elicitation** and **knowledge.**

Key questions

1 What do I want the pupils to learn?
2 What concepts are essential to this?
3 Do the learners possess these already?
4 Do they possess them in sufficient detail to be usable?
5 How can I best sequence learning for concept acquisition and development?

References

Bruner, J., Goodnow, J. and Austin, G. (1999) The process of concept attainment, in E. Margolis and S. Laurence (eds) *Concepts: Core Readings*, pp. 101–23. Cambridge, MA: MIT Press.
Jackendoff, R. (1989) What is a concept, that a person may grasp it? *Mind & Language*, 4(12): 68–102.
White, J. (2002) *The Child's Mind*. London: Routledge.

Further reading

Margolis, E. and Laurence, S. (eds) (1999) *Concepts: Core Readings.* Cambridge, MA: MIT Press.

Confidence

Teaching is unforgivingly complex. It is not simply good or bad, right or wrong, working or failing. Although absolutes and dichotomies such as these are popular in the headlines and in campaign slogans, they are limited in their usefulness. They tacitly assume there is consensus across our diverse society about the purposes of schooling and what it means to be engaged in the process of becoming an educated person as well as consensus about whose knowledge and values are of most worth and what counts as evidence of the effectiveness of teaching and learning.

(Cochran-Smith 2003: 4)

This extract from an article by Marilyn Cochran-Smith neatly details some of the issues associated with teaching, and with being a teacher in contemporary society. The teacher not only has to deal with the reality of their classes day in, day out, but of having to handle governmental and societal expectations too. Developing confidence to do this takes time.

There are stages towards the development of competence which all teacher training programmes recognize. The stages towards mastery move from being focused on the self to being focused on the learners. The early stages of being a teacher rely on relatively small successes. As time passes by, though, this is no longer enough, and concern shifts from a focus on teaching to a focus on learning. This is right and proper. The point of a being a teacher is to teach, and the outworking of this lies in the development of students as learners.

The key areas that occupy teacher concerns tend to be those associated with classroom management and behaviour. In primary schools there are concerns about delivering the full range of curriculum subjects, including PE, music and technology. Confidence is a key issue in all of these. Warnings about appearing confident whilst not being so, that many new teachers are given, are only part of the story. The development of confidence is something that teachers can work at, and much of this comes down to planning. The possibility for any lesson to go badly wrong always exists, but good planning can help prevent this. Behaviour issues can occur at any time, but an ill-conceived or hastily thrown together lesson from a beginning teacher is a sure-fire recipe for disaster. Yes, there are teachers who have been teaching for years who can teach anything to anyone at the drop of a hat, but this comes from a confidence with the elements of successful pedagogy, built on years of experience.

Every new teacher needs to work at confidence. Each lesson or class will be novel, and the experiences contained with these early experiences need to be reflected on and learnt from. One of the key ways of doing this is by being what Schön (1983) refers to as a 'reflective practitioner'. Positive and structured written reflection is encouraged on many training and CPD programmes, and it is from these that learning takes place. Reflection does not mean having a moan over coffee in the staffroom, but of thinking through the issues. One way of doing this is via critical incident reflection. As David Tripp observes: 'Incidents happen, but critical incidents are produced by the way we look at a situation; a critical incident is an interpretation of the significance of an event' (Tripp 1993: 8). Using these as the basis for a structured reflection is a good way of developing confidence, and also enables you to develop your repertoire of pedagogic techniques for future use.

Key questions

1 What am I good at in the classroom?
2 Where am I less confident (be honest with yourself!)?
3 What can I do about this?
4 Do I know anyone who is good at what I'm not? Could they help?

References

Cochran-Smith, M. (2003) The unforgiving complexity of teaching: avoiding simplicity in the age of accountability. *Journal of Teacher Education*, 54(1): 3–5.

Schön, D. (1983) *The Reflective Practitioner*. Aldershot: Academic Publishing.

Tripp, D. (1993) *Critical Incidents in Teaching: Developing Professional Judgement*. London: Routledge.

Further reading

Tripp, D. (1993) *Critical Incidents in Teaching: Developing Professional Judgement*. London: Routledge.

Creativity

Perhaps one of the most famous definitions of creativity comes from the National Advisory Committee on Creative and Cultural Education (NACCCE) report (NACCCE 1999), where creativity is discussed in terms of students' learning displaying four primary characteristics: 'First, they always involve thinking or behaving imaginatively. Second, overall this imaginative activity is purposeful: that is, it is directed to achieving an objective. Third, these processes must generate something original. Fourth, the outcome must be of value in relation to the objective' (NACCCE 1999: 29). In this entry, we'd like to focus on three main points.

First, and most importantly, creativity is something that all students have and can develop further. Every time a child paints a picture, comes up with a new idea, plays a new arrangement of notes on a piano, thinks of a new way of assembling their science experiment, makes a new construction with lego bricks, or a myriad of other everyday creative acts, they can be said to be being creative, not along the lines of composing a Beethoven symphony, but in a smaller, more personal way. Anna Craft calls this 'little c creativity' (Craft 2000: 3); 'the kind of creativity which guides choices and route-finding in everyday life, or what I have come to term "little c" creativity'.

Second, creativity is normally thought of as a process. This is inherent in the NACCCE definition. However, much earlier pieces of work done by writers and thinkers in this area have explored what this process might look like. For example, Wallas, in 1926, broke down the creative process into four stages:

1 Preparation
2 Incubation
3 Illumination
4 Verification

The first stage, preparation, represents the consideration of an issue. This is followed by incubation, which is defined as a period of time where the issue and its ramifications are considered, mulled over and thought about. Illumination involves arriving at a point of realization where a solution presents itself, or becomes apparent. Finally, verification involves some form of testing of that which has happened. Guiding your students through this process will be an important part of your work as a teacher.

Third, and finally, creativity is something that can be developed through all subjects and all activities. It does not have any limits. Whilst some may argue that certain subjects (e.g. the arts) facilitate a broader range of creative thought than others, we would argue that this is not the case at all. Dwelling on the history of any subject reveals that key individuals and groups have worked creatively and imaginatively in numerous ways.

This also means that creativity applies to your teaching as well as to your students' learning. As we have briefly considered, creativity involves thinking and action within a particular domain that is purposeful and novel to the individual or group. Teaching can be a 'site' for creativity just like anything else in life.

Key questions

1 What would teaching creatively look like?
2 How can my creativity as a teacher be developed further through a structured process of development that is meaningful for me?

References

Craft, A. (2000) *Creativity Across the Primary Curriculum: Framing and Developing Practice*. London: Routledge.

NACCCE (1999) *All Our Futures: Creativity, Culture and Education*. Sudbury: DfEE. Also available from http://sirkenrobinson.com/skr/pdf/allourfutures.pdf (accessed 1 July 2012).

Wallas, G. (1926) *The Art of Thought*. London: Watts.

Further reading

NACCCE (1999) *All Our Futures: Creativity, Culture and Education*. Sudbury: DfEE. Also available from http://sirkenrobinson.com/skr/pdf/allourfutures.pdf (accessed 1 July 2012).

Cross-curricular approaches

Cross-curricular approaches to teaching and learning are often collaborative (Ofsted 2008). These collaborations may be informal, led by pairs or small groups of interested teachers. But in the majority of cases, cross-curricular work is initiated by a curriculum manager and is developed within a larger framework (a 'collapsed' timetable day, a special project of some sort, etc.).

But there is another way that cross-curricularity can be imagined. This relates to the development of your own, personal pedagogy that is infused with a cross-curricular disposition or way of thinking. This has been defined as follows:

> A cross-curricular approach to teaching is characterized by a sensitivity towards, and a synthesis of, knowledge, skills and understandings from various subject areas. These inform an enriched pedagogy which promotes an approach to learning which embraces and explores this wider sensitivity through various methods.
>
> (Savage 2010: 8–9)

In this definition, the emphasis is placed firmly on your subject-based pedagogy. It includes a number of key ideas and terms:

1 *Sensitivity, synthesis and subjectivity* These words refer to the ways in which teachers could approach the knowledge, skills and understanding inherent within every curriculum subject. These are exemplified in curriculum documents but also have a historical legacy that is underpinned in various ways, not least in teachers' and others' conceptions about a particular subject and how it should be taught. Understanding this is a vital step that needs to be taken whilst considering moving into collaborative curriculum ventures or developing a cross-curricular approach within your own subject pedagogy.

2 *Enriching, embracing and exploring* The new, enriched pedagogy of cross-curricular teaching will embrace and explore the teacher's sensitivity towards, and synthesis of, the different knowledge, skills and understanding within curriculum subjects.

There are a number of principles that could define this alternative approach. These include cross-curricular teaching and learning being:

- based on individual subjects and their connections through authentic links at the level of curriculum content, key concept or learning process, or through an external theme/dimension;
- characterized and developed by your excellent subject knowledge, a deep understanding of their subject culture and a capacity to re-conceptualize this within a broader context of learning beyond their subject, and with sensitivity towards other subject cultures;
- coherent in its maintaining of links with students' prior learning and experience;
- contextualized effectively, presenting opportunities for explicit links with students' learning outside the formal classroom;
- underpinned by a meaningful assessment process that is explicitly linked to, and informed by, the enriched pedagogical framework.

The purposes of cross-curricular teaching and learning include:

- motivating and encouraging students' learning in a sympathetic way in conjunction with their wider life experiences;
- drawing on similarities in and between individual subjects (in terms of subject content, pedagogical devices and learning processes) and making these links explicit in various ways;
- promoting students' cognitive, personal and social development in an integrated way;
- allowing you the opportunity to evaluate and reflect on their teaching and be imaginative and innovative in your curriculum planning;
- facilitating a shared vision amongst your school through meaningful collaborations at all levels of curriculum design.

Teaching in this way will be challenging, but the potential benefits for yourself and your students are considerable.

Key questions

1 To what extent can I strengthen the cross-curricular or collaborative elements within my teaching? What strategies of professional or curriculum development could I employ to do this?
2 How can I broaden my knowledge of other subject areas, including their subject pedagogies, to ensure that I treat them with the respect and dignity that they deserve?

References

Ofsted (2008) *Curriculum Innovation in Schools*. London: Ofsted.
Savage, J. (2010) *Cross-curricular Teaching and Learning in the Secondary School*. London: Routledge.

Further reading

Savage, J. (2010) *Cross-curricular Teaching and Learning in the Secondary School*. London: Routledge.

Curriculum

In common language use, we use the word curriculum to mean a set of arrangements for a course of study. It might include specific subjects, themes that span across subjects (e.g. globalization), specific ways of thinking (e.g. creativity) or even ways of learning (e.g. visual, auditory and kinaesthetic).

In education, we talk about the 'National Curriculum' which, until relatively recently, meant the over-arching curriculum of subjects and other elements that all schools, regardless of their foundation or status, were required to provide as a core offering for all students.

For many, the curriculum equates to the organization of subjects in varying degrees of rigidity within a school timetable. The precise amount of time or resource that a particular subject receives is based on decisions made about the relative importance or not of that particular subject. In the past, schools have often reflected the broader structures of the National Curriculum and examination specifications in the ways in which their curriculum was organized. This is changing rapidly as schools are given greater degrees of autonomy.

Recently, many have argued that the 'curriculum' is becoming increasingly politicized. Decisions made by Government ministers, e.g. the retrospective imposition of the English Baccalaureate, have resulted in schools making arbitrary decisions about the organization of their curriculum and the prioritization of particular subjects within it.

Others take a more reflective view of the term 'curriculum'. Like Lawrence Stenhouse, we like to position it alongside the work of the teacher. An over-emphasis on the external dimensions of the 'curriculum' as a set of subjects, themes, ways of thinking or learning can lead to what Stenhouse viewed as the 'over-objectification' of the curriculum itself. This, he argued, leads to the teacher as a disempowered labourer, being told what to do and where to do it. More prosaically, this concept of the curriculum: 'rests on an acceptance of the teacher as a kind of intellectual navvy. An objectives based curriculum is like a site-plan, simplified so that people know exactly where to dig their trenches without having to know why' (Stenhouse 1980: 85).

For Stenhouse, such a definition of the word 'curriculum' and the resulting imposition of centralized prescriptions of GCSE specifications or national curricula de-professionalized teachers. Throughout his career he developed alternative ideas that reasserted the teachers' role in curriculum planning and development. If, as he wrote, 'it seems odd to minimise the use of the most expensive resource in the school' (Stenhouse 1975: 24), it would be better, he argued, to 'reinvest in the teacher and to construct the curriculum in ways that would enhance teachers' understanding and capability' (Ruddock 1995: 5).

For Stenhouse and ourselves, teachers are central to the creation and delivery of a curriculum for their students. In this philosophical sense, teachers embody the curriculum that they deliver. It is ideas such as this that led Stenhouse to make one of his most famous statements, 'No curriculum development without teacher development' (Silbeck 1983: 12).

As we have seen, the term 'curriculum' can be understood in varying ways. From the simple notion of it being a collection of subjects that are taught in a systematic way, to the philosophical and conceptual relocation of the curriculum to the pedagogy of individual teachers, it is vital that all of us who care about education do not allow the 'curriculum' to be hijacked by our politicians.

Key questions

1 If there is no curriculum development without teacher development, how can I develop my pedagogy in order to enrich and extend the curriculum opportunities my students will receive?
2 Although National Curriculum requirements and GCSE specifications have an important role to play, how can I ensure that they do not become prescriptions of content or pedagogy and undermine my own professionalism?

References

Ruddock, J. (ed.) (1995) *An Education that Empowers: A Collection of Lectures in Memory of Lawrence Stenhouse*. Clevedon: Multilingual Matters.

Silbeck, M. (1983) Lawrence Stenhouse: research methodology. *British Educational Research Journal*, 9(1): 11–20.

Stenhouse, L. (1980) Product or process? A reply to Brian Crittenden, reprinted in Ruddock, J. and Hopkins, D. (eds) (1985) *Research as a Basis for Teaching*. London: Heinemann Educational.

Stenhouse, L. (1975) *An Introduction to Curriculum Research and Development*. London: Heinemann Educational.

Further reading

Stenhouse, L. (1975) *An Introduction to Curriculum Research and Development*. London: Heinemann Educational.

D

Data

An enormous amount of data is available to teachers in schools, from whether a pupil has forgotten their shoes, to their statistically derived examination score predictions. It is the latter form of data that tends to be the most important to schools, and the term 'data' has now come to be almost synonymous with assessment information. So what is it, what does it mean, and what should you do with it?

Assessment data comes in one of two basic forms, attained and predicted. Attained data consists of test grades and examination results which students have actually scored. Predicted data is derived from how cohorts of similar students, based on socio-economic and other information, have performed in the past. This sort of prediction is a highly specialized activity, and is undertaken in many cases by external agencies, the Fischer Family Trust and the Centre for Evaluation and Monitoring at Durham University being two of the most well known in the UK.

Worthy of note is that these data sets are not concerned with individual students, whereas you will be! You will know the names of your students, and you will know exactly why Darren's predicted grades did not materialize, or why Danielle did not do so well in her GCSE examination. Predictions cannot do this. It is, however, not an excuse for low attainment if your students do not meet their targets. The reason for the statistical averages being employed is to give the school, you, your students and their parents an idea of what they are aiming for.

In your own teaching it is important to maintain details of assessment data that students produce. We are working in an educational climate where success in education is not measured by 'soft' means, such as how students feel, or whether they enjoy school, but by 'hard' statistics of test scores, assessments and examination grades. You will need to show, given the starting points your students were at, how they have improved and developed in their learning over time. To do this you will use National Curriculum levels, GCSE (or other external examination) predicted grades, and will want to be as accurate as you can. You will also be required to demonstrate comparability with other subject areas. Are students in art achieving at similar standards in maths? If not, why?

Another point to bear in mind is that data should be of use to you in planning. If you find that a class you are going to be teaching contains high attaining students, then you should be using this information to plan lessons so that you can take into account their prior attainment, not, as one sixth former observed, 'we sat in a classroom for two years and did exactly the same thing as everyone else in the year' (TES 2012). The purpose of you knowing the data is so that you can tailor your teaching accordingly. You should be using available data to work out what to do with the classes you teach, as well as using it to find out what the analyses show ought to be their appropriate attainment levels.

Data will figure highly in your life as a teacher, but it is important for you not to lose sight of the fact that you are teaching students, not spreadsheets.

Key questions

1 What statistical evidence do I have for the attainment of my students?
2 How can I use data on their prior attainment to help inform my current teaching?
3 Are students in my classes attaining results broadly in line with my colleagues?
4 How can the school data manager help me with my teaching?

Reference

TES (2012) Let's Break Free of GCSE Constraints! http://www.tes.co.uk/article.aspx?storycode=6287794 (accessed 12 July 2012).

Further reading

Centre for Evaluation and Monitoring at Durham University: www.cemcentre.org (accessed 12 July 2012).
Fischer Family Trust: www.fischertrust.org (accessed 12 July 2012).
Gardner, J. (ed.) (2012) *Assessment and Learning*, 2nd edn. London: Sage.

Development

In education the notion of *development* carries with it a number of different meanings. In psychological terms it refers to the ways in which maturation occurs at different speeds within different students. Development can refer to curriculum development, and the ways in which teaching and learning materials change over time. It can also refer to the ways in which a curriculum offers the potential for learning development, which is the sense in which this entry will look at it.

One of the key questions to ask of your programmes of study is 'How do they show development over time?' There was a time when resource books of lesson materials used to say 'these units can be taught in any order'. This begs the question of how they offer developmental learning potential. It is clear that during the course of a Key Stage learning should develop. A useful follow up to this question is 'what can they do/know at the end of the Key Stage that they couldn't do/didn't know at the start of it?' This key planning question can be turned on its head to ask, 'What do I want the class to do/know at the end of the Key Stage?'

It is also useful for a whole Key Stage to consider this issue. In primary schools, where one teacher can be responsible for a large proportion of the students' education, it might be less of a problem; but in a secondary school where responsibility is spread over a large number of teachers, then joined-up developmental planning is important. Far better for the Key Stage team to concentrate their resources on covering multiple topics in many subjects, than the same topic over and over again.

So, what does develop in developmental learning? One possible way to think about this in relation to teaching and learning units is in terms of *breadth* and *depth* of learning. You will want to cover more topic areas, to give breadth to the units of work, but you will also want to study some topics in greater depth. This is not only a matter of professional judgement, but also depends on having a sound overview of the curriculum requirements of your topic area, as you will want to have a view as to the long term developmental potential of what you are teaching; in other words, you are able to take a long term view of what concepts, skills and knowledge will be required later in this, or another Key Stage, and ensure that your students are appropriately prepared.

The notion of the *spiral curriculum* is a useful one to consider in terms of breadth and depth. There are many topic areas which can be usefully taught to younger children, but which can also be studied in greater depth in higher education settings. In the school context, having a spiral curriculum in mind when planning for learning means that you can introduce the essential features of a topic area at early stages, and then revisit them in more depth later on.

Key questions

1 What knowledge, skills and understandings develop during the course of a Key Stage in the areas which I teach?
2 How can I plan for developing breadth *and* depth in my teaching?
3 How does what I teach fit in with what other people are teaching in the same Key Stage?

Further reading

Capel, S.A., Leask, M. and Turner, T. (2009) *Learning to Teach in the Secondary School: A Companion to School Experience*, 5th edn. London: Routledge.
Hart, S., Dixon, A., Drummond, M.J. and McIntyre, D. (2004) *Learning Without Limits*. Maidenhead: Open University Press.

Differentiation

The term *differentiation* covers a whole host of meanings. In essence, differentiation is about how organizations, schools and individual teachers create conditions whereby the curriculum is made accessible to individual learners in ways which are appropriate to their needs, and which allow the learners to function to the fullest potential.

Differentiation is commonly encountered in two formats, by *task,* and by *outcome.* Differentiation by task involves the teacher choosing different tasks within an overall learning lesson plan for different students or different groups of students. This can be a fairly major commitment, and involves the teacher in a considerable degree of planning. As Diana Burton observes:

> Differentiation by task requires a great deal of forward planning by teachers and a thorough knowledge of each learner's needs. Whilst commercially produced material can be of some value, case-study research . . . has shown that teachers still need to devise their own differentiated support materials to meet each student's needs.
>
> (Burton 2003: 59)

Differentiation by task requires the teacher to have planned carefully what the overall learning aims and objectives will entail, and then have worked out pathways through this for groups of students within the class.

Differentiation by outcome occurs when students all undertake the same task, but produce different pieces of work from this. Whilst this is a much more manageable form of differentiation, it really needs to be handled as part of a structured package of teaching and learning resources, as there is an inevitability about classroom work tending to produce differentiation by outcome anyway!

Other forms of differentiation include the following:

1   *Differentiation by teaching resource*   Different worksheets, materials, software packages or other forms of instructional materials are used at the same time in the class with different students or groups. In a way this a variation on differentiation by task, but with the notable difference that the students can be doing the same thing, but using different materials.

2   *Differentiation by support*   Learners receive different levels of aid from the teacher, or from a teaching assistant. This can be an inclusion strategy, and involves making the curriculum accessible to all the class.

3   *Differentiation by questioning*   We discuss elsewhere in this book the vital role that questioning plays in developing learning. As a differentiation strategy it can be used to focus specific learning possibilities onto individuals or groups of students, by asking questions that lead to higher-order thinking, or to different aspects of learning.

Carol Ann Tomlinson delineates stages involved in effective differentiation merging a number of these strategies:

> [E]ffective differentiation is not random. Rather, it is based on a clear cycle of: (a) articulating what is essential in a topic or discipline, (b) assessing a student's standing relative to those essentials, (c) providing feedback and adapting instruction to ensure that each student progresses in the most effective ways possible to master the essentials, (d) assessing outcomes, and (e) making additional adaptations as needed.
>
> (Tomlinson 2005: 264)

She also points out that differentiation is not about producing different lesson plans for each individual in the class:

> [W]hile it is true that differentiated instruction offers several avenues to learning, it does not assume a separate level for each learner. . . . Effective differentiated classrooms include purposeful student movement and some purposeful student talking.
>
> (Tomlinson 2001: 2)

What differentiation is not, then, is an overbearing requirement to personalize everything to the nth degree, making the work of the teacher impossible. Nor is it a recipe for classroom disorder, and individuals undertaking unrelated tasks or activities. Differentiation is an approach to teaching and learning which uses materials, resources, plans or tasks to help students achieve their individual potential.

Key questions

---

1   What do I want *named* students to get from my lesson? How can I best go about this?
2   What do I need to do to help them to achieve their individual potentials? How can I do this in a manageable fashion?

References

Burton, D. (2003) Differentiation of schooling and pedagogy, in S. Bartlett and D. Burton (eds) *Education Studies: Essential Issues*, pp. 42–71. London: Sage.

Tomlinson, C.A. (2001) *How to Differentiate Instruction in Mixed-ability Classrooms*. Alexandria, VA: Association for Supervision & Curriculum Development.

Tomlinson, C.A. (2005) Grading and differentiation: paradox or good practice? *Theory Into Practice*, 44(3): 262–9.

Further reading

Tomlinson, C.A. (2001) *How to Differentiate Instruction in Mixed-ability Classrooms*. Alexandria, VA: Association for Supervision & Curriculum Development.

E

Elicitation

Elicitation is a component of good formative assessment practice. In this entry we look at ways in which elicitation of student information forms a part of classroom practice, and how it can be included into teaching and learning routines. Wiliam and Black (1996) talk about a three stage cycle in the assessment process:

elicitation > interpretation > action

Some issues for the teacher to consider occur in the process of eliciting information from learners:

> One way of asking a question might produce no answer from the student, while a slightly different approach may elicit evidence of achievement. We can never be absolutely sure that we have exhausted all the possibilities, so that we can never be sure that the student does *not* know something, but some assessments will be better than others in this respect.
> (Wiliam and Black 1996: 541, original emphasis)

This is problematic. Let us take a common example which occurs in the process of baseline assessment. There is often a tacit correlation in the mind of the teacher between concept and vocabulary, so that if a student lacks the vocabulary, they also lack the concept. Take this example, from a report on a secondary school music lesson:

> The teacher took a large suspended cymbal and a soft beater. First she hit the cymbal softly at the rim. Second, she hit the cymbal as hard as she dared. She asked the [11-year-old] students if they could tell her in what way the second sound differed from the first one. One student volunteered that the second sound was longer than the first sound. No, that was wrong. Another student ventured that the second sound was more metallic, and the first more wooden. No, that was wrong too. A third student suggested that the pitch

of the second sound wavered, whereas that of the second sound was higher, and more constant in pitch. No, that was still not right. Eventually, a student pointed out that the second sound was louder than the first. When she evaluated this lesson at the end of the day, the teacher wrote that most of the class had not grasped the concept of loud–soft, and were consequently still working towards the achievement expected of [7-year olds in the National Curriculum].

(Mills 2005: 109)

It is clearly nonsense to think that a child can get to the age of 11 years and not have worked out that some sounds are louder than others. Besides the rather bizarre way in which the activity in the lesson that Janet Mills described was conducted, this is an example of the teacher confusing vocabulary with concept. The elicitation process was clearly at fault here. As Wiliam and Black said above, 'we can never be sure that the student does *not* know something'; this music example is a clear case of that.

Moving from *elicitation* to *interpretation*, an example would be if a science teacher assumed that because a pupil did not write up details of an experiment properly, they lacked understanding. This interpretation may be wrong – perhaps the student simply could not be bothered! We have recommended a number of times in this book that *feedback* is an essential component of the teaching and learning process, and it is important to note that feedback is not a teacher monologue, it involves discussion with students about their learning.

True formative assessment involves the teacher being prepared to take action with regards to student learning, and being able to formulate jointly with the student what the next stages in the learning process should be.

Key questions

1   What do the students know/what can they do already? How do I know this? How sure am I?
2   Am I clear on the differences between vocabulary and concept?
3   How can I best elicit information from the students in my classes?

References

Mills, J. (2005) *Music in the School*. Oxford: Oxford University Press.
Wiliam, D. and Black, P. (1996) Meanings and consequences: a basis for distinguishing formative and summative functions of assessment? *British Educational Research Journal*, 22(5): 537–48.

Further reading

Assessment Reform Group (2006) *The Role of Teachers in the Assessment of Learning*. London: Institute of Education, University of London.

Gardner, J., Harlen, W., Hayward, L., Stobart, G. and Montgomery, M. (2010) *Developing Teacher Assessment*. Maidenhead: Open University Press.

English as an Additional Language (EAL)

Teaching students for whom English is an additional language raises a number of specific challenges. However, right at the outset, it is important to recognize that many of these challenges can be solved through the basic application of the principles of good teaching that we are exploring through this book.

However, there are specific challenges for these students. Each school needs to recognize these and seek to support these students and help them integrate meaningfully into school life. Our focus here will be on what you can do as an individual teacher to help these students in your lessons.

Before we discuss some practical advice, try and take that imaginative leap into the position of someone who is a 'linguistic stranger' (Gershon 2011). Perhaps you have been in this position when on holiday in a foreign country. It can be highly unsettling. How much more unsettling can it be when you are expected to learn things in a language that is unfamiliar?

As a teacher, there are a range of things that you can do to help these students. First, be prepared. Find out as much as you can about these students. What English language ability do they have, if any, and what can they be expected to understand and do? What key language types are they working towards? This groundwork will pay dividends for you later on. Do not rush your work here.

Second, remember that teaching effectively is much more than the words you speak. These students will rely on the visual elements of your teaching to a much greater extent than others. This will include the images that you use to introduce or model a new idea or ask a question, as well as the way that you yourself 'act' in the classroom and use your body to exemplify key learning. Hand gestures, how you stand, how you move and the 'performance' of teaching become especially important. They all convey key messages about learning that students will recognize and remember even if the words are not fully understood.

But third, although teaching is more than words, the language that we use as teachers is very important. Teaching students for whom English is an additional language provides a useful check for your use of speech in your classroom. How do you introduce new technical vocabulary? How do you vary the tone or intonation of your voice throughout a lesson? When and how do you ask questions? What about the pace of your delivery? All of these things are important for your general pedagogy but will be essential aspects of how a student with EAL is able to begin to understand a new language. So, for instance, new technical vocabulary may be introduced alongside a specific visual aid; the pace of your delivery may need to be slightly slower at key moments of the lesson; and perhaps your use of analogy and metaphor needs to be checked on occasions to avoid misunderstandings.

Alongside these general pedagogical approaches, there will be a range of other practical elements that you might want to consider, including:

- buddying up an EAL student with a strong native language speaker for certain activities;
- providing foreign languages dictionaries or specific flash cards with bi-lingual definitions for key vocabulary;
- providing scaffolded framework for writing tasks (e.g. the use of sentence starters to help students with EAL begin a piece of writing);
- giving more time and space for EAL students' responses, including the provision of 'rehearsal' time before requesting a response to a specific question;
- modelling approaches to language use, both in your own language and with other native language speakers, to help facilitate the types of interactions you want EAL students to develop;
- when appropriate, allowing the EAL student to use their first language with the support of another adult or other students who can help translate for them.

Key question

1 What practical strategies can I develop in my teaching to help ensure that the students for whom English is an additional language can make good progress through my teaching?

Reference

Gershon, M. (2011) How to Succeed with EAL Students in Your Classroom. Available from: http://www.guardian.co.uk/teacher-network/2011/nov/07/eal-students-classroom-teaching-resources (accessed 10 July 2012).

Further reading

Gershon, M. (2011) EAL Toolkit. Available from: http://teachers.guardian.co.uk/teacher-resources/5419/EAL-Toolkit-by-Mike-Gershon (accessed 14 July 2012).

Haslam, E., Kellett, E. and Wilkin, Y. (2005) *English as an Additional Language: Meeting the Challenge in the Classroom*. London: David Fulton.

Evaluation

Educational evaluation is a means of understanding the activities that go on within your classrooms. It is a tool that you can use to investigate your own practice in a systematic and self-critical way. Evaluation involves many things and activities. It includes looking at things, asking questions, listening to others, describing events and making interpretations about the value of what you see.

As a beginning teacher, you will be asked to evaluate your lessons. What does this mean? How can you begin to do it? How can you learn to do it better?

Evaluate the lesson objectives and teaching activities

Most lessons have learning objectives and activities. These may well be drawn from your longer term planning and relate closely to the units of work that underpin your curricula. It is a good idea to start your lesson evaluation by considering both of these elements.

Look back on your learning objectives in light of the lesson you have taught. Were they met? If so, were they challenging enough? If not, were they too far removed from students' current level of understanding? Did all students meet them? Who did? Who didn't? Why not? These questions can help you chart the progress of your students' learning week by week.

Similarly, the activities of the lesson are worthy of careful description. Typical activities may include various pedagogical elements that are being brought together within the project. These might cover aspects such as the application of different technological tools, a different approach to language and communication or a new approach to grouping students drawn from another subject pedagogy that you have identified. Either way, the activities of the project are as important as the learning objectives. They frame the teaching and learning that takes place.

Evaluate your own performance

Teaching is a skilful activity that, over time, you should improve in. However, this improvement does not occur by accident. It is the result of a deliberate process of practice and reflection. In each phase of your teaching, you will have key areas for improvement (perhaps identified at the start of your teaching placement) that you will want to reflect on. Your lesson evaluation is an ideal place to start this process.

So, use these documents as a way to discuss the nitty gritty of your teaching. Try and think in detail about specific elements of your pedagogy (e.g. how you questioned a student, how you modelled a specific process, how you used a new behaviour management strategy, where you stood in the room, your body language, your tone of voice – the list really is endless!) and discuss it, briefly in your evaluation. And, most importantly, use this opportunity to set yourself another target in that area (for reflection on and evaluation later on).

Or, alternatively (or as well), perhaps your subject mentor has asked you to focus on a particular aspect of your pedagogy. They may have done this explicitly (i.e. you really must improve X or Y) or implicitly (i.e. you've sensed this might be an issue in their mind). Either way, the evaluations that you complete lesson by lesson are an ideal time to show a positive response to their advice and guidance. Done well, they can provoke constructive discussions in your mentor meetings and create a positive impression of your engagement and progress.

Evaluate your students' learning

Finally, it will be crucial to evaluate the learning that your students have engaged in during the lesson. Hopefully, part of this will be covered in your evaluation of the learning objectives and teaching activities. But here, it is helpful to be even more specific. You might want to highlight the progress made by one or two students specifically (i.e. name them and what they have managed to achieve). It would certainly be appropriate here to talk about strategies of differentiation and personalization (and how these are different) and how they have been applied to particular students (perhaps those with SEN or on the G&T register).

> **Key questions**
>
> 1 To what extent is evaluation different from assessment? Are there links between the two that I could usefully exploit?
> 2 What could I do with the products of my evaluation work? Who will read them?
> 3 What are the benefits of keeping a teaching journal, with regular pieces of evaluative writing done week by week?

Further reading

Altrichter, H., Posch, P. and Somekh, B. (1993) *Teachers Investigate Their Work*. London: Routledge.

Holly, M.L. (1989) *Writing to Grow: Keeping a Personal-professional Journal*. Portsmouth, NH: Heinemann Educational Books, Inc.

Examinations

> Does education mean anything beyond passing tests? . . . England's children are now the most tested in the world . . . Teachers and students are now judged almost exclusively on their ability to get students through their next assessment.
>
> (Mansell 2007: xiv)

Examination results have become, in the minds of many, what education is all about. It is not the place for this book to debate this, but to deal with it as a reality of contemporary schooling, not only in England, which the quote from Mansell referred to, but across the world.

Let us begin by taking a step back, and asking what an examination is. Paul Black observes that the written examination in the UK began in universities: 'in Oxford in 1702, and in Cambridge in 1800, but general abandonment of oral in favour of written tests became widespread only after 1830' (Black 1998: 10).

From these early beginnings examinations spread to schools, and went through a series of mutations over the years, from School Certificates, O levels, A levels, and Highers to Btec, AS levels, and many more. What is important, in the UK context, is that these examinations are operated externally to the school. They are not set and marked by teachers who have been teaching the students who will be taking the examinations, but externally, by examination boards, who may or may not be operating for profit, but are certainly established as businesses. This causes regular debates in the national and local press about whether standards are fall-ing, and whether businesses should be involved at all. Back in 2008, the Association of School and College Leaders looked into the costs of exter-nal examinations, and produced case-study examples:

> In a 1,500-student comprehensive school with a sixth form in Wales, the cost of examination fees is approximately £100,000. Administration of the external examinations is over £17,000 and support staff for invigilation costs approximately £13,000. The total is £130,000.
>
> (ASCL 2008: 2)

In some schools they reported the cost of examinations is the second highest cost after staffing salaries; in other words it costs more to enter the students for external examinations than the school spends on materials to prepare them for these exams. Whatever the debates are (and they are worth you looking into) it is the case that examinations are operating an ever-increasing role in the lives of teachers and students alike.

But what does this mean for you, the teacher? A major part of your role is to prepare your students for examinations. Experienced teachers will tell you that there are at least two main aspects to this; there is teach-ing the knowledge, skills and understandings required, which will be laid out in the examination specification, and then there will be examina-tion technique. In the 'performance driven' world in which education operates, it is likely to be the latter that causes standards to improve over time. It is not necessarily the case that students have got smarter, but that teachers have got better at preparing students for external examinations. This means the use of trial questions, past papers, taking mock examina-tions under exam conditions and helping students refine answers accord-ing to mark schemes, so that they know which key words or phrases trigger marks, and what model answers should contain. It can be argued that this is, in effect, 'gaming' the system, in that teachers are focusing as much on process – doing well in the exam – as on product – knowledge to be tested. As Gordon Stobart observes: 'obsession with aspirational targets based on test scores invites playing the system and encourages a focus on results rather than what has been learned' (Stobart 2008: 137).

What will be important for you, the teacher, is to ensure that you are fully conversant with both syllabus and questions, that you have prepared the students not only in terms of knowledge, skills and understanding required for the examination, but also in ensuring that the students have done plenty of past questions, know what examiners will be looking for, and understand how to phrase their answers to this end.

Key questions

1   What will examiners be looking for? Have I studied model answers?
2   Do I have past papers? Have I asked colleagues for their interpretations of model answers?
3   Have I been to examination board training sessions?
4   How can I collaborate with colleagues so as to maximize opportunities for my students?

References

ASCL (2008) *The Future of Assessment*. Leicester: Association of School and College Leaders.

Black, P.J. (1998) *Testing: Friend or Foe?: The Theory and Practise of Assessment and Testing*. London: Falmer Press.

Mansell, W. (2007) *Education by Numbers: The Tyranny of Testing*. London: Politico's Publishing.

Stobart, G. (2008) *Testing Times: The Uses and Abuses of Assessment*. Abingdon: Routledge.

Further reading

Revision guides for subjects you teach.

McMillan, K. and Weyers, J. (2011) *How to Succeed in Exams and Assessments*, 2nd edn. Harlow: Prentice Hall.

Explanations

Being able to explain something effectively is one of the most important skills that all teachers need. Almost every lesson that you teach will have a period of explanation within it at some point. Some people are born with an innate ability to explain things well. But for most of us, explaining things is a skill that can be learnt, practised and developed.

There are a number of characteristics or features of a successful explanation. In no particular order of priority, these include:

- using a hook of some sort to grab your students' attention and
  interest;
- having a key concept or idea which is at the heart of the explanation;
- varying your language, intonation and posture to emphasize specific points throughout your explanation;
- using signposting statements that signal a new direction within
  the explanation or help to summarize key points;
- using humour (which may or may not come naturally) to help a
  key idea remain with the student long after the explanation itself
  has finished;
- using examples from real life that help illustrate the key concept and establish students' understanding within a particular
  context;
- connecting new ideas to students' previous experience or exist-
  ing knowledge;
- utilizing props or resources of various kinds to help add power
  and/or illustrate key ideas within the explanation.

An explanation is a vitally important part of most lessons. In the early
days of teaching, you would be well advised to script your explanations,
perhaps even writing them down word by word. Whilst we do not advise
you to read them out from a physical script, this mental preparation for
this part of your lesson will be invaluable. Many of the points above
(e.g. generating a hook for the explanation, incorporating contextual
examples, signposting techniques, etc.) will all be difficult to do 'off the
cuff' and need careful preparation. Explanations, like every aspect of your
pedagogy, need careful thought and preparation in the vast majority of
cases. Do not leave your explanations to chance. They will be ineffective
and, at worse, will only serve to confuse your students.

So far, we have positioned the explanation as something that is under
your control, delivered in a scripted way with little, if any, student
involvement. This is only part of the story. Explanations can be dynamic,
entertaining, interactive and inclusive if you are able to think through
how students will not only receive new knowledge or information, but
how they will then go on to process that throughout the rest of your lesson. Much of this comes down to effective planning on your part. You
will need to consider how your learning objectives for the lesson are not
only explored within your explanation, but also developed through the
teaching activities you have designed.

Explanations are mediated through your spoken language. Your ability to use language skilfully is essential. You will need to empathize with students, ask purposeful questions about the process of their learning (perhaps even within the explanation itself), consider the timing and pace of your delivery (are students able to keep up with you?), as well as the performance aspects of delivery (intonation, posture, etc.) that affect, at a fundamental level, how we communicate with each other.

It is interesting to reflect on the nature of teacher talk. The modern way is to discourage teachers from talking too much. Teacher talk is seen as a monological process and the antipathy of interaction and inclusion. However, nothing is really further from the truth. Teacher talk can be captivating, engaging, inspirational and motivational, done in the right way. Not many of us are born with these skills, but it is worth pursuing them in a structured way.

Key questions

Reflect back on an explanation that you have delivered to a class recently. Ask yourself the following questions:

1 Were the key points of my explanation linked to the learning objectives of the lesson? Was this mentioned to the students?
2 Where were the students sitting during my explanation? What were they doing? Was I able to actively engage them in any way during the explanation?

Further reading

Roehler, L. and Duffy, G. (1986) What makes one teacher a better explainer than another. *Journal of Education for Teaching: International Research and Pedagogy*, 12(3): 273–84.

F

Facilitation

Teachers are facilitators of learning. In this entry we explore what this involves.

As with many aspects of teaching and learning we explore in this book, the notion of facilitating learning depends to some extent upon which learning theories the teacher is employing at the time. To be a learning facilitator often involves some form of constructivist approach, where students construct their own meanings from learning materials. One aspect of facilitation is also known as *discovery learning*. In Mosston and Ashworth's continuum of teaching styles (Mosston and Ashworth 2002) three variants of this are described:

1   Guided Discovery: where the teacher guides the students, but remains in charge of the teaching programme;
2   Convergent Discovery: where there is only one answer, and the teacher helps the students to reach it;
3   Divergent Discovery: where there is more than one outcome, and the teacher supports the students in the process of working.

In each of these cases the students are working towards finding out answers, solutions or responses by themselves, and the teacher steers them towards the desired goals.

There are many cases where the teacher-as-facilitator is a logical way of working. Take the case of an art lesson, in which students are required to draw a still-life of everyday objects that the teacher has assembled in the classroom. In this case the teacher will have worked with students in advance on shape, perspective, shading, tone and many other aspects. The purpose of the task is to use these in a picture that demonstrates the students can do the task required. Clearly there will be more than one outcome, although the students are all looking at the same collection of objects.

Teacher-as-facilitator also occurs when there is an element of skill involved in a learning task. If a teacher wants the students in PE to learn to throw the discus, the teacher will demonstrate, but then the students need to have a go themselves.

Facilitation enable learners to construct their own meaning. It does require some thinking on the part of the teacher, as when working in this fashion 'teaching is a problem-solving context in which they must come to understand the meaning of students' ideas rather than just correct them' (Hmelo-Silver and Barrows 2006: 21). And this is the point of facilitation. As we say many times in this book, if teaching was just telling, then it would be a unidirectional flow from teacher to student. As it is not, then there needs to be the possibility of multiway flow of information. For teachers to act as facilitators, they need to respond to the ways in which learning develops in their students.

Key questions

1 What do I want the students to learn? How can I facilitate them learning it?
2 How much can they find out for themselves?
3 How much information do I need to give them before they can start?
4 What sorts of topics in the areas I teach would respond well to this sort of pedagogy?

References

Hmelo-Silver, C.E. and Barrows, H.S. (2006) Goals and strategies of a problem-based learning facilitator. *Interdisciplinary Journal of Problem-based Learning,* 1(1): 21–39.

Mosston, M. and Ashworth, S. (2002) *Teaching Physical Education.* San Francisco, CA: B. Cummings.

Further reading

Capel, S.A., Leask, M. and Turner, T. (2009) *Learning to Teach in the Secondary School: A Companion to School Experience.* London: Routledge.

Moore, A. (2000) *Teaching and Learning: Pedagogy, Curriculum and Culture.* London: RoutledgeFalmer.

Folk pedagogy

As everyone went to school as a child, many people make the assumption that they are now educational experts! This is also true, in many cases, of politicians. Kelly's magisterial book on the curriculum (Kelly 2009) devotes a whole chapter to 'what the average politician understands about education'; the chapter is entirely blank!

Jerome Bruner writes about *folk pedagogies*:

> Watch any mother, any teacher, even any babysitter with a child and you'll be struck by how much of what they do is steered by notions of 'what children's minds are like and how to help them learn', even though they may not be able to verbalise their pedagogical principles.
>
> (Bruner 1996: 46)

Folk pedagogies are theories and ideas that lay people have about how learning takes place, the best ways of teaching and of how schools should be organized. The folk pedagogies are rooted in the educational experience of an individual, and possibly the ideological stance they take.

> Folk pedagogies, for example, reflect a variety of assumptions about children: they may be seen as willful and needing correction; as innocent and to be protected from a vulgar society; as needing skills to be developed only through practice; as empty vessels to be filled with knowledge that only adults can provide; as egocentric and in need of socialization. Folk beliefs of this kind, whether expressed by laypeople or by 'experts', badly want some 'deconstructing' if their implications are to be appreciated. For whether these views are 'right' or not, their impact on teaching activities can be enormous.
>
> (Bruner 1996: 49)

Let us endeavour to do some deconstructing, as Bruner requests. We know that a commonly held view of teaching is that teachers have 'the knowledge', and the purpose of teaching is to pass on this knowledge to the students: 'Think of teaching as a simple and straightforward activity that results in learning. Teachers teach; students learn. Teaching is telling. Learning is listening to what the teacher says and giving it back more or less intact' (Feiman-Nemser et al. 1987: 3). This very simplistic view of pedagogy prevails in some of our daily papers! This is teaching as 'chalk and talk' – the teacher expounds, the children sit and listen. It is fair to say that for many of the traditionalists holding these views, 'chalk and talk' is rather mild; they would probably prefer what they recall from their own schooling: 'shout and clout'!

The reason for this political diversion is that:

> [If] you as a pedagogical theorist are convinced that the best learning occurs when the teacher helps lead the student to discover generalizations on her own, you are likely to run into an established cultural belief that a teacher is an authority who is supposed to *tell* the child what the general case is, while the child should be occupying herself with memorizing the particulars.
>
> (Bruner 1996: 46)

The implications of this are that being involved in educational activity which involves change, you will not only need to convince the students who hold folk pedagogies of their own, but others in and beyond the school.

As Bruner observed in a quotation above, 'whether these views are "right" or not, their impact on teaching activities can be enormous'. Indeed, the whole way that a system of pedagogy is articulated can depend on the view of those who are organizing it. If the view that 'teaching is telling' is the dominant paradigm, then the programme will be organized in this fashion. If, however, the prevailing view is that children learn best through discovery learning, then the curriculum will be put together so as to enable the students to do this.

Folk pedagogies are often rooted in a past modality, and may not be suitable for twenty-first century young people. As much human knowledge is now contained in the Internet, knowing how to find things out becomes more important than it was before. Pedagogy needs to be appropriate for its context, and fit for purpose.

Bearing in mind that folk pedagogies will continue to exist in the population at large, it also becomes important for those engaged in education to couch discussions of their innovations in ways which those who are not directly involved can understand.

Key questions

1 What folk pedagogies do I hold about education? Are these different from, say, my parents?
2 What folk pedagogies do politicians seem to hold?

References

Bruner, J. (1996) *The Culture of Education.* Cambridge, MA: Harvard University Press.

Feiman-Nemser, S., Williamson McDiarmid, G., Melnick, S.L. and Parker, M. (1987) Changing beginning teachers' conceptions: a description of an introductory teacher education course. Paper presented to the American Educational Research Association Annual Meeting, Washington, DC, 20–24 April.

Kelly, A.V. (2009) *The Curriculum: Theory and Practice*, 6th edn. London: Sage.

Further reading

Fautley, M. and Savage, J. (2010) *Secondary Education: Reflective Reader.* Exeter: Learning Matters.

G

Gender

The issue of gender is felt quite significantly in schools. This can start with differences in school uniform for boys and girls, and move to differences in examination attainment at 16 and 18 years of age. Indeed, there are many schools which are separated entirely on the basis of gender, with boys and girls in different institutions. There are also gender differences in the ways students act in the classroom, and the ways in which teachers deal with this. Finally there are gender differences in the proportion of males and females employed as teachers.

We know there are differences in the ways in which teachers view boys and girls in the classroom, and that in many cases these fall back on stereotypical standpoints concerning the different ways in which male and female students act and react. As Jones and Myhill observe:

> [Boys] face a constant barrage of negative representations of masculinity – they are seen as emotionally inadequate, while girls are seen as emotionally and socially adept. Boys compete while girls cooperate; boys argue but girls share and facilitate; boys make commands, girls make requests; boys cannot concentrate, girls can; boys are concerned with objects, girls with people.
>
> (Jones and Myhill 2004: 534)

Although boys and girls can seem to behave and react differently, there are dangers of falling back onto stereotypes and assuming that these things are always true. Another danger is assuming that there is somehow a neurological difference between brains of boys and girls. Usha Goswami writes of a number of 'neuromyths', one of which is this idea of the gendered brain:

> One is the idea that a person can either have a 'male brain' or a 'female brain'. The terms 'male brain' and 'female brain' were coined to refer to differences in cognitive style rather than biological differences (Baron-Cohen 2003). Baron-Cohen argued

that men were better 'systemisers' (good at understanding mechanical systems) and women were better 'empathisers' (good at communication and understanding others). He did not argue that male and female brains were radically different, but used the terms male and female brain as a psychological shorthand for (overlapping) cognitive profiles.

(Goswami 2004: 11)

Whilst it is clearly true that there are biological differences between the sexes, and that these can contribute to the ways in which actions then follow, neuroscience is making rapid advances (see the entry **brain**), and doubtless there is more research to be done in this important area.

Another aspect of education in which gender figures is that of the feminization of the teaching profession. According to UNESCO figures, the percentage of female primary school teachers in North America and Western Europe stands at over 80 per cent, and has been rising steadily. In secondary schools in the same areas, the proportion is over 50 per cent, and again is rising (UNESCO 2012: 98–9). This is another contentious issue, based on the notion that boys have suffered due to the lack of male role models at school, and who, in contemporary fractured societal structures, may not be present in their home lives either. The students themselves may be not a useful source of information on this, as Francis et al. observed: 'Asked, "Do you think it makes any difference whether you have a man or a lady teacher?", an overwhelming majority of the students (198 students; two thirds of the sample) said that it does not. Only 81 (just over a quarter) said that it does make a difference' (Francis et al. 2008: 24). This relates to key research findings of Drudy, who noted that:

Gender balance in teaching remains an important equality issue. Gender needs to be embedded in policy thinking on teaching and teacher education. Discourses on teaching are increasingly drawn from the perspective of performativity, arguably more compatible with a culture of hegemonic masculinity than with a culture of femininity … research to date suggests that the policy direction should be towards attracting high quality people into the profession irrespective of whether male or female.

(Drudy 2008: 319)

Issues for you in the classroom with regards to your students are likely to centre around addressing their learning needs and treating them as individuals. Whilst gender matters will be obvious at times, adopting stereotypical viewpoints and treating any group of students as being entirely homogenous in viewpoint and outlook is problematic.

> **Key questions**
>
> 1 Do I treat boys and girls differently? Is this a good thing?
> 2 Who gets the majority of my attention in the classroom? Why is this?

References

Baron-Cohen, S. (2003) *The Essential Difference: Men, Women and the Extreme Male Brain.* London: Allen Lane.

Drudy, S. (2008) Gender balance/gender bias: the teaching profession and the impact of feminisation. *Gender and Education,* 20(4): 309–23.

Francis, B., Skelton, C., Carrington, B. et al. (2008) A perfect match? Students' and teachers' views of the impact of matching educators and learners by gender. *Research Papers in Education,* 23(1): 21–36.

Goswami, U. (2004) Neuroscience and education. *British Journal of Educational Psychology,* 74(1): 1–14.

Jones, S. and Myhill, D. (2004) Seeing things differently: teachers' constructions of underachievement. *Gender and Education,* 16(4): 531–46.

UNESCO (2012) *World Atlas of Gender Equality in Education.* Paris: United Nations Educational, Scientific and Cultural Organization.

Further reading

Gurian, M. (2011) *Boys and Girls Learn Differently.* San Francisco, CA: Jossey-Bass.

Governors

Each school within the state education sector is required by law to have a governing body. Individual governors are drawn from different parts of the local community and could include parents, teachers, local employers, representatives of the local authority and others. Every governor has an equal standing on the governing body, with the exception of the Chair of Governors and Vice-Chair of Governors who are normally elected by the other school governors.

The governing body of a school has a serious job to do in being held legally responsible for the conduct of the school. The precise responsibilities that any individual governing body may fulfil do vary, but normally include most of the following:

1   setting targets for student achievement;
2   managing the finances of the school;
3   reviewing the curriculum arrangements in place at the school;
4   appointing and rewarding staff, including the headteacher;
5   reviewing staff performance and dealing with any disciplinary matters;
6   maintaining the school building and any grounds that the school owns;
7   managing student exclusions from the school.

The governing body will normally meet at least once each school term. Governors will arrange their work within various committees with a particular focus on one dimension of their responsibilities. There may be a curriculum committee, a staffing committee, an exclusion committee, etc. These committees will normally have their own schedule of termly meetings.

Governors are not paid for their role. They represent the United Kingdom's largest voluntary group with approximately 300,000 school governors in total contributing to the strategic development of schools. The best way that governors can be described is as 'critical friends' for the school and its staff. Whilst the vast majority of governors are not professional educators, they do have expertise drawn from many different areas of life and are willing to apply this in support of your school.

Within the new academies, there is a twin tier of governance. The conventional element of this follows the arrangements described above; however, the academy will also have to have established a legal trust that owns the assets of the school (these will have normally been transferred from the local authority). This trust is formed between key governors, the headteacher and representatives drawn from the academy's sponsor (if applicable). This twin tier of governance means that individual school governors are not legally responsible or liable for the assets of the school.

From the perspective of a teacher in a school, it is highly likely that you will have two main points of contact with a governing body. First, you will have colleagues who are governors and represent the staff as a whole on the governing body. These governors can be approached for advice and support and can act as 'critical friend' when required. Second, in the majority of schools governors are normally assigned a curriculum area or two to 'look after'. This might mean that they come and chat to staff in that area, watch some lessons and generally take an interest in what you are up to in your work. They are not there to judge you, tell you what to do or interfere. Rather, use your school governor as a useful source of advice and support within the school as a whole. They can be a great source of ideas for new ventures or initiatives that you might want to develop.

Key questions

1   Which members of staff represent me on my school governing body? Which governor has a responsibility for my curriculum area or year group?
2   How can I use the governors to help support the work I am doing in the school? What practical steps can I take to help inform them about my work?

Further reading

Department for Education (2012) Categories and Roles of School Governors. http://www.education.gov.uk/schools/leadership/governance/a0056694/categories-and-roles-of-school-governors (accessed 12 June 2012).
National Governor's Association: http://www.nga.org.uk/ (accessed 27 June 2012).

Grading

Grading of students occurs during assessment. This can be complex, and it is worth spending some time thinking about what the options are. Popham (2011) suggests three common grade-giving approaches. These are:

Absolute grading
A grade is given based on a teacher's idea of what level of student performances is truly necessary to earn, for instance, an A. Thus, if . . . in a given class no student performs at the A level of proficiency, then no student will get an A.

Relative grading
. . . a grade is given based on how students perform in relation to one another. Thus for any group of students there will always be the *best* and *worst* performances.

Aptitude grading
. . . a grade is given to each student based on how well the student performs in relation to the student's academic potential . . . if a particularly bright student outperforms all the other students in the class, but still performed well below what the teacher believed the student was capable of the student might get a B.

(Popham 2011: 397)

There are problems with aptitude grading, including: 'the difficulty of deciding on just what each student's academic potential is' (Popham 2011: 397), but it is interesting to give some thought to how it might be applied in your classroom.

In the UK, we tend to refer to absolute grading as *criterion referenced* assessment. This is where students are assessed against a set of criteria, often in the form of statements. National Curriculum levels are one example of this approach. Relative grading is known as *norm referencing*, and here the results often approximate to the bell curve of normal frequency distribution. This is harder to deal with when the cohort is small; it tends to work best for larger populations.

For classroom grading schemes where you, the teacher, are in charge, you have some choice over what grades you will give. Before you can do this though, you need to give some thought to the issue of how you will allocate your grades, and therefore what grading scale you will be using. For many teachers in the UK, there is a default position of using National Curriculum levels. As these were never intended to be used for individual pieces of work there can be a problem of application. Another difficulty is the use of subdivided National Curriculum levels. We know that for many subjects these do not exist officially; schools have essentially invented them (Fautley 2011). If you are using subdivided National Curriculum levels, are you clear on what performance the student is required to demonstrate in order for you to arrive at a decision? To do this you need to have clearly delineated grade boundary statements, so what makes a level 4c distinct from a level 4b is clear. In some schools, the delineation is:

A: met the level requirements at a high standard, but not yet met next level requirements;
B: met the level requirements;
C: partially met the level requirements, but better than the previous level.

If this is the case in your school, then it may be a matter of professional judgement as to how you apply the grading criteria. Some questions you will want to ask yourself include:

- Am I criterion referencing?
- If so, what are my criteria?
- How clearly delineated are the boundaries?
- What grading scale am I going to use?
- What grades will I give?
- Do I want to encourage some students?
- Do my grades link to external examination grades and criteria?

However, this criterion referencing process can be further confused as some schools have added a degree of pseudo-norm-referencing into the mix, and given teachers targets of what percentage of students should get, say, a level 5A. In these cases, the figures are based on a statistical projection of broadly similar cohorts' performance. These figures tend to be least accurate when a degree of talent is involved, say in PE or the Arts. If your school requires this then you should be given some guidance on how suitable the statistical progression figures are for the students you teach. After all, Darren is a person, not a statistic, and you teach Darren, not a spreadsheet! (See also the entry on X – positive approaches to marking.)

Key questions

1 What does a good criterion statement in my subject look like?
2 How can I clearly delineate between criterion statements?
3 What do I do about the student who always tries hard, but constantly gets a low grade?
4 What do I do if my results do not match my externally-set target grades?

References

Fautley, M. (2011) Problems of teacher assessment and creativity: the case of music in the English National Curriculum at Key Stage 3. Paper presented at the British Education Research Association Conference, IOE, London, September.

Popham, W. (2011) *Classroom Assessment: What Teachers Need to Know*, 6th edn. Boston, MA: Pearson.

Further reading

Fautley, M. and Savage, J. (2008) *Assessment for Learning and Teaching in Secondary Schools*. Exeter: Learning Matters.

Gardner, J., Harlen, W., Hayward, L., Stobart, G. and Montgomery, M. (2010) *Developing Teacher Assessment*. Maidenhead: Open University Press.

Grouping

We look at some aspects of grouping in the entries on **ability** and **mixed ability**. In this entry we consider other aspects of grouping, paying particular attention to in-class modalities. Groupwork in class settings is an important and useful way of organizing the class, and so the approaches outlined here give a choice, and some flexibility, to the ways in which you can organize this as a teacher.

In the UK, the national literacy strategy (DfES 2001) classified strategies for organizing groupwork. These are still useful, and to this we shall add some more recent ideas.

1 Pair talk
Setting up classes to talk in pairs is fairly straightforward. Many classes are set up with paired desks, and so for pupils to talk to their neighbour does not take a great deal of additional organization. How pupils sit in the class may need some thought, and teacher-established seating plans may well be helpful here.

2 Snowballing
Here the pairs that were established in the previous example come together in groups of four to discuss things further, and to compare and contrast ideas. Fours can then become eights, and then, if needed, report back to the whole class.

3 Listening triads
Pupils are grouped in threes, with specific roles assigned: talker, questioner or recorder: 'The talker explains something, or comments on an issue, or expresses opinions. The questioner prompts and seeks clarification. The recorder makes notes and gives a report at the end of the conversation. Next time, roles are changed' (DfES 2001: 60).

4 Envoys
Here different numbers of people can be involved in a group. Once the task is completed one person from the group goes to another group and explains what their group did. This can be used with groups discussing the same topic, or different ones.

5 Rainbow groups
Individual pupils are assigned a colour (although we have also seen this done with foodstuffs). Either after working in pairs or other small groups, pupils with the same colour nomenclature get together to discuss the original issue and take it further. Food labels can combine again further

to create third and fourth tiers, for instance 'apples and pears' groups work together, and so on.

6 Spokesperson

After discussion, one person is nominated to talk back, possibly with the aid of a flipchart page. Variations on the flipchart include the use of 'sticky notes' which are displayed, and possibly grouped thematically, on the wall.

7 No hands up/randomized responses

In a variation of the spokesperson mode, here the teacher picks at random an individual pupil to give feedback to the class. This can be done by allocating numbers, or by drawing names in some way. For those teachers with interactive whiteboards, randomized name display software is available to do this task.

8 World Café (Brown and Isaacs 2005)

Groups are organized around a table, with a large sheet of paper, or paper tablecloth, upon which ideas are written. Groups then rotate around the room looking at different ideas from the tablecloths.

9 Charrette/mantle of the expert

This is somewhat more complex and takes some setting up. This builds on the *mantle of the expert* notion of Dorothy Heathcote (1991). In this the pupils take on various roles, and become, as it were, the experts in particular situations. For instance, in one secondary school in Birmingham some Year 7 pupils were working as though they were members of a witness protection unit (WPU), taking on the roles of members of the police and courts, but also roles from the community:

> They role-played the gang members because we started to look at the gang and what it's like to be part of the gang. They also played members of their families because we're looking at migration of people into Birmingham and a look at the generation gap between the gang members and their parents and grandparents. So they are considering ritual, religion and behaviour and manners and etiquette. As members of the WPU we're making files on individual gang members and using drama to uncover key moments.
>
> (Fautley et al. 2011: 48)

A Charrette is when a group of people come together in a relatively unstructured format to work on an issue. This can be done without the mantle of the expert work described above, but in this case the pupils use their own views, ideas and opinions to arrive at a solution.

Finally, do not forget that whole class teaching and learning do not preclude social constructivist activity taking place. The class can be involved conjointly on tasks and learning, and then split into groups, and then back to the whole class again, as the occasion requires.

Key questions

1 What groupings are there that would suit the work I want the pupils to be engaged in?
2 How can I organize the space in the most effective fashion?
3 What is the learning that I expect to be taking place?
4 How can I ensure that groupings work out well?

References

Brown, J. and Isaacs, D. (2005) *The World Café: Shaping our Futures Through Conversations that Matter*. San Francisco, CA: Berrett-Koehler.

DfES (2001) *Literacy Across the Curriculum: Key Stage 3 Strategy*. London: Department for Education and Skills.

Fautley, M., Hatcher, R. and Millard, E. (2011) *Remaking the Curriculum: Re-engaging Young People in Secondary School*. Stoke-on-Trent: Trentham.

Heathcote, D. (1991) *Collected Writings on Education and Drama*. Evanston, IL: Northwestern University Press.

Further reading

Fautley, M., Hatcher, R. and Millard, E. (2011) *Remaking the Curriculum: Re-engaging Young People in Secondary School*. Stoke-on-Trent, Trentham.

H

Homework

Homework, every pupil's favourite! For many schools homework is a compulsory component of the teaching and learning programme. Teachers are expected to set it, and pupils are expected to do it. The purpose of homework is to raise standards of attainment. As Hargreaves (1984) noted, 'over the five years of secondary education, appropriate homework can add the equivalent of at least one year of full-time education'. Research evidence for the effectiveness of homework is somewhat mixed, however. A meta-study of research, primarily from the UK and the USA, found that 'The research findings on the impact of homework on students, their attitudes and their achievements were mixed, with both positive and negative effects indicated. (Queensland Government Department of Education and the Arts, 2004: 3). And another international study based in Germany looking at maths homework based on PISA (programme for international student assessment) scores reported that:

> Multilevel analyses found a positive association between school-average homework time and mathematics achievement in almost all countries, but the size of the association decreased considerably once socioeconomic background and school track were controlled. At the student level, no clear-cut relationship was established between homework time and achievement across the 40 countries.
> (Dettmers 2010: 73)

However, homework tends to be considered a good thing, and so schools encourage it! But what, as a teacher, can you do to make homework purposeful and relevant? One of the commonest homework tasks is to finish off work that was started in the class, yet as Julian Stern observes, this may not necessarily be a good idea:

> 'Finish off' homework tasks are unfair and unreasonable. They are unfair because they penalise slower workers and reward quicker workers, which usually (though by no means always) penalises

the lower achieving pupils and rewards the higher achieving pupils. They are unreasonable because the pupils (notably the slower-working pupils) are likely to need a teacher's support . . .

(Stern 2009: 23)

So what can, and should, you do? According to the American academic Cathy Vatterott, 'Homework shouldn't be about rote learning. The best kind deepens student understanding and builds essential skills' (Vatterott 2010: 10). She suggests that there are five characteristics which good homework should demonstrate:

First, the task has a clear academic purpose, such as practice, checking for understanding, or applying knowledge or skills. Second, the task efficiently demonstrates student learning. Third, the task promotes ownership by offering choices and being personally relevant. Fourth, the task instills a sense of competence – the student can successfully complete it without help. Last, the task is aesthetically pleasing – it appears enjoyable and interesting.

(Vatterott 2010: 4)

These are helpful suggestions, and translate readily into a number of contexts. Planning for homework should ideally be done at the same time as the lesson plan, and with the same attention to detail. If teachers treat it as an afterthought, then it is hard for students to take it seriously too. Good homework extends learning, whereas bad homework just breeds resentment.

Key questions

1 What homework am I setting this week? Why am I setting it? What do the pupils get out of it?
2 Can I explain (to myself, to my colleagues, to the pupils, to the parents) what the purpose of this homework is?
3 How can I take account of Vatterott's five characteristics of good homework in my daily practice?

References

Dettmers, S. (2010) Effektive Hausaufgaben: Untersuchungen zu einem psychologischen Rahmenmodell (Effective homework: studies submitted to a psychological framework model). PhD thesis. Department of Educational Studies and Psychology. Berlin: Freien Universität Berlin.

Hargreaves, D.H. (1984) *Improving Secondary Schools: Report of the Committee.* London: Inner London Education Authority.

Queensland Government Department of Education and the Arts (2004) *Homework Literature Review: Summary of Key Research Findings.* Queensland: Queensland Government Department of Education and the Arts.

Stern, J. (2009) *Getting the Buggers to do their Homework.* London: Continuum.

Vatterott, C. (2010) Five hallmarks of good homework. *Educational Leadership*, 68(1): 10–15.

Further reading

Stern, J. (2009) *Getting the Buggers to do their Homework.* London: Continuum.
Vatterott, C. (2010) Five hallmarks of good homework. *Educational Leadership*, 68(1): 10–15.

Humour

Our experiences of life generally prove that some people are just funnier than others. The same is probably true of our teachers. As I write this section, I can recall those teachers who made me laugh regularly with a greater degree of detail and fondness than the myriad of others who did not!

The educational literature reinforces something that I suspect many of us know to be true from our own experiences of education already: the use of humour creates a positive atmosphere, reduces anxiety and facilitates the learning process (Berk 1996, 1998; Hill 1988).

So, can you learn to be funny in your teaching? To the extent that some people have a natural affinity towards humour as part of their individual personality, probably not. But all of us can learn to use humour in a constructive way within our teaching. According to Garner (2005), humour is most effective when it is appropriate to the audience, targeted within a specific topic, and placed in the context of the learning experience.

His article illustrates how humour can be linked to the use of metaphor and analogy in our teaching to help create positive associations in our students' minds that result in a greater chance of them remembering information, improve their critical thinking and create a positive and engaging classroom environment. It is available freely and well worth a read (see further reading).

Of course, everyone finds different things funny. One of the dangers of trying to be too humorous in the classroom is that you may alienate as many students (who do not find you funny) as those that you engage (and think you are the next great stand-up!). But, and perhaps you will not be surprised by this, educational researchers have even examined the appropriateness or inappropriateness of various types of humour in the classroom setting (Wanzer et al. 2006). This research identified four main types of appropriate humour:

1   Related humour: this included using media or other objects to enhance learning, jokes, stories, stereotypes, teacher perform-ance, creative language usage;
2   Un-related humour: similar to the above but un-related to the curriculum context being presented;
3   Self-disparaging humour: making fun of yourself, telling embar-rassing stories, etc.;
4   Unintentional or unplanned humour: unintentional puns or slips of the tongue.

In terms of inappropriate humour, the researchers document offensive humour, disparaging humour aimed at individual students related to their intelligence, race, gender or appearance, and disparaging humour at 'other' targets as well as self-disparaging humour.

Whilst all this is probably extremely unfunny, it does illustrate the breadth of possible humour in the classroom. So, whilst our personalities are difficult to change (and there is a good argument in favour of not trying to be someone else when teaching!) it seems that it is possible to integrate humour of various types into our pedagogy. As with any new strand to your pedagogy, do not make drastic changes too quickly. Stu-dents see through thin-veiled and inauthentic pedagogical approaches very quickly. The best advice is probably to be yourself!

Key questions

1   Can you remember any good jokes? Why not look out some suitable con-tent that is related to your subject and try a few out in a forthcoming lesson?
2   Metaphor and analogy are two related areas that fit well with humour in the classroom. Why not try bringing unusual ideas or concepts together in new ways and see how they spark off each other?

References

Berk, R. (1998) *Professors are from Mars, Students are from Snickers.* Madison, WI: Mendota Press.

Berk, R. (1996) Student ratings of ten strategies for using humor in college teaching. *Journal on Excellence in College Teaching,* 7(3): 71–92.

Garner, R. (2005) Humor, analogy, and metaphor: H.A.M. it up in teaching. *Radical Pedagogy,* 6: 2. Also available from http://radicalpedagogy. icaap.org/content/issue6_2/garner.html (accessed 14 January 2013).

Hill, D. (1988) *Humor in the Classroom: A Handbook for Teachers.* Springfield, IL: Charles C. Thomas.

Wanzer, M., Frymier, A., Wojtaszczyk, A. and Smith, T. (2006) Appropriate and inappropriate uses of humor by teachers. *Communication Education,* 55(2): 178–96.

Further reading

Hill, D. (1988) *Humor in the Classroom: A Handbook for Teachers.* Springfield, IL: Charles C. Thomas.

ICT

ICT stands for 'information and communication technologies'. This term has been used for several years to describe any form of digital technology that is used within the classroom. It includes computers, cameras, interactive whiteboards, scanners, iPads, etc.

There are a number of ways that ICT can be used within your teaching.

First, they can be used by you to help you teach more effectively. You might use an interactive whiteboard to present information, a spreadsheet to keep track of student attainment, YouTube video clips to help illustrate key concepts, or a digital camera to help record students' work.

Second, you can include ICT within the teaching activities that your students are undertaking in your lesson. They might use a scanner to create frameworks for their own artwork, a digital recorder to reflect on their musical compositions, a piece of design software to experiment with alternative designs for a particular product, or presentational software such as Prezi to prepare a class presentation.

Third, social collaborative tools might be used by you and your students to help connect together their learning inside and outside your classroom. This might include the provision of homework tasks through a school network, the sharing of student work within secure social spaces (e.g. NUMU[1]) or the use of curriculum content from remote sources around the world or provided by talented 'experts' from a specific curriculum field.

Teaching and learning with ICT is not the same as teaching and learning without it. Many of the technologies we have mentioned above are very powerful and can transform the processes of teaching and learning in fundamental ways. These may not always be desirable. So, it is important to experiment and explore different approaches to the use of ICT in education. Teachers should not buy into the rhetoric that continuous technology change is always an improvement. Socio-cultural theorists such as James Wertsch (1998) have provided us with frameworks and tools such as mediated action that allow us to explore the benefits or affordances that ICT can bring, whilst also exploring the limitations that they impose on our thoughts and actions.

In terms of practical advice, here are a few tips from our experiences of working with ICT in various teaching and learning contexts:

1   Always work with the technology yourself before using it with your students.
2   Maintain a critical approach to any piece of ICT, exploring both the possible benefits and limitations of any particular given piece of technology.
3   Resist the temptation to replace or upgrade technologies for the sake of it. Tried and tested ICT are often better than the latest innovation.
4   Remember that most pieces of technology are not designed for the educational space. So, your pedagogy with any specific technology will need to be skilful and refined in order to get the most out of it.

Key questions

---

1   What does digital competence, usage and transformation look like in my subject area?
2   What ICT do I currently use in my classroom? Are they effective? What new tools could I bring in and how might they change my approach to teaching or the opportunities students have to learn?

Note

1. NUMU is a moderated social media space for the sharing of students' musical compositions.

Reference

Wertsch, J.V. (1998) *Mind as Action*. New York and Oxford: Oxford University Press.

Further reading

The Futurelab resources page (http://www.futurelab.org.uk/resources/) contains a range of fascinating reading on these topics. All resources are available electronically and free of charge. For example, why not start with:

Futurelab (2012) *Digital Literacy Across the Curriculum Handbook*. http://www.futurelab.org.uk/resources/digital-literacy-across-curriculum-handbook (accessed 22 June 2012).

Identity

> Good teaching cannot be reduced to technique; good teaching
> comes from the identity and integrity of the teacher.
>
> (Palmer 2009: 10)

Teaching should always be challenging and is often exciting! Whilst it
may not always feel exciting, the challenges of various types – intellectual, practical, physical and emotional – are always there. We are all constantly learning about teaching. Within this process of learning, there
are a broad range of life skills and experiences that we can draw on to
help us develop. Whilst this may be true in a practical sense (i.e. you may
have been able to establish and maintain good, professional relationships
with young people through helping out at a local youth club), it is also
true in a psychological sense. The person that you are today has been
formed through a mixture of your genetic disposition and your life experiences, relationships and activities. These have shaped your personality,
your speech, body language and ways of thinking and acting. Teaching
is a new type of mental and physical activity. But 'you' do it! Every part
of you will be challenged by it and, if you are doing it properly, it will be
physically and psychologically demanding.

Palmer's quote suggests that good teaching is firmly based in the identity of the teacher. But what does that really mean? How can you begin
to understand your 'identity' and use that knowledge to help ensure that
your teaching is really built upon a firm foundation?

Our dictionary gives a range of definitions for the term 'identity'.
These include:

1   the collective aspect of the set of characteristics by which a thing
     is definitively recognizable or known;
2   the set of behavioural or personal characteristics by which an
     individual is recognizable as a member of a group;
3   the quality or condition of being the same as something else;
4   the distinct personality of an individual regarded as a persisting
     entity; individuality.

There are a number of important, basic points to note here. First, identity
is about something being known or recognized. For our discussion, it is
what makes you the person you are (physically, emotionally, intellectually,
spiritually, etc.). It may also be elements or characteristics that other people can recognize in you. Second, identity is often linked to a relationship.
An object's identity may be related to or distinct from another object
within a particular group. The particular aspects of your identity are best

understood when one contextualizes them in different ways (e.g. your actions in a particular context could be seen as being representative or demonstrative of a specific element of your identity, which can be perceived by others and, therefore, mark you out as a particular individual). This is particularly important when you seek to develop a new identity for a new type of activity (e.g. teaching).

These thoughts have some important consequences for our work as teachers:

1   Whilst undergoing a process of initial teacher education, it is important to reflect on the contextualization of aspects of your 'pre-teaching' identity within the new activity of teaching that you are undertaking.

2   For more experienced teachers, your identity – both as a teacher and more widely in our adult lives – continues to change and develop. Important life experiences, e.g. having your own children, will change your perspective about life and be reflected in your identity as a teacher.

3   Identities are formed through relationships. As we meet significant people in our lives (personally or professionally), our own sense of identity is reinforced, challenged or sometimes changed. Again, these developments will all impact on our perception of ourselves as a teacher (and the ways in which are students perceive our identity).

Key questions

1   How has my identity changed and developed in recent years? Can I chart significant changes at key moments (e.g. training to be a teacher, becoming a parent, getting married)?

2   How were these changes reflected in my identity as a teacher?

Reference

Palmer, P. (2009) http://www.newhorizons.org/strategies/character/palmer.htm (accessed 2 February 2010).

Further reading

Palmer, P. (2009) http://www.newhorizons.org/strategies/character/palmer.htm (accessed 2 June 2012).

Interest

Why are you a teacher? There are many answers to this question! Commonly given will be one or both of these:

- you like your subject area;
- you want to help the next generation on its way.

Of course, there are lots of other reasons too, but these are bound to figure somewhere, and we would be worried if they did not. Despite what the tabloid press say, very few people become teachers for the money or the holidays!

What this means, therefore, is that you have an interest in your subject, and you have an interest in helping students learn it. So, how can you make your teaching as interesting as possible?

We know that each of us finds some things more interesting than others. Some people are trainspotters, some people collect teapots, and some people knit. There is no universal recipe for interestingness! We need therefore to distinguish between two things: *interesting content* and *interesting presentation*. The former can depend very much on the age of the students, so whilst early years students may be fascinated by some things, by the time they are 15 they are likely to be interested in very different ones! You will know your students, and so you will know what topics are of themselves likely to hold their attention.

We have talked elsewhere of content, of not being an entertainer, and of planning your lessons carefully. In terms of maintaining interest we know that the concentration span of people varies according to a number of factors, including age, environment, time of day, and so on. Good teaching involves spotting when it is time to alter the activity, or to change tack. Spending too long on one thing can get tedious, and so planning does not just need to be about content, it also needs pace and activity during the course of a lesson.

Good planning is not in and of itself always sufficient though. It is the skill of the teacher which brings the plan alive, and makes it leap off the page! Many beginning teachers worry about deviating from their planned lesson, and think this will be seen as a bad thing. The converse, however, is normally true. A good teacher knows when to deviate from their lesson plan because the students are getting restless, or because they have mastered it already, or because they need more help with the basics. All of these factors rely on the teacher's professional judgement in order to happen.

Key questions

1 What can I do to make my lessons interesting?
2 How do I distinguish between interesting content and interesting presentation?
3 Do I deviate from my lesson plan when necessary?

Further reading

Brooks, V., Abbott, I. and Bills, L. (2007) *Preparing to Teach in Secondary Schools: A Student Teacher's Guide to Professional Issues in Secondary Education*, 2nd edn. Maidenhead: Open University Press.

Wallace, I. and Kirkman, L. (2007) *Pimp Your Lesson!: Prepare, Innovate, Motivate, Perfect*. London: Continuum.

J

Judgements

There are many occasions where you will be required to make professional judgements. Indeed, it is possible to regard the whole process of teaching and learning as involving a series of judgements. These occur in a number of basic formats:

- judgements you make on the spur of the moment;
- judgements you make with time to reflect;
- judgements you make alone;
- judgements you make as part of a team.

Spur of the moment judgements can be further subdivided:

- spur of the moment judgements regarding teaching and learning;
- spur of the moment judgements regarding behaviour management.

Teaching and learning judgements tend to evolve over time. After you have been teaching for a while you will add to your repertoire of what to do in a given situation. This type of judgement making relates very closely to what Shulman (1986) called *pedagogic content knowledge*: 'The most useful forms of representation of those ideas, the most powerful analogies, illustrations, examples, explanations, and demonstrations – in a word, the ways of representing and formulating the subject that make it comprehensible to others' (Shulman 1986: 9). Judgements you make of this nature will be taken during the course of the lesson, and often involve reframing ideas and concepts so that all of the students gain an understanding of the issues in question; these can be a key part of assessment for learning.

Spur of the moment judgements regarding behaviour management also develop over time, but for beginning teachers often involve a degree of emotional involvement. In the entry on **behaviour** we offered a number of ways of thinking about this issue, but it will be in the heat of a classroom that you will put these ideas into practice and use your judgement.

Judgements made as part of a team will involve pastoral and curriculum issues. Your input to these is important, and your status as a team member means you will need to think about how you enact judgements which have been reached in this fashion.

Alongside teaching and learning judgements, you will also be called upon to exercise your professional judgement with regards to your personal life, as well as your professional one. The teaching standards state that: 'Teachers uphold public trust in the profession and maintain high standards of ethics and behaviour, within and outside school' (DfE 2012). This means that there will be personal situations in which you may find yourself where you need to think about your behaviour. Examples include being with friends in the pub when a student arrives with their parents, or being at a party where a student arrives as the son/daughter of another invitee. It also encompasses how you react when, say, you are shopping in the supermarket and a parent wants to 'have a word' about their child's performance in your classes. The effect of this is that there is no such thing as an off-duty teacher, and it is the judgements you make, again in the heat of the moment, that can have far-reaching consequences.

Sometimes you will want to try things out. For example, you may feel that the physical classroom layout could be altered in order to improve teaching and learning. These are things that are worth trying, and sometimes you may find that your judgements were wrong, and other times they were right. This is all part of the developing experience. Remember the proverb that some people have ten years' experience, and others have one year's experience ten times. The former is clearly better in teaching!

Some of the hardest things to deal with in teaching are when your judgement is questioned, when you need to account for your actions, or when you face a difficult decision unexpectedly. There are times when it is important to think through what happened. For example, if you have a behavioural incident in your class, you need to write down what happened and report it. If a pupil wants to tell you something 'in confidence' you need to be clear with the pupil that you may have to take further what they tell you.

Making judgements in the heat of the moment is a key teacher skill, and as time passes teachers are able to build on their knowledge and experience, and this is an essential part of being a good teacher.

Key questions

1 What judgements do I make in my teaching?
2 What opportunities are there for me to reflect on these?
3 Who should I share key information with?

References

DfE (2012) Teachers' Standards. https://www.education.gov.uk/ publications/eOrderingDownload/teachers%20standards.pdf (accessed 1 July 2012).

Shulman, L. (1986) Those who understand: knowledge growth in teaching. *Educational Researcher*, 15(2): 4–14.

Further reading

Brooks, V., Abbott, I. and Bills, L. (2007) *Preparing to Teach in Secondary Schools: A Student Teacher's Guide to Professional Issues in Secondary Education*, 2nd edn. Maidenhead: Open University Press.

K

Kinaesthesia

Kinaesthesia means 'the sensation by which bodily position, weight, muscle tension, and movement are perceived'. Within education, the term 'kinaesthetic' relates closely to this definition and has been commonly used to describe a student who likes to learn about something by doing something physically, rather than thinking, listening or reading about it in other ways. Kinaesthetic learners are 'doers'. According to this approach, those students who display an excess amount of energy, get easily distracted or bored or cannot sit still might be 'kinaesthetic' learners.

Drawing on this idea, various models of learning that attempt to categorize students according to their preferred style of learning have sprung up in recent years and have been adopted in some schools. One of these, VAK, argues that students are either visual, auditory or kinaesthetic learners. Through the use of various questionnaires and observation, teachers are able to identify which of these styles of learning (or blend of them) any individual student prefers and they can then design their teaching activities to facilitate their learning most effectively.

This type of approach to learning should be treated with a great degree of suspicion. There is very little robust educational research that shows that it is a successful categorization of students' psychological preferences, and there is plenty that shows that it has little benefit (in fact, some argue it has substantial dangers) when implemented within schools.

Many commentators on these approaches refer back to the work of Howard Gardner, in particular his theory of multiple intelligences. Within this, Gardner wrote about certain people, like dancers or surgeons, who exhibit a high degree of kinaesthetic intelligence. In other words, they use their bodies to create or do something very skilful. However, many educational researchers believe that we are on dangerous ground if we take Gardner's work too literally. Burton writes that a simplistic understanding and application of multiple intelligence theory is dangerous to educational practice yet understandable given various contextual factors such as the way curricula are organized around subject cultures and knowledge boundaries. She continues:

It is easy to see how Gardner's model could gain currency at a common-sense level since people often display particular talents or tendencies. Indeed, the school curriculum and Hirst's (1975) forms of knowledge use similar categorisations. However, if one sees cognition as the processing of information using fairly universal sets of mental strategies it is difficult to conceive of separate, discrete intelligences. Sternberg (1999) points out that although Gardner cites evidence to support his theory he has not carried out research directly to test his model.

(Burton 2007: 13)

Burton's view is that Gardner's model has become a popular educational 'device' in many schools around the world because if offers an alternative to the common view of a single intelligence that pupils exhibit to different extents. Rather, Gardner's model encourages a focus on multiple capabilities that an individual might exhibit and allows them to develop them independently.

Our view is that the careless imposition of models of learning such as VAK do more harm than good. Rather than seeking to understand each student as an individual, they de-personalize approaches to teaching and learning through a simplistic and spurious framework. In our experience, the vast majority of students enjoy learning about something by engaging with it in a practical way. We all have a body and enjoy using it to experience the world around us. We are all kinaesthetic learners whether we like it or not. It makes no conceptual, philosophical or educational sense to divorce the body from the mind, the ears or the eyes. Burton's work clearly shows that the development of a skilful pedagogy is central in ensuring that each student is given an appropriate opportunity to fulfil their learning potential. This is where your attention should be focused.

Key questions

---

1 How can I develop my own pedagogy to include a greater degree of skilful differentiation?
2 Beyond differentiation by task and outcome, what other forms are there?

References

Burton, D. (2007) Psycho-pedagogy and personalised learning. *Journal of Education for Teaching*, 33(1): 5–17.

Hirst, P.H. (1975) *Knowledge and the Curriculum*. London: Routledge.
Sternberg, R. (1999) Intelligence, in R.A. Wilson and F.C. Keil (eds) *The MIT Encyclopedia of the Cognitive Sciences*, pp. 409–11. Cambridge, MA: MIT Press.

Further reading

Burton, D. (2007) Psycho-pedagogy and personalized learning. *Journal of Education for Teaching*, 33(1): 5–17.

Knowledge

Knowledge is a problematic construct. The notion of knowledge has occupied psychologists and philosophers alike for many centuries. How do we know what we know? Are there different types of knowledge?

Let us start with types of knowledge. Knowing how to ride a bike involves a different form of knowing than knowing what happened in Hastings in 1066. A common way of differentiating between these two knowledge types is to refer to the one as *procedural* and the other as *declarative*. Procedural knowledge involves knowing how to do something, what the procedures involved in doing it are, and, importantly, being able to actually do it. Declarative knowledge is knowledge which can be spoken. Another way of describing knowledge was proposed by Bertrand Russell (1911), and involves *knowledge by acquaintance* and *knowledge by description*. These terms have found their way into schools, and are often now referred to as 'knowing about', 'knowing of', and 'knowing that'. 'Knowing about' is factual knowledge, 'knowing of' is knowledge by direct acquaintance, and 'knowing how' involves being able to do something.

However, knowing this alone is not sufficient to be able to demonstrate facility in something. As a student once told their music teacher, 'Playing the piano is easy, you've only got to push the keys in the right order'. As a piece of declarative knowledge the student is essentially correct, but as anyone who has ever tried to play the piano will tell you, in practice it is not quite that simple! So procedural knowledge needs to be developed and needs to be worked at. This is why budding pianists spend many hours practising scales and pieces. They may just be pressing the notes in the right order, but they are developing their facility to do this well. The same is true in sport, in the performing arts, and in anything which involves skill. We want our dentists to have done lots of practice drilling before we let them near our mouths, for example!

How we know what we know is a different matter. Although knowledge is clearly contained in the brain there are questions about how this transfers. The pianists and dentists we described have highly developed sensory-motor skills which transfer information from brain to fingers, but the fingers themselves have been doing the practice. Expert athletes have highly developed facilities too, so the question of how we know what we know becomes a little more complex.

For the teacher, knowing (but what sort of knowledge is this?) that there are different types of knowledge is useful when thinking about planning for learning, and for developing assessment schemes. We saw in the entry for **assessment** that it can be a category error to mistake sound command of English for subject knowledge in assessments. In the same way we want to devise ways of capturing attainment in the various areas of knowledge that our subjects involve. After all, the dentist we spoke of above does not only need to have drill practice, she needs to know what sort of dental problems drilling is a component of solving. So in working out what attainment levels pupils have we need to have thought about the various types of knowledge that are involved in reaching those levels, and how we can best assess them. See also entries on **learning** and **concepts**.

Key questions

1 What types of knowledge does my subject area involve?
2 How can I best develop the various types of knowledge in my teaching?
3 What are the most appropriate ways of assessing the various types of knowledge that will exist in my pupils?

Reference

Russell, B. (1911) Knowledge by Acquaintance and Knowledge by Description. *Proceedings of the Aristotelian Society* (New Series), Vol. XI (1910–1911), pp. 108–28.

Further reading

Bernstein, B. (1971) On the classification and framing of educational knowledge, in M. Young (ed.) *Knowledge and Control*. London: Collier-Macmillan, pp. 47–51.
Greeno, J.G., Pearson, P.D. and Schoenfeld, A.H. (1999) Achievement and theories of knowing and learning, in R. McCormick and C. Paechter (eds) *Learning and Knowledge*, pp. 136–53. London: Paul Chapman.
Hargreaves, A. (2003) *Teaching in the Knowledge Society: Education in the Age of Insecurity*. Maidenhead: Open University Press.

L

Language

All teaching involves language, spoken and written. Educational types of language and patterns of usage relate to:

- the act of teaching itself;
- the subject(s) we are teaching about;
- our own personal background, values and heritage and the way that these are communicated within the classroom.

For example, at the curriculum level every subject exhibits certain language types or words that are designated as being important and which your students need to gain fluency with. Drawing on these, the language patterns within your classroom will mediate your and your students' engagement with particular concepts or forms of knowledge. You are a key person in this environment. How you use language, both formal curriculum language and informal natural language that you bring into the classroom, shape the teaching and learning that occurs. The same will apply for your students too. The structures that you create in your teaching that allow them to use their own informal language will help them make links to the more formal curriculum language that you are hoping they will assimilate.

If this sounds formulaic and prescriptive, it is worth pausing and considering the provisionality and ambiguity of language. These things are at the core of its importance as a tool for thinking and learning:

> The fact that language is not always reliable for causing precise meanings to be generated in someone else's mind is a reflection of its powerful strength as a medium for creating new understanding. It is the inherent ambiguity and adaptability of language as a meaning-making system that makes the relationship between language and thinking so special.
>
> (Mercer 2000: 6)

By becoming aware of this inherent ambiguity you can begin to play with language in your teaching. The richness of language, and the possibilities for multiple meaning making, can be exploited for educational benefits in a range of contexts. Mercer gives us an obvious example from the English curriculum perspective:

> When we are dealing with complex, interesting presentations of ideas, variations in understanding are quite normal and some- times are even welcomed; how otherwise could there be new interpretations of Shakespeare's plays, and why else are we inter- ested in them? . . . The act of reading any text relies on the inter- pretative efforts of a reader, as well as on the communicative efforts and intentions of the author.
>
> (Mercer 2000: 5)

The points that Mercer makes here in relation to the exchange of ideas and development of thought between the author and the reader apply just as forcefully to the relationship between the teacher and the student. So, in summary:

- Be careful what you say in the classroom and be aware that because of the inherent ambiguity of language this will not result in the same meaning or understanding in every student's mind.
- Acknowledge the various language types that exist within the classroom. Allow space for some creative interplay within them.
- In particular, welcome students' natural/informal language within your classroom. Do not seek to impose formal, curriculum language too quickly. Rather, build on their spoken or written responses to teaching activities and nurture their development of a new language type gently.
- Model approaches to the adoption of new language types within your teaching. Do not be afraid of using key terms or phrases in your own language and do not feel the need to interrupt the flow of your language to explain them. Like young children, stu- dents often understand the flow of a full sentence or paragraph without necessarily understanding the meaning of every word or phrase within it.
- Value diverse understandings that emerge from specific teaching activities, and use these diverse understandings to explore the richness of human thought rather than seeking to impose a sim- plistic account for the sake of the curriculum requirements that you are working within.

Key questions

1 How can I broaden my use of language within my teaching to help students engage more effectively with my subject?
2 What practical approaches can I develop to help students use their natural language to explore key concepts or ideas within my lessons?

Reference and further reading

Mercer, N. (2000) *Words and Minds: How we Use Language to Think Together.* London: Routledge.

Leadership

Leadership is a key part of every teacher's work. Whilst some teachers will have specific leadership responsibilities within a school structure, every teacher is required to be a leader in a more fundamental way. Within your classroom, you are the leader of your students! All the models of leadership that you can find out there will be applicable to your role as a primary or secondary school teacher. You will need to be organized, supportive and visionary. You will need to communicate effectively, delegate responsibly, assess regularly and reflect carefully – and much more besides!

That said, of course, there are key roles within a school structure where staff have specific leadership roles. Traditionally, it has been the case that teachers can take on leadership responsibilities within their subject areas or in the pastoral care structures within the school. If you are a young teacher within a typical secondary school, looking out for opportunities to work as an assistant to the Head of Department or Head of Year would be a useful way to gain experience of leadership. Within most primary schools, there will be leadership positions in respect of particular curriculum areas across the school. Larger primary schools may also have a year group structure to help with the leadership of the pastoral care system.

If you have an aspiration to lead a school by becoming a headteacher at some point in your career, then you would be well advised to study for a higher degree early in your teaching career. There are a number of different courses that you can choose from, some of which are sponsored by schools or teaching unions. Finding time to study for a Masters degree or a Doctorate in Education is a major personal commitment and it is unlikely that you will get time off work to do this. You may have to pay for it too. However, it is time and money well spent and will help you immensely as you develop your career.

One of the often forgotten applications of leadership within the school is that provided by students themselves. There are numerous ways in which this can occur:

1   In traditional school structures there will be opportunities for students to develop their leadership skills through Head of House, Head of Year, Prefect, Head Boy/Girl type roles.
2   Sporting teams will promote leadership opportunities such as team and assistant team captains and by providing coaching opportunities for senior students.
3   Drama and musical performances will include key leadership roles such as leader of the school orchestra, responsibilities for front of house, management of props, etc.

However, beyond these types of opportunities, there are many ways that pupils can take on leadership roles within your own classroom. Finney and Tymoczko (2004) describe five ways in which students take on leadership roles within the classroom when they are:

1   selected to model appropriate behaviour, demonstrating and leading others by example;
2   invited to make positive contributions to planning and practice, offering their insights and analysis of teaching and learning to individual teachers in the process of learning;
3   as older and more experienced students, taking the role of teacher's apprentice to support well-defined learning tasks;
4   acting in the role of researcher into some aspect of teaching and learning on behalf of their peers and in collaboration with their teacher;
5   given opportunities for positive curriculum leadership with peers within school and in ways that will be of benefit to other students.

Of course, developing your students' leadership skills is something that you can focus on within your own curriculum planning. However, being an effective leader yourself is the best way that you teach your students these important skills.

> **Key questions**
>
> 1 To what extent does my subject area allow students to develop their own areas of responsibility and leadership?
> 2 How can I build opportunities within my own teaching that allow for students to develop their leadership skills in imaginative ways?

Reference

Finney, J. and Tymoczko, M. (2004) Secondary school students as leaders: examining the potential for transforming music education. *Music Education International*, 2(1): 25–41.

> **Further reading**
>
> Bowen, M. (2011) *Brilliant Subject Leader: What You Need to Know to be a Truly Outstanding Teacher*. Harlow: Pearson Education Limited.

Learning

Learning is complex and multifaceted. There are no simple ways of establishing what a good learning programme looks like, otherwise it would have been done by now, and books such as this would be redundant!

We'll start by thinking about the nature of learning itself. Anna Sfard (1998) has helpfully conceptualized two metaphors for learning, the *acquisition metaphor* and the *participation metaphor*. In the acquisition metaphor, learning is seen as something which an individual acquires: 'This approach, which today seems natural and self-evident, brings to mind the activity of accumulating material goods. The language . . . makes us think about the human mind as a container to be filled with certain materials and about the learner as becoming the owner of these materials' (Sfard 1998: 5). This is unproblematic, and is a relatively straightforward way of looking at things: the teacher has the knowledge, and their job is to pass it on to the pupils.

In contrast, however, in the participation metaphor: 'learning a subject is now conceived of as a process of becoming a member of a certain community. This entails, above all, the ability to communicate in the language of the community and act according to its particular norms' (Sfard 1998: 6). In other words, what takes place here is that 'the permanence of *having* gives way to the constant flux of *doing*' (Sfard 1998: 6, original emphasis). Participation can be conceived of as taking part in a learning activity, and of becoming a member of a community of practice (Lave and Wenger 1991) where practitioners of that activity, whatever it may be, can be seen to cohere as a group. It is also useful to extend the metaphor to think about certain types of learning as participatory. We discuss in the entry on **knowledge** that playing the piano involves a different kind of knowledge to knowing the capital of France. Indeed, using Sfard's metaphors we can classify learning to play the piano as a participatory event. The learner participates in the community of pianists. If someone says that they are learning to play the piano, the usual reaction is 'play us a tune then'; they are not asked to describe the process of playing a tune. This participation is also clearly evidenced in a number of other active pursuits as well, from sport to fine art. But participation is also evidenced in other subjects. Sfard's background is as a researcher in maths education; there are clear links to participation in the ways in which certain maths activities are undertaken, and this holds true across a whole range of other subjects too.

One of the key factors concerning the way in which Sfard conceived these two metaphors can be deduced from the title of her article, 'On two metaphors for learning and the dangers of choosing just one'. What she is saying is that neither one of these metaphors is sufficient in and of itself to account for learning; we need to operate both at the same time.

The implications of this for the teacher are manifold. It is, for instance, really helpful to think about what sorts of knowledge you will be wanting the pupils to acquire and participate in. Whilst this may seem fairly obvious, what is less so is how you break it down so that the stages are clearly delineated. Participatory knowledge may also involve some acquisition *en route* for it to be successful. We would not want pupils learning about science experiences without some form of health and safety knowledge acquisition first, for example. The task for the teacher is to think about which metaphor describes the learning they will be dealing with, and then work out the most appropriate ways of teaching and learning. This extends to assessment too. Our piano learner is likely to take examinations on the instrument which involve playing pieces and scales: the assessment of the participation in the process of playing the piano is evidenced in achievement. This is important. Attainment which is evidenced in achievement is of a different nature to attainment which is evidenced in description, and it is here that the skill of the teacher comes in in devising appropriate ways in which these various forms of learning can be assessed.

Key questions

1 What do I want the pupils to learn? What sort of learning is it?
2 How do I know how much of this learning they have acquired/participated in?
3 How can I think about assessing these different types of knowledge?

References

Lave, J. and Wenger, E. (1991) *Situated Learning: Legitimate Peripheral Participation*. Cambridge: Cambridge University Press.
Sfard, A. (1998) On two metaphors for learning and the dangers of choosing just one. *Educational Researcher*, 27(2): 4–13.

Further reading

Illeris, K. (2007) *How We Learn: Learning and Non-learning in School and Beyond.* Abingdon: Routledge.

Lesson planning

In the entry on **planning** we consider long and medium term planning; here we focus on the requirements of the individual lesson.

We need to disentangle the notion of lesson planning from that of filling in lesson plan documentation, such as that provided by schools, universities and training providers. The lesson plan document is the result of thinking which has taken place; the planning is the important part, the document is simply a way of making that planning visible!

The most important part of a lesson plan is the learning that pupils will do. We describe in the **planning** section how planning for activity is much easier than planning for learning; the same is true of lesson planning. The key questions for lesson planning are:

1 What do I want the pupils to learn?
2 Why do I want them to learn it?
3 What is the best way to go about doing this?

The question of what the pupils should be learning ought to be derived from the medium and long term plans already made. In the case of an individual lesson this should be for how this particular class will enact this particular component of the learning journey. In schools where more than one class will be undertaking the same unit of work it is quite likely that different classes will progress through the learning at different speeds, thus although 9A and 9Z are doing the same topic, 9Z may be racing ahead, in planning terms, whilst 9A are covering the same route a lot slower. This means that lesson plans need to be *differentiated* to suit the unique case of the specific class who will be doing them. This is not a point of worry, it is a normal part of teaching. It also explains why it can be problematic to write lesson plans for a whole term in advance. The medium term planning should give an overview of the journey, the lesson plan plotting the specific route for each class.

The question 'why do I want the pupils to learn X?' is not a trivial one. Of course, in many cases the answer may be that the topic is on the examination syllabus, but for classes where this is not the case it is worth regularly reviewing why the learning is being undertaken. The pupils will certainly not be afraid to ask 'why are we doing this?', and if the answer is 'because I said so' that will hardly satisfy them. The purpose of learning should be to undertake a sequential and progressive journey, where topics interlink in a clear fashion, and where concepts are developed so as to be useful for subsequent stages in the course of a unit. This is where discussions between teachers are useful, as the novice teacher may have only a limited grasp initially of the progression required between short, medium and long term plans, whereas those who have been teaching for a while will have to deal with these interrelationships as they play out over the course of a Key Stage.

Key questions

1 What are the differences between *learning* and *doing* in my lessons?
2 How does this lesson link with others in the medium/long term plan?
3 How will I develop the learning from this lesson?

Further reading

Beere, J. (2010) *The Perfect Ofsted Lesson*. Bancyfelin: Crown House.
Moon, B. and Murphy, P. (eds) (1999) *Curriculum in Context*. London: Paul Chapman.

Listening

Listening is clearly an important skill for learners, and in this entry we consider some of the issues concerned with listening, and ways in which you can foster it in your students. Listening can be met as part of National Curriculum assessment for English, modern foreign languages and music. Our concern here is not so much with these as with ways in which listening is encountered in all subjects, as part of the normal everyday interaction between teacher and learners.

Listening involves hearing. We know that in unimpaired individuals hearing involves perception, but that there is significant mental processing involved too. Michael Rost (2010) discusses listening as involving

> overlapping types of processing: neurological processing, linguistic processing, semantic processing, and pragmatic processing . . . neurological processing [involves] consciousness, hearing, and attention . . . linguistic processing [is] the aspect of listening that requires input from a linguistic source – what most language users would consider the fundamental aspect of listening to language . . . semantic processing [is] the aspect of listening that integrates memory and prior experience into understanding events . . . While closely related to semantic processing, pragmatic processing evolves from the notion of relevance – the idea that listeners take an active role in identifying relevant factors in verbal and non-verbal input and inject their own intentions into the process of constructing meaning.
>
> (Rost 2010: 9)

Whilst it is the case that there is very little that you as a teacher can do about the perception of verbal information by students, there is something you can do about the processing of that information, and that is to consider the effects of what you say upon how it is received. From their work with young children Spooner and Woodcock suggest four basic rules for promoting good listening in students:

- Look at the person who is talking.
- Sit still.
- Stay quiet so that everyone can listen.
- Listen to ALL of the words.

(Spooner and Woodcock 2010: 7)

Although designed for the early years, there are clear spin-offs for use in primary and secondary schools, where we know listening can be a problem.

In particular, the examples they give for the last of their rules seem particularly apposite in much older settings too; this is the notion of listening to all of the words. They describe some problems here:

1   Children may not follow instructions given to the whole class and will only listen if they are called by name.
2   Children may listen to the first part of an instruction, think they know what to do, and then stop listening.
3   With a familiar activity, children may not listen at all as they have already experienced the task and think they know what to do.
4   Some instructions may contain a 'trigger phrase' such as 'Line up at the door' or 'It's nearly dinnertime'. When children hear this, they don't pay attention to anything else.

(Spooner and Woodcock 2010: 8)

These are clearly relevant to older students too. So, what can you as a teacher do about this? One of the first things is to think about *what* you are saying, and, second, *how* you are saying it. If you are going to use a 'trigger phrase', then try to think about giving instructions in a different way. When observing student teachers, for example, a common example of this is for the student teacher to start a sentence with 'It's nearly home time . . .': anything important that follows will be lost. If the instruction was to be about finishing off, organizing homework or packing away, all of these subsidiary instructions have been lost behind the trigger phrase. We appreciate that it is difficult to monitor in advance every word you use in the teaching situation, but some phrases like this are best avoided. The sequencing of giving verbal information is a key skill for beginning teachers to work on.

Beall et al. made the observation that 'effective listeners are generally more successful in school' (Beall et al. 2008: 126). With this being the case, it is clearly worthwhile to spend time developing students' listening skills. One of the effects of the national literacy strategy has been to focus whole-school attention onto this. As should be apparent by now, we hope that developing the listening skills of learners is not seen as something which is wholly the responsibility of the English department.

Key questions

1   What is the message that I want to impart? What is the best way of phrasing this?
2   Am I inadvertently using 'trigger phrases'?
3   Is there a whole-school policy on listening? If so, who is responsible for enacting it?

References

Beall, M.L., Gill-Rosier, J., Tate, J. and Matten, A. (2008) State of the context: listening in education. *The International Journal of Listening,* 22(2): 123–32.

Rost, M. (2010) *Teaching and Researching: Listening.* Harlow: Longman.

Spooner, L. and Woodcock, J. (2010) *Teaching Children to Listen: A Practical Approach to Developing Children's Listening Skills.* London: Continuum International Publishing Group.

Further reading

Spooner, L. and Woodcock, J. (2010) *Teaching Children to Listen: A Practical Approach to Developing Children's Listening Skills.* London: Continuum International Publishing Group.

Literacy

Teaching students literacy is not solely the role of the English teachers in a school. It is expected that everyone has a part to play in this important activity. As the DfE observes:

> Students should be taught in all subjects to express themselves correctly and appropriately and to read accurately and with understanding. Students should be taught the technical and specialist vocabulary of subjects and how to use and spell these words. They should also be taught to use the patterns of language vital to understanding and expression in different subjects. These include the construction of sentences, paragraphs and texts that are often used in a subject.
>
> (DfE 2012)

Literacy across the curriculum, often abbreviated to LAC, is likely to figure as a policy in the school in which you work. There may be some common guidance which is designed to help students achieve consistency in the ways in which they work with text both in and across subjects. A common example of this is to be found in the headings for work. Many schools have adopted the LAC premise that all subjects in the school will adopt a common format for headings, dates, underlining and margins. This relatively simple and low-level literacy strategy is helpful both for saving time in lessons in that there is a common format, and is also helpful for students who have specific learning difficulties, as they only need to master one set of instructions which will work everywhere, rather than knowing to do it like this for Mrs Jones, and like that for Mr Singh.

Literacy also involves the way in which you treat subject-specific vocabulary. For example, are there words which are used in a specific subject which might not be used, or used as much, elsewhere? Are you able to compile a list of words which are specific to your subject? Many schools have these words put up on the classroom walls as part of the learning display. Does your school have examples of this?

Or there are words which have a specific meaning in one subject, and may mean something different in another subject? Here are some possible examples:

Higher: means what in PE? Art? Music? Science?
Composition: means what in English? Music? Art? Drama? Geography?
Texture: means what in . . . ?
Pitch: means what in . . . ?
Form: means what in . . . ?
Compass: means what in . . . ?
Flow: means what in . . . ?

Do you need to make sure you explain how the words you are using in your subject might not have the same meaning as the same word in another subject?

Literacy involves more than words and text. As James Britton observed, 'reading and writing float on a sea of talk' (Britton 1983: 11). It is worth thinking about whether you need to explain to the pupils that a word you are using in your subject may not have the same meaning as the same word in a different subject.

In thinking about developing writing, it is useful to model how you would like the students' writing to take shape. If there are ways of expressing ideas which are pertinent to your subject, then these will benefit from attention being paid to them in class time. LAC policies might involve commonalities, but specificities remain very much in the realms of subjects.

Key questions

1   What aspects of learning involving literacy do I want to develop?
2   How can I best model the thinking, subject-specific terminologies and means of expression that I want the students to adopt?
3   What do I understand literacy to entail in my curriculum area?

References

Britton, J. (1983) Writing and the story of the world, in B.M. Kroll and C.G. Wells (eds) *Explorations in the Development of Writing: Theory, Research, and Practice*. pp. 3–30. New York: John Wiley & Sons.

DfE (2012) Use of Language. www.education.gov.uk/schools/teaching-andlearning/curriculum/a00199695/use-of-language (accessed 12 September 2012).

Further reading

DfES (2001) *Literacy Across the Curriculum: Key Stage 3 Strategy*. London: Department for Education and Skills.

Goodwin, P. (ed.) (1999) *The Literate Classroom*. Abingdon: Routledge.

Literature

In this entry we want to argue that your engagement with the literature about teaching is a cornerstone of your work as an effective teacher. By literature, we mean:

- published materials including books about education;
- academic research published in peer-reviewed educational journals;
- government publications;
- materials produced by professional subject associations;
- web-based materials, including blogs, forums and other websites.

The precise ways in which you engage with these is clearly a matter for you alone. But we believe that the work that you do as a teacher can be usefully enhanced and developed through an engagement with the established educational literature. Elsewhere (Savage and Fautley 2010), we have written about the ABC of critical reading for education. This is summarized below.

1   *Associate with ideas and apply them to your work*
    First, at any stage of your career it is important to associate your own thinking and pedagogy with the many schools of thought that have considered and dwelt on the huge themes related to educational practice over the years. But reading in and of itself is not enough. You will need to apply these ideas to your work too.

2   *Be broad and balanced*
Second, be broad and balanced in your range of reading. Try to avoid becoming overly dependent on one author and, importantly, on one 'type' of literature. For example, if you only read Government reports on behaviour management and policy then you fall into the trap of ignoring the wider contextual and historical considerations that might have informed these political decisions. Similarly, an overdependence on published educational research within academic journals *may* make it difficult to associate with ideas and apply them within your day-to-day work as a teacher.

3   *Challenge and connect*
Just because something is in print, do not assume it is correct! This applies to everything that you read. You will need to challenge ideas and test them out. This testing process may involve you discussing ideas with other colleagues, your mentor or other students. It may involve you broadening your range of reading through considering other sources. But, and this is vitally important, your own thinking will also be challenged by the ideas that you encounter. Connecting your own teaching with ideas drawn from the reading you undertake should result in you becoming a more articulate, confident, skilful and reflective teacher.

So, for all these reasons we believe that a proactive engagement with the 'literature' of education is a vital component at all stages of your teaching career.

Key questions

1   How can I make time in a busy schedule to ensure that I read an appropriate blend of the education literature?
2   Realistically, what targets can I set myself here?

Reference

Savage, J. and Fautley, M. (2010) *A Reflective Reader for Secondary Education*. Exeter: Learning Matters.

Further reading

Kincheloe, J. (2012) *Teachers as Researchers: Qualitative Inquiry as a Path to Empowerment*. London: Routledge.

M

Management

In our entry on **leadership** we discuss how all teachers are leaders in one way or another. Here, we will be discussing the management of schools, the people involved and the skills they need.

Schools are managed by two main groups: a senior leadership or management team and a group of governors. The senior leadership team is led by the school's headteacher and normally contains other senior members of staff; the governing body is led by the Chair of Governors. The role of governors has been discussed elsewhere in this book, so our focus here will be on the role of the headteacher and senior leadership team.

The management of schools is a serious business. Many schools have a budget of hundreds of thousands, if not millions, of pounds of public money that needs to be handled responsibly. And, much more important than the money, the lives of hundreds of children can be affected, for better or worse, by the way in which a school is managed.

For these reasons, headteachers and others on a school's senior leadership team need to be trained and equipped with a range of skills in order to fulfil their responsibilities to their school and wider community. Key skills that school managers need include the ability to:

- Set out the strategic vision, direction and development of the school. This will include the ability to plan for the school's future needs and how it will develop to fulfil these within the local and national context.
- Manage the teaching and learning throughout the school, monitoring and evaluating its effectiveness by various methods including benchmarking and target-setting.
- Lead and manage staff, including all teaching and non-teaching staff. In particular, school leaders need to implement an effective performance management or appraisal system to ensure that all teachers are working to the highest possible standards.
- Deploy staff and resources effectively to meet specific objectives in line with the school's strategic plan.

- Communicate well, be trustworthy and accountable. Headteachers and others need to be transparent in their dealings with parents, staff, governors, local employers and the wider community.
- Be financially competent and able to deal with the prioritization and monitoring of school finances, together with the ability to develop and implement fund raising strategies when needed.

Although the vast majority of headteachers came into the teaching profession as teachers, a significant degree of training is required before one can develop from a teacher into a senior leader. Fortunately, if this is something that you are interested in doing the progression from teacher to senior leader and ultimately headteacher is a well travelled journey. There will be opportunities in most schools to gain experience in managing a department, including staffing and resources, before moving onto a larger role such as Head of Year or a Deputy Head position with certain responsibilities (e.g. continuing professional development or curriculum management). Ultimately, having gained experience at department level and higher up the school structure you can apply for headship positions.

However, at some point in this process, you will be well advised to undertake further training such as the National Professional Qualification for Headship. This training programme follows a modular curriculum based on Master's level criteria and focuses on giving you the knowledge, skills and attributes to be a successful headteacher. It can be completed 'on the job' and takes between six and 18 months in total. In order to access the programme, you will need the endorsement of your current senior line manager (normally your headteacher). The programme is run by the National College for School Leadership.

Thankfully, the days of falling into a headship at the end of a teaching career are well and truly gone. Being an effective manager requires a different, but related, set of skills to being an effective teacher. The two roles are not the same. However, if you aspire to fulfilling a management position at some point in your teaching career do make this known to your immediate line manager and/or headteacher. They should be able to support you in the development of an appropriate skill set and give you opportunities to exercise these new skills in an appropriate way.

Key questions

1 Which of the skills I currently have as a teacher will be useful for me in a management position?
2 What new skills will I need to develop in order to be an effective manager?

Further reading

National College: http://www.education.gov.uk/nationalcollege/index (accessed 16 July 2012).
National Professional Qualification for Headship (NPQH): http://www. education.gov.uk/nationalcollege/index/professional-development/ npqh.htm (accessed 16 July 2012).

Mixed ability settings

In the section on **ability** we explore why the notion of ability is itself a problematic construct, and in the section on **streaming and setting** we examine ways of organizing pupils. In this entry we concentrate on mixed ability teaching, why its proponents argue that it is a good thing, and ways in which you can teach appropriately in mixed ability settings.

In **streaming and setting** we observe that according to government figures the majority of English, maths and science lessons in UK secondary schools are taught in classes which are set for ability. The figures for other subjects are harder to obtain, but many teachers of non-core subjects view their teaching as being essentially mixed ability anyway. As one secondary school art teacher observed, 'although they come to art lessons in their modern language sets, they may as well be mixed ability for all the difference that makes'. One of the conundrums of mixed ability grouping is that some say that it benefits the lower ability students, whilst ability grouping is good for those of higher ability:

> There do, however, appear to be differential benefits for students in selective and unselective systems. Selection and ability grouping tend to work to the advantage of students in the higher attaining groups, while unselective systems and mixed ability grouping tend to benefit those in the lower attaining groups.
> (Ireson and Hallam 2001: 17)

Mixed ability teaching means that students of all abilities within the intake of the school will be present in classes. Of course, this has a different meaning in schools which select according to ability, such as grammar schools, but the essential feature remains the same: students have not been organized into approximately homogenous groupings. For teachers this means that teaching mixed ability classes involves preparing and delivering lessons with differentiation, which challenge the most able whilst being suitable for lower abilities. One of the criticisms levelled at mixed ability teaching is that it tends to aim for the middle and in doing so misses the upper and lower ability bands. However, personalizing learning means all teaching should be aimed at real, named, students, not at some mythical 'average' group, and so this should alleviate some of these issues.

What does tend to differ between mixed ability and setted groups are the attitudes and expectations of teachers towards them:

> The great majority of teachers teaching sets expected a faster rate of work from the more able students (89%). In mixed ability classes there was less expectation that able students would work at a faster rate (69%). Whether students were in mixed ability or set classes, the majority of teachers expected greater depth of work from the more able students (86%). In mixed ability classes teachers expected more independent thought from the higher ability students (84%) than in set classes (76%). Most teachers expected the more able children to take greater responsibility for their own written work whether they were in mixed ability (71%) or sets (76%).
>
> (Ireson and Hallam 2001: 139)

If you are faced with mixed ability groups, there are a number of actions you can take, depending on age, phase and subject. Primary school teachers are likely to be involved with mixed ability classes across the board, whereas secondary school teachers are more likely to meet them in non-core subjects. The essential features of good teaching remain the same, though, however the groupings are arranged.

One of the first actions you should take is to find out about the prior attainment of *all* of the students in your class. Having established this you can then begin to plan for the students in the class. This may entail having different plans for parallel groups in the same year group. You can also think about stretching the most able, in ways which do not solely involve helping other students; this is an inadequate form of differentiation. You will also want to be stretching the less able, and doing so not just using 'keep them busy' tasks. Finally the middle ability range of a class covers a wide spectrum; these students also need stretch and challenge.

As we have said elsewhere, breadth and depth are different areas of educational attainment, and you will need to think about which is appropriate for you to work on, and it may well be that these differ at times within the mixed ability grouping.

> **Key questions**
>
> 1 How are my classes set/streamed? Are all my classes mixed ability, even if set/streamed, because that is the nature of my subject?
> 2 What does 'mixed ability' mean in the specific cases of the classes I teach?
> 3 How can I plan so as to ensure I am stretching the most able, challenging the middle, and supporting the least able?

Reference

Ireson, J. and Hallam, S. (2001) *Ability Grouping in Education.* London: Paul Chapman.

Further reading

Boaler, J., Wiliam, D. and Brown, M. (2000) Students' experiences of ability grouping: disaffection, polarisation and the construction of failure. *British Educational Research Journal*, 26(5): 631–48.

Dillon, J. and Maguire, M. (eds) (2011) *Becoming a Teacher: Issues in Secondary Teaching*, 4th edn. Maidenhead: Open University Press.

Modelling

We saw in the entry for **brain** that learning from observation is more straightforward than learning from a set of instructions. This is one aspect of modelling as it is applied in schools. When we are learning a new skill or preparing to undertake a challenging task, it helps if we can:

- see someone else do it first;
- hear them 'thinking aloud' about the decisions they are making;
- hear them explaining what they are doing at each stage;
- ask questions about the process as it is happening;
- identify problems as they arise and think aloud about how to solve them;
- slow the process down to look in detail at the most difficult part and ask for further clarification;

- see the process demonstrated visually, sometimes repeated more than once if it is difficult to grasp;
- be given time to discuss what has been done and predict next steps.

(DfES 2004: 4)

This gives a good overview of what is involved when engaged in presenting a new idea, skill, concept or technique to the class. It is especially important to notice the emphasis on slowing down and thinking out loud.

Thinking out loud is a key aspect of modelling, and it need not apply only to when doing something for the first time. It is a useful pedagogic skill to demonstrate the steps that you, the teacher, are undertaking when you work through a process to arrive at an answer. It is particularly useful when there is a series of stages which need to be gone through in order for the students to be able to do this by themselves. In many subjects the 'show your working' notion is an important one in written tasks; in modelling the equivalent is thinking out loud.

In psychology literature the idea of 'think out loud protocols' is well established. These are used when people are asked to talk through the thought processes they are engaged in when undertaking a task of some sort. This has a clear application in education, and it is useful for you, the teacher, to employ this technique.

Another appropriate way the teacher can employ modelling in the classroom is in the use of subject-specific terminologies. This is particularly helpful when discussing topics from the standpoint of a subject-specific approach. In the **thinking** section of this book we discuss what is involved in thinking like an artist. Modelling involves not only thinking like an artist, but in talking like one, and using the vocabulary appropriately too.

Modelling can be applied throughout all teaching and does not have to apply to subject-specific areas. Many generic skills can also be modelled. For instance, note-taking is a key component of many aspects of education, and is also one which may be missing from a taught programme. Modelling what constitutes good note-taking would be one way for this to be developed.

Key questions

1 Am I modelling learning?
2 Am I modelling domain-specific thinking?
3 Do I model thinking out loud?

Reference

DfES (2004) *Pedagogy and Practise: Teaching and Learning in Secondary Schools (Unit 6: Modelling)*. London: DfES.

Further reading

Bransford, J.D., Brown, A.L. and Cocking, R.R. (eds) (1999) *How People Learn: Brain, Mind, Experience and School*. Washington, DC: National Academy Press.

Motivation

Everyone involved in education needs to be well motivated! Motivation is characterized in two main ways: *intrinsic motivation* and *extrinsic motivation*. The vast majority of successful people comment on the importance of motivation, e.g. geniuses such as Newton and Darwin had a great degree of perseverance and motivation as well as extremely high intelligence (Cox 1926).

Intrinsic motivation is the desire to carry out an activity for the sake of the activity itself. It has three main characteristics:

1   *Interest* Anyone is more likely to be motivated by something that has captured their interest rather than being of no perceived value.
2   *Competence* The motivating effects of increasing competence in a particular domain are considerable. Students will seek out activities and persist in them for longer if they feel they are mastering something, particularly if they are doing this on their own.
3   *Self-determination* This moves students beyond the need for success in a particular activity. To be intrinsically motivated, they have to feel that they are pursuing the activity because they have chosen to do so. They have to feel that they are working on an activity, in a particular subject area, for their own reasons rather than for yours.

Intrinsic motivation is contrasted with extrinsic motivation. Extrinsic motivation could be associated with external rewards such as praise, prizes, grading, positive testing or even the avoidance of punishments. Extrinsic rewards can lead to enduring improvements in a student's work if they are appropriately targeted and their delivery does not undermine that student's own sense of intrinsic motivation. For example, Starko comments that:

Classrooms that operate under threat of tests and grades are centering on controlling extrinsic motivation. Praise that is doled out to good pupils without a clear indication of what they did well can have a similar effect. . . . Praise that gives pupils information about what they did well and enhances their sense of competence is less detrimental. The more obvious the external motivation, the more problematic it is.

(Starko 2001: 325–6)

In your pedagogy, it is important to consider the balance between intrinsic and extrinsic motivation. Some writers suggest that extrinsic motivation might be more beneficial early in the learning process, with intrinsic motivation taking over at a later stage:

Teachers can provide extrinsic forms of motivation, e.g. incentives or rewards, but it is also important that children are encouraged to develop intrinsic forms of motivation, e.g. curiosity. The former will aid the immediate acquisition of knowledge of skills at school, but the latter will sustain a person's interest in a field and encourage an individual to become a lifelong learner. Once children have developed or found their individual forms of intrinsic motivation, extrinsic motivation should be applied cautiously, as it might stifle creativity.

(Craft et al. 2001: 23)

The manner in which you apply intrinsic and extrinsic motivation will depend on the individual students and classes that you teach. You will have to draw on these ideas and see what does or does not work. There is no correct 'balance' between in any particular pedagogical approach intrinsic and extrinsic motivation.

Key questions

1 What specific techniques for intrinsic and extrinsic motivation can I identify within my own teaching?
2 To what extent should I balance these approaches in my teaching? At what particular moments should I be expecting students to be intrinsically motivated? When can I constructively reward them through extrinsic motivational techniques?

References

Cox, C. (1926) *Genetic Studies of Genius: The Early Mental Traits of Three Hundred Geniuses*. Palo Alto, CA: Stanford University Press.

Craft, A., Jeffrey, B. and Leibling, M. (2001) *Creativity in Education*. London and New York: Continuum.

Starko, A. (2001) *Creativity in the Classroom*. London and New Jersey: Lawrence Erlbaum Associates.

Further reading

Gillet, N., Vallerand, R. and Lafrenière, M. (2012) Intrinsic and extrinsic school motivation as a function of age: the mediating role of autonomy support. *Social Psychology of Education*, 15(1): 77–95.

Schunk, D., Pintrich, P. and Meece, J. (2008) *Motivation in Education: Theory, Research and Applications*. London: Pearsons.

Myths

There are many myths about teaching; in this section we look at some of the most common.

1 Teachers finish at half past three and go home

By the time you have done your post-school clearing up, done bus duty and seen the students off the premises, it will then be time to go and get your marking for the evening, see some parents, take a rehearsal, go to a meeting . . . and that is before you get home, with marking and preparation for the next day. There are few quiet evenings in teaching! Legally teachers are required to work for 1 265 hours per year. However, surveys regularly find that teachers work around 50 hours per week on average, more than in many other professions.

2 Teachers get long holidays

For some people, work is what you do at work. For a teacher, work is not just standing in front of classes; there is preparation, marking, pastoral matters, trips, and so on. For non-teachers holidays are when you are not working. For teachers, school holidays are when the students are not in school. This does not mean there is no work to be done, nor that teachers are not doing it. This significant difference needs to be carefully explained to people who equate working at home with idling.

3 Teachers get paid well

Teaching is, at the moment, still a graduate profession. Pay can compare well with some jobs, but there is no overtime, no weekend payments for sports, plays, trips, etc. And teaching is full-on: there is no opportunity to coast in teaching. It is a high-demand, high-stress occupation. And teachers have no opportunity for earning a bonus, unlike bankers!

4 Teachers get good pensions

But they have been paying into them since starting work, and for many teachers, a good pension is compensation for what they see as not such good salaries during the course of their career. Assuming they make it to the end, of course, pensions are favourable but Government policy in this area may make them less so in years to come.

5 Teachers get to go on free holidays

I think you'll find that's a school trip. And if you think taking 40 teenagers to a foreign country, preventing them drinking, snogging, smoking or worse, when it's 2.30 a.m. and you have spent all day wandering around a museum is a holiday, you're welcome to try. School trips are good learning, social and educational activities. But free holidays, no. And because of exam pressures, most schools will only allow such trips in school holidays (see above) with, if lucky, a Friday afternoon off to dash to the port for a cheap crossing (which you spend helping the sick, those who ate all their food *en route*, and trying to keep the older-looking ones from the alcohol in the bars).

6 Those who can, do; those who can't, teach

Actually those who can often make the worst teachers, as they cannot understand why anybody cannot do what they can. In a survey of students in a youth orchestra the young players much preferred the teachers, rather than the professional musicians, helping them, as the teachers showed them what to do whereas the professionals said 'just do it like this', which if you can't do it, doesn't help.

7 Teachers' unions are all Marxists

As in any group of people, teaching employs a wide range of participants, and their political beliefs are spread across the spectrum. True, some like to get involved more than others, but the odd five-minute soundbite from an annual conference of a 'loony leftie' is no more typical than to assume all policeman say "'ello, 'ello, 'ello, what's goin' on 'ere?'! Teachers unions do good work developing learning materials, researching current events and providing a safety net for their members. Their legal departments look after the teachers falsely accused by mendacious students. They also provide buffers against unscrupulous employment practises.

8 Good discipline is easy, you just have to shout a lot

In some cases shouting is what students hear at home. SHOUTING IS NORMAL. Shouting at these students will probably not help, and anyway, what will you do if they shout back? Good discipline is not an easy thing to establish, it takes time and is relationship dependent. Shouting may work in some schools, and with some classes, but it pays a heavy toll on a teacher's health to be shouting all day. Other ways are better.

9 I got the cane, didn't do me any harm

It's been illegal now for many years. So has hanging.

Key questions

1 How will I deal with the common myths when I encounter them?
2 What would I add to this list?
3 What annoys me most about non-teachers' attitudes to teachers?
4 What do my non-teaching friends think I do?

Further reading

The *Times Educational Supplement*

N

Networking

Networking is an important part of many careers. Despite the time intensive nature of teaching, and the obvious fact that you have to be in a particular place at a specific time, there are plenty of ways to network effectively and ensure that you are up to date with what is going on. So, if you have not done so already, why not:

1   Join a teaching union. Apart from the obvious legal benefits, your union will run a range of national and local events for its members where you will get to meet other teachers, discuss a range of current issues and get access to a plethora of support materials.
2   Join a subject association. These exist for the vast majority of subjects being taught in our schools (some have more than one!) and, like a union, you will get the opportunity to meet up with other teachers who share a passion for your subject both in your local area and at national events such as annual conferences.
3   Use online forums to network. There are lots of these. Two of the largest are those run by the *Times Education Supplement* (http://www.tes.co.uk/forums.aspx?navcode=14) and *The Guardian* (http://http://teachers.guardian.co.uk/). Both of these sites allow you to network virtually with teachers across a range of subject or other themed education forums.
4   Utilize LinkedIn, Twitter, Facebook and other social media to help your networking. Whilst these tools might not be for everyone, it is important to recognize that they are playing an increasingly important part in contemporary life. We would urge you to be cautious about setting up a personal account in any social network and using this for both your private life and work simultaneously. However, the benefits of networking through social media can be immense.
5   Create a link to your local higher education institution. Many of these run teacher education programmes, both for initial teacher training and continuing professional development, and welcome

the input of teachers within these programmes. You may also be interested in hosting a student teacher within your department or school. This can have very positive benefits for your work as well as the student's.

6 Prioritize making some links to teachers in other local schools. These links used to be developed by local authority education officers but this is seldom the case any more. The local links being established by schools as part of broader education networks can help you, as an individual teacher, find out about what is going on in the school down the road and lead to the development of productive networking opportunities at a personal level.

Effective networking has many positive benefits. As we discuss in our entry on **collaboration**, one of the dangers of teaching is becoming professionally isolated. You need to be proactive about the establishment of an appropriate network of support for yourself and your work. Not only will this help you teach better but it will also make teaching a more rewarding activity that will sustain your interest and motivation throughout your career.

Ultimately, any one kind of networking is only as good as the amount of time and effort that you put into it. So, make a positive effort to choose an appropriate networking mechanism and then be proactive about contributing to it fully. What you get out of it will probably be equal to the amount you put in.

Key question

How can I make best use of the time and resources I have available to network effectively and ensure that I do not become professionally isolated?

Further reading

There are many resources out there about how to network effectively. A lot of these are focused on the business community but there are important lessons here for all professionals, including teachers. Why not start with:

Robinson, L. (2012) Top 10 Tips for Effective Networking. Available from http://www.law.ed.ac.uk/careers/files/Top%2010%20tips%20for%20effective%20networking.pdf.pdf (accessed 17 July 2012).

Vermeiren, J. (2007) *Let's Connect!: A Practical Guide for Highly Effective Professional Networking*. New York: Morgan James Publishing.

Numeracy

As with literacy and the obvious association with English teaching, there can be a temptation to think that numeracy is the right and proper work of the maths department, and that teachers of other subjects need not concern themselves with it. However, again as with literacy, there are many aspects of numeracy which figure in every subject. Numeracy across the curriculum, often abbreviated to NAC, is going to impact upon you and your teaching.

For example, consider the topic of *measurement*. It is clear that this is going to appear in a number of different curriculum areas. Here are a few examples:

1 Geography: map scales, distances;
2 PE: distances run, jumped, thrown, timings;
3 Science: weighing, size, mass, speed;
4 D&T: precision, sizes, weighing;
5 History: changing roles of units of measurement over time;
6 RE: measurements in other cultures;
7 Drama: stage settings, lighting;
8 Music: sound levels, timings, beats;
9 Art: perspective, scale;
10 . . . and many more besides!

This is just a simple look at a complex topic, and doubtless you can think of many more examples from your own subject area.

From this list, questions that arise include:

1 Who should teach measuring?
2 When should they teach it?
3 How much detail should they go into?

These are clearly pertinent to NAC. In both primary and secondary schools there will be different requirements for measuring in different subjects. Weighing tiny amounts of chemicals in science is similar to weighing ingredients in food technology, but differs by degree. Measuring how far a pupil has achieved in the long jump is similar to measuring a distance on a map, but again differs in scale.

For an integrated NAC approach the school will have considered this from a curriculum-mapping exercise, where topics taught across a range of subjects will have been looked at for their interlinking. What this will mean is that there will be a basic level of measurement pedagogy, perhaps taught in maths, and then more subject-specific aspects will be taught in the subjects concerned. This helps address the issue that in some cases the only people who know the full extent of curriculum mapping in a school are the students! Undertaking this type of approach has two main benefits: it prevents duplication of effort in a cramped curriculum, where learners are essentially taught the same thing twice, and it helps prevent the converse of this, where teachers assume someone else has taught it when they have not, and thus there are gaps in pupil knowledge. Doing this also goes some way towards Jo Boaler's concern that 'mathematics can be learned in school, embedded within any particular learning structures, and then lifted out of school to be applied to any situation in the real world' (Boaler 1993: 12). However, it is often the case that this does not necessarily happen without some assistance.

NAC can play a part in much smaller ways too. One school found that students had to draw margins in their books using four different widths. This seemingly inoffensive issue was causing unnecessary headaches for special needs students, and for those for whom simply remembering was problematic. By having a school standard of margin-width this problem was solved. Sometimes it can be surprising how the smallest things can cause considerable anxiety among students, and these can often be ones which are relatively marginal (pun intended!) to the learning experience.

What is useful for you as a teacher is to think about what aspects of numeracy you will want the students to employ in your subject, and then endeavour to ascertain whether they have done something similar to this before, with another teacher, or in another subject, and then plan for your delivery of it accordingly.

Key questions

1 What aspects of numeracy do I want the students to engage with in my teaching and learning plans?
2 Do I know whether this has been taught anywhere else in the school?
3 Do I know how well the students are able to do this?
4 Do they need some practice exercises beforehand, or are they able to do it well enough already?

Reference

Boaler, J. (1993) The role of contexts in the mathematics classroom: do they make mathematics more real? *For the Learning of Mathematics,* 13(2): 12–17.

Further reading

Ellis, V. (ed.) (2007) *Learning and Teaching in Secondary Schools*, 3rd edn. Exeter: Learning Matters.

Grigg, R. (2010) *Becoming an Outstanding Primary School Teacher.* Harlow: Longman.

O

Objectives

In many people's minds *aims* and *objectives* are linked closely together. In our aims section we concentrated on broad aims for schools and for teaching generally. In this objectives section we are going to focus on specific learning intended to take place over the short and medium term. This section also links with those on lesson planning and planning.

There is no universal language for lesson planning statements, so the way in which we are going to use the terminology 'objectives' here may be different from the one in which you work. We are going to use objectives to mean the specific things that you want students to learn during a programme of study or scheme of work. In some cases these are called lesson objectives, learning outcomes, or intended learning statements. The important thing for us is that objectives are about *actual and intended* learning activity. Whilst it is very laudable that you feel your objective for a series of lessons is that all the students will learn to love the music of Beethoven, this is unlikely to be achieved! But it is realistic for the students to learn the context in which the *Pastoral Symphony* was written, and gain some understanding of the notion of imagery in music. Writing lesson objectives which are specific is a difficult task. Elsewhere in this book we discuss how it is much easier to plan for activity than it is for learning. The same holds true for objectives: it is simpler to write task objectives than learning ones.

Thinking about being specific in objective writing, some schools advocate the use of SMART objectives, SMART being some variation on the following terms:

- specific
- measurable
- attainable
- relevant
- timely

One of the reasons for being specific in producing lesson objectives is that it focuses attention onto what will be learned. So, consider these two examples:

1   In this lesson the students will learn about World War I.
2   In this lesson the students will learn about trench warfare on the opening day of the Somme battle.

These two lesson objectives were for the same lesson, yet the second one is much more specific. It also has the advantage, which the first one lacks, that the teacher can use it to discover whether or not the objective has been met.

In many schools there is a requirement for lesson objectives to be broken down according to ability. These are often along the lines of all-most-some, must-should-could, or some similar form of differentiated statements. Here is an example from a music lesson:

1   All students will be able to play the bass line of the chord sequence for a 12-bar blues.
2   Most students will be able to play the chord sequence using triads.
3   Some students will be able to play the bass line and the triads together.

Jackie Beere gives an example from an English lesson:

By the end of this lesson you will be able to:

1   Note how the writer has used language effectively;
2   Comment on how the writer uses language to engage the writer using quotations.
                                                    (Beere 2010: 19)

What is important here is that in each of the cases the learning is developmental.

The use of objectives for planning in this way is useful, but we have seen examples where instead of being used as a component of the production of useful lesson material, the learning objectives have become ends in their own right. In these cases the objectives are written up, the class copy them down, and then at the end of the lesson the objectives are revisited. This formulaic (and, frankly, tedious) repetition does nothing to help learning. The point of the learning objectives as we have described them is for the teacher's benefit in planning. Indeed, we see a lot of value on occasion in the students not knowing what they are going to learn, and it coming as a revelation to them! In a similar vein the attaching of National Curriculum levels to learning objectives may not necessarily be helpful, in that the levels were originally meant to be used at the end of a Key Stage only.

A further useful characteristic of a good learning objective is that it is *measurable* (the M from SMART). A well-crafted learning objective can become its own assessment criterion. This is helpful when determining whether or not the students have met the requirements of the learning objective. In assessment for learning terms this is far more useful than the formulaic approach outlined above, as the teacher is then able to prepare and adapt future lessons and learning sequences to take account of individual differences, and by doing so ensure that all students are able to progress at their speed, not one determined in advance.

Key questions

---

1 What do I want the children to learn *specifically* in this lesson?
2 Am I going to provide differentiated learning objectives?
3 Are they SMART objectives?
4 Can I use them as assessment criteria during the lesson?

Reference

Beere, J. (2010) *The Perfect Ofsted Lesson*. Bancyfelin: Crown House.

Further reading

Fautley, M. and Savage, J. (2008) *Assessment for Learning and Teaching in Secondary Schools*. Exeter: Learning Matters.
Wiliam, D. (2011) *Embedded Formative Assessment*. Bloomington, IN: Solution Tree Press.

Observation

Observation is a common stage in most beginner teachers' work. You may observe experienced teachers working or you may be asked to observe other students on your course. But here we would like to consider how you might observe students learning within your own lesson. Effective teachers make time during their lessons to take that step backwards from the complexity of classroom interactions to observe what is going on. Here are three tips for learning to observe your classroom more effectively.

First, learn to live with uncertainty in your observations. The notion of 'truth' is highly contestable. What you are watching is framed by notions

of objectivity and subjectivity, which you could spend a lifetime exploring. You do not have time to do that now! Rather, look for examples of
activities which are 'credible and defensible rather than true' (Kushner
1992: 1). Whilst you are observing, use your instincts as a teacher to look
out for interesting responses that students make within the lesson, unusual responses within particular activities, or that spark of creativity that
a pupil may show at a given moment. Accounting for these in a simple
way through your observation notes will be important, even if it is a brief
comment in your teaching journal that can be returned to at a later date.

Second, use a range of technology to help you with your observations.
This could include audio or video recording. The analysis of these materials can also reveal interesting points that you may miss in the busyness
of a lesson. Whilst this can be a timesaver and very beneficial, beware
of relying too much on this. It takes a long time to review recorded
materials. But the benefits can be significant if you have the time. If
you want to explore and analyse your own pedagogy, why not consider
video recording yourself? After you have got over the initial embarrassment of watching yourself on film (or is that just me?), this can be a
very enlightening activity. If you are able to use a laptop computer with
an in-built web camera directed at the position where you are standing,
then your students may not even know that you are video recording
yourself. Recording yourself as a teacher is no different from those disciplines such as acting, dancing or athletics where video analysis is central
to improving performance. Why should it be any different for teachers?

Finally, be focused in your observations. Your lesson has specific learning objectives and activities. Try and focus on these in the early stages
of your observation. But, as we discussed above, remember that these
should not be thought of as being fixed in stone. Your understanding of
the planned learning objectives and teaching activities will develop as
the lesson unfolds; try to give an account of this process of development
in any evaluation that you write about your lesson.

Key questions

1 How can I structure my lesson to ensure that I get time to complete the kind
of observation described above?
2 What tools could I adopt and use to help me observe my classroom, and the
activity within it, more effectively?
3 Are there opportunities to work collaboratively with other students or
teachers to help develop critical and formative observations of my own and
others' teaching?

Reference and further reading

Kushner, S. (1992) *The Arts, Education and Evaluation: An Introductory Pack with Practical Exercises*, Section 5: Making observations. Norwich: Centre for Applied Research in Education, University of East Anglia.

Ofsted

Ofsted is the Office for Standards in Education, Children's Services and Skills. Although it reports directly to Parliament, it is an independent and impartial organization.

Ofsted inspects and regulates a range of organizations throughout the United Kingdom. This includes schools, early year child care providers, colleges and courses of initial teacher education within universities or school-centred training groups. Ofsted works collaboratively with a range of other education consultancy groups to provide a trained workforce of inspectors that conduct inspections and regulatory visits to these organizations. The reports from these visits are published on the Ofsted website (www.ofsted.gov.uk).

The aim of this inspection process is to promote improvement across the educational system as a whole as well as to ensure value for money. As a result of this, all children, young people, parents and carers, adult learners, employers and employees (i.e. you!) should benefit.

As a teacher, you will most likely come into contact with Ofsted inspectors when they come to inspect the school within which you are teaching. Whilst is is probably true to say that no-one likes the thought of an Ofsted inspection, it is important to try not to worry about this too much. If you have been working hard and doing your job responsibly with the support of your head of department or school leadership team alongside you, then the best attitude you can have is that you have nothing to hide and it is business as usual. In reality, of course, this is seldom the case. Schools are given prior warning of an Ofsted inspection and there will be additional demands placed on all teachers to help prepare the school for the inspection. The weeks or days before the inspection will be a stressful time.

There is lively debate among teachers and the wider educational community about Ofsted and whether it does a worthwhile job. It is not difficult to poke holes in their various inspection frameworks, and the quality of their inspectors varies immensely mainly because they generally come from a large range of external companies. There are clearly issues of inspector training, monitoring and quality assurance that could be tightened up. Every teacher has a tale to tell about an Ofsted inspector who has done a bad job!

But having said all that, it is now hard to imagine the educational system in the United Kingdom without Ofsted (although you could try!). It would probably be naïve in the extreme to imagine that Ofsted has had no role in the general rise in educational standards across the country as a whole. Clearly, with the vast number of schools that exist in our country there are going to be some schools, and some teachers, who are not doing the job as they should and those institutions and individuals need challenging.

However, with the recent abolishment of the General Teaching Council for England, the role of the teacher unions has become increasingly important for individual teachers. When faced with challenges to their competence by Ofsted or others, individual teachers will need the support of a professional organization now more than ever. We strongly advise every teacher to join one of the teaching unions.

Key question

How can I ensure that I am always doing my very best so that I have nothing to fear when that Ofsted inspector knocks on my classroom door?

Further reading

Didau, D. (2012) Myths: What Ofsted Want. Available from http://learningspy. co.uk/2012/03/17/myths-what-ofsted-want/ (accessed 14 July 2012).

Outdoor learning (or learning beyond the classroom)

Whilst your first concern as a teacher will be the teaching and learning that goes on within your classroom, it is important to remember that your students' learning does not stop the moment they walk out of your classroom door! Many of the structural systems that schools adopt compartmentalize learning into manageable chunks. We have timetabled days with set periods of time for particular activities or lessons; teachers with a specialism in a particular subject; tailored spaces for particular types of learning, etc. All these can unhelpfully limit our understanding of the broader processes of learning that span beyond the school boundary.

So, there are various ways in which learning carries on 'outside' the classroom. The most obvious of these is the use of homework activities. We have covered these in more detail elsewhere in this book.

Some subject areas of the curriculum have a tradition for utilizing outdoor spaces as part of the regular teaching and learning opportunities. Curriculum areas such as history or geography will often include field trips or visits to interesting sites to allow students to investigate, in a different way, a particular set of learning objectives. Other curriculum areas, such as physical education, could not really be conceived as being able to operate effectively without regular and sustained access to outside spaces for various sporting activities. For other curriculum areas, perhaps, the choices of outside learning locations or opportunities are not so obvious.

There are strong arguments in favour of all students having a regular opportunity to learn outside the classroom as an integral part of their mainstream schooling. The Council for Learning Outside the Classroom believe that:

> Learning outside the classroom is about raising young people's achievement through an organized, powerful approach to learning in which direct experience is of prime importance. Meaningful learning occurs through acquiring skills through real life hands-on activities. This is not only about what we learn, but most importantly, how and where we learn.
>
> (LOTC 2012)

Their website provides a range of further evidence about the benefits of outside learning which are well worth reading in more detail.

As teachers, there are a number of things that you will need to think about before taking your students outside your classroom on a school trip. First, be imaginative about your choices of outside learning opportunities. Organizing a trip to an outside location can be very time consuming and expensive. It is important to have a clear objective for the trip and to be able to justify this in terms of time and money.

Second, use the opportunity to engage in learning outside the normal classroom environment to help structure the teaching and learning opportunities prior to the trip and after it. Think about the various curriculum links and opportunities that such a trip will facilitate and integrate these in your broader unit of work.

Third, consider the various risks involved and seek the support of the member of staff at your school with a responsibility for health and safety issues when students are taken outside the normal school environment. There are also various legal responsibilities that you, and other teachers going on the trip, will need to ensure are met.

Fourth, your school with have a 'charging policy' for school trips and you will need to find out what this is and how the trip can be costed properly to ensure all students can access it fairly.

Finally, you will need to communicate with your students' parents and carers well in advance of the trip itself. You will need their permission and you will want to ensure that they have a full understanding of the purposes for the trip in terms of the curriculum opportunities it offers their child.

Don't forget that every school has an outside environment of its own that you can exploit imaginatively. Whilst it may not be as exciting as a trip to a remote location, it would certainly prove to be less demanding in terms of your time and organization, and less expensive to the school or parents, but could be equally rewarding. All it takes is a bit of creative thinking.

Key questions

1   How can I provide opportunities for learning outside the classroom in my curriculum area(s)?
2   How can I exploit my school environment to help develop these opportunities in an imaginative and creative way?

Reference and further reading

LOTC (Council for Learning Outside the Classroom) (2012) http://www. lotc.org.uk/ (accessed 18 July 2012).

P

Parents

What can we say about parents? Well, we should probably start by saying that as parents ourselves, our views about 'parents' changed significantly when we started parenting! Parenting is one of the most challenging and rewarding things you can do. You are constantly learning, frequently surprised by your children and their insights, pretty regularly humbled by their responses to life and their achievements, and the fleeting nature of your influence on their lives. That said, as teachers, we often said that once you met a student's parents their manner, work and personality suddenly made sense. For good or bad, our parents are a massive influence on our lives.

Educating a child is a partnership between the child, the school and the parents. We believe that this is a simple truism that has profound implications for the way in which formal schooling is structured. At various levels, schools and individual teachers need to ensure that parents are constructively included within this partnership in appropriate ways.

At the whole school level, policies need to be in place which ensure that parents are communicated with regularly about all aspects of their child's progress. This is done in various ways. Paper-based forms of communication, such as newsletters and formal school reports, are very common; but, increasingly, schools are making use of 'real-time' monitoring of pupil progress through software solutions, included as part of the school website or VLE, that allow parents to check on their child's attendance, progress, eating habits, homework tasks and more besides!

Schools also need to facilitate effective face-to-face meetings with parents. These are often done through 'parents' evenings' where individual members of staff get to meet parents and discuss their child's progress. These can be organized in different ways. Perhaps the most common format is an appointment system where parents either meet their child's form tutor or, in the case of secondary schools, they get the chance to meet their child's subject teachers (or a selection of them) to discuss their progress in that subject. These occasions can be very beneficial for all involved although careful thought needs to be given to the location of staff, the timings allocated for individual appointments, and the type, quality or quantity of information that you want to share with parents in what is normally a short period of time.

More broadly, of course, parents have a vital supportive role. As an individual teacher you can engage with parents in a range of different ways to help support your students' learning. These could include:

- designing homework tasks that help draw and engage the parents' into their child's learning;
- inviting parents to come to specific events within the school where your subject, or class, is doing something interesting;
- making use of parental expertise within your curriculum area (as parents, we have been asked to play the piano at school events, bring dogs and babies into class and answer questions about how to look after them, and provide advice about pieces of technology!).

Alongside parental engagement, community engagement is also a key part of many schools' work. The local environment and community can become a very useful resource for schools in all kinds of ways, including an inspiration for curriculum planning and inter-generational dialogue as well as creating a good sense of social and civic engagement within our local communities.

Key questions

1 How do I, and my school, engage with parents?
2 Are there subject- or class-specific things I can organize to help promote engagement with parents or other members of the local community in a more effective manner?

Further reading

Crozier, G. (2000) *Parents and Schools: Partners or Protagonists?* Stoke on Trent: Trentham Books.

Pedagogy

The *Oxford English Dictionary* defines 'pedagogy' as 'the profession, science, or theory of teaching'. Other definitions of pedagogy extend this to cover the practice and process that underpin the activity of teaching. For example, Popkewitz develops a broad based definition of pedagogy:

> Pedagogy is a practice of the social administration of the social individual. Since at least the 19th century pedagogical discourses about teaching, children, and learning in schools connected the scope and aspirations of public powers with the personal and subjective capabilities of individuals. This administration of the child embodies certain norms about their capabilities from which the child can become self-governing and self-reliant.
>
> (Popkewitz 1998: 536)

Bernstein picks up on this notion of pedagogy as process, defining it as:

> A sustained process whereby somebody(s) acquires new forms or develops existing forms of conduct, knowledge, practice and criteria, from somebody(s) or something deemed to be an appropriate provider and evaluator. Appropriate either from the point of view of the acquirer or by some other body(s) or both.
>
> (Bernstein 1999: 259)

Note the ethical dimensions of a pedagogical approach in the above definition. The teacher, as an appropriate provider, acts in the role of evaluator (by valuing knowledge, skills and understanding) and developing appropriate forms of practice and conduct. This goes much further than just viewing pedagogy as the uncritical delivery of pre-packaged knowledge!

In recent years, one of the most influential figures in discussions surrounding pedagogy has been Robin Alexander. As a Fellow of Wolfson College at the University of Cambridge and Director of the Cambridge Primary Review, Alexander defines pedagogy as: 'the act of teaching together with its attendant discourse. It is what one needs to know, and the skills one needs to command, in order to make and justify the many different kinds of decisions of which teaching is constituted' (Alexander 2008: 11). Alexander makes the key, and by now familiar, point that pedagogy is not the same as teaching. In resonances to Bernstein's quote, Alexander highlights the important justificatory elements of pedagogy that are often ignored within contemporary educational discourses.

So, pedagogy involves teaching, but it is much more than that. It also involves an 'attendant discourse' that comprises of the knowledge and skills which inform, justify and value the decision making processes within teaching. Pedagogy is both a 'practice' and a 'process' through which certain things can be acquired or through which certain capabilities can be developed, justified and valued. In all definitions, references are made to something 'outside' the obvious context of an educational exchange (i.e. a teacher and pupil). In Popkewitz's definition, this is seen in the phrase 'scope and aspirations of public powers'; in Bernstein's by 'an appropriate provider or evaluator'; in Alexander's by his phrase 'attendant discourse'.

Skilful teachers embody a skilful pedagogy. They are responsible for its development and application. This skilful pedagogy does not appear by accident. It develops over a long period of time and needs constant nurturing through critical reflection and analysis.

In Alexander's words, 'it is schooling that has reduced knowledge to "subjects" and teaching to mere telling' (Alexander 2008: 141). Pedagogy is much more powerful than this. Our students' education is much more important that this! Your pedagogy is the most important and powerful element of your work as a teacher. Treasure the pedagogy that you develop. It is the most sophisticated tool you have to inspire the students that you teach.

Key questions

1 How would you characterize your own pedagogy? What particular strengths does it have? What areas need to be improved further?
2 How do I know if my pedagogy is effective? Is the sole measure of its effectiveness in my students' achievements? If not, what else would I look towards in gaining a broader understanding about the impact of my pedagogy?

References

Alexander, R.J. (2008) *Essays on Pedagogy*. London: Routledge.
Bernstein, B. (1999) Official knowledge and pedagogic identities, in F. Christie (ed.) *Pedagogy and the Shaping of Consciousness*, pp. 246–61. London: Cassell.
Popkewitz, T. (1998) *Struggling for the Soul: The Politics of Schooling and the Construction of the Teacher*. New York: Teachers College Press.

Further reading

Alexander, R.J. (2008) *Essays on Pedagogy*. London: Routledge.

Personalization

Personalization is about ensuring that every individual child is given the best possible chance to succeed. Gilbert defined it as:

> taking a highly structured and responsive approach to each child's and young person's learning, in order that all are able to progress, achieve and participate. It means strengthening the link between learning and teaching by engaging students – and their parents – as partners in learning.
>
> (DCSF 2007: 6)

As teachers, we will encounter students with many different educational needs. We will need to make adjustments to our own pedagogy in order to respond positively to them. There are a large number of other aspects of your pedagogy that can be adapted and developed to help achieve a stronger approach to personalized learning.

One of the most important elements will be your curriculum planning. This is not just about planning in terms of your subject, or the knowledge that you want to try and impart. It is about planning the personalized processes of learning that the students are going to engage in during the lesson. This is an important distinction to get hold of. Although with any group of students of a similar age there will be a certain amount they have in common, planning the learning and the types of engagement that you are hoping students will have within the classroom involves you considering their ability levels, the structure of tasks (open or closed), the types of presentational approaches you might adopt (e.g. explanations or modelling), the progression routes within the learning, the particular tools you want to use (or get them to use), and much more besides.

One of the terms that used to be very popular in the debate prior to 'personalization' was 'differentiation'. You will find an entry for *differentiation* in this book that discusses it in more detail. At the heart of differentiation as a pedagogical strategy are two notions; first, that children are all different; second, that teachers need to make different pedagogical choices depending on what they think is the best way that students can learn. The choices you make as a teacher have consequences. Learn to reflect on these choices in the evaluations drawn from your lessons.

Over the coming years there will be a increasing range of top-down, business-led initiatives which claim to personalize learning and result in more effective student engagement, cognitive acceleration, personalized VAK learning styles, mental processing or whatever the latest educational catch-phrase might be. We would urge you to maintain a critical approach to what seem like quick-fix solutions to something as complex as personalization within teaching and learning. Whilst there may be valuable components within some of these types of initiatives much of the psychology and neuroscience behind them is at best only particularly understood by some of those advocating these approaches and at worst deliberately manipulative. There may also be commercial agendas at play here which one should always be wary of. The motivation for financial profit behind many of these initiatives is very questionable.

For us, effective teaching and learning is centred on a strong relationship between the individual teacher, their emerging pedagogy and their students. All students deserve an education that is appropriately personalized to their educational needs. Every child matters and their education is too important to be sold or manipulated by careless handling of complex ideas. Focus on your role in the classroom, hone and craft your pedagogy and listen carefully to your students. These are the keys to an effective, personal approach to teaching and learning.

Key questions

1 What pedagogical approaches have I seen used to help provide a personalized learning opportunity or environment for students?
2 How can I plan for an inclusive, personalized set of learning opportunities for all my students?
3 What do strategies such as differentiation by outcome, or differentiation by process, look like in my subject teaching?

Reference

DCSF (2007) *Pedagogy and Personalisation*. London: DCSF. http://www.teachfind.com/national-strategies/pedagogy-and-personalisation-O (accessed 31 January 2013).

Further reading

Burton, D. (2007) Psycho-pedagogy and personalised learning. *Journal of Education for Teaching*, 33(1): 5–17.
Wilmot, E. (2006) *Personalising Learning in the Primary Classroom: A Practical Guide for Teachers and School Leaders*. Carmarthen: Crown House Publishing. (Please do not be put off by the word primary in the above book title. There is much of value in this book for all teachers, regardless of the age of students they are teaching.)

Planning

This entry needs to be read in conjunction with the section on **lesson planning**, to which it strongly relates.

Planning is often considered under three headings, long term, medium term, and short term. Short term planning is associated closely with lesson planning, and so is dealt with in that entry; here we concern ourselves with long and medium term planning. The amounts of time which are involved in long and medium term planning vary between schools. We are treating medium term planning as being for a term or less, and long term planning as being for a term or more.

Long term planning takes an overview of teaching and learning, and is concerned with directionality of learning, and the goals which learning will be aiming for over time. In many schools long term planning includes an overview of the expectations of attainment that students will accomplish during the time frame, with suitably differentiated outcomes to account for ability. To think about long term planning it is useful to begin with some key questions, including:

1   Where do I want the students to be at the end of this period?
2   Where are they now?
3   What do I want them to have learned and/or be able to do?

Starting from these questions the programme of study can then be devised to facilitate this movement from where the learners are now, to where they are required to be later on.

Medium term planning involves a more broken-down standpoint, derived from the long term plan, and aiming to show an overview of the route the students will take. The same questions as were asked of long term planning can be asked here, alongside some additional ones:

4   What is the best way for the required learning to be achieved?
5   What do the class require in order to do this?
6   What range of activities will facilitate this learning?

Notice that the final stage of medium term planning is to think about activity. A common error novice teachers make is to think about activity before learning. Whilst keeping the class busy and occupied is good, this is not in and of itself an end. The aim of planning should be learning; treadmills kept nineteenth-century prisoners occupied, but they did not learn much! The starting and finishing point for planning needs to be learning, and so there naturally follows a further question:

7   vill I know when they have learned what I want them to?

This seemingly innocent question takes us into the realm of assessment for learning (AfL), and so when planning for learning it is useful to have *learning outcome* statements, which delineate the intended learning clearly. Written well, these statements can be used as assessment criteria in their own right, and so careful planning of these statements is worthwhile as it will facilitate AfL. Just as starting with activity rather than with learning is problematic for novice teachers, planning for learning is much harder than planning for activity, and involves careful thought and reflection.

Key questions

1 Will all classes in the school be equally able to access the intended learning?
2 What evidence of mileposts en route will I want to show me progress is being made?
3 Why do I want the students to learn this in the first place?
4 What is the best way of ordering the planning for sequential learning to take place?

Further reading

Hattie, J. (2012) *Visible Learning for Teachers: Maximizing Impact on Learning.* Abingdon: Routledge.
Wiliam, D. (2011) *Embedded Formative Assessment.* Bloomington, IN: Solution Tree Press.

Plenary

The plenary is commonly held to be the final part of a lesson, but this need not necessarily be the case. The word 'plenary' has its origins in the Latin term for full, or fullness, and it is in the sense of showing the complete lesson that it has come to be associated with the end.

There is a popular mythology that the three-part lesson, consisting of starter, main body of lesson and plenary, is the only way that lessons should be taught, and that Ofsted will look unfavourably upon any-thing else. This is not true. Good teaching is good teaching, and structure is less important than quality of teaching and learning. Unremitting emphasis on three-part lesson structures will not auto-matically guarantee quality teaching and learning. But in general, it is good practice to have a structured finish to a lesson. One headteacher observed that if you are still teaching when the bell goes, then you are not in complete control of your lesson. Being a professional means knowing what you are doing, so losing track of time is not conducive to this.

Mini plenaries as the lesson progresses are a perfectly reasonable way to proceed. There is something to be said for the teacher drawing all the various strands together, and checking that understanding has taken place so far. So, a plenary is a moment of summary, and of drawing together, and can happen at any point in the lesson.

In designing opportunities for teaching and learning, it is helpful for all teachers to think about the notion of structure. To do this it is useful to divide up the lesson into a series of episodes. This means that each episode within a lesson can be devoted to a different activity, or segment of learning. Breaking down learning into a series of small steps or stages is clearly of benefit. This is what is meant by planning for learning. The episodic format allows the teacher to be in control of the flow of the lesson, and to place a variety of structured learning opportunities into a logical schedule.

Another use for a plenary is as a focusing activity. In periods of whole class activity on practical aspects of learning, it can prove useful to have ongoing mini plenaries as focusing elements for the class. This will involve monitoring the levels of activity and, possi-bly, noise, that the class is engaged with, and using the mini plenary to think about key aspects of the task in hand, and to quieten them down too.

The end plenary does not have to be a teacher-led activity. Through-out this book we emphasize the importance of formative assessment, and so the plenary gives an opportunity for the teacher to find out what progression in learning the students have made. Whilst it can seem easy for the teacher to sum up for the students what they have learned during the course of the lesson, it is clearly better for the students concerned to do this themselves. Choosing students to do this in advance, at the start of the lesson, say, allows the students con-cerned time to think about what they will say. Equally valid, though, is to choose students to undertake this on the spur of the moment, which can then reveal the sorts of learning which have really taken place!

Key questions

1 What learning do I want to consolidate in the plenary?
2 What is the best way to undertake this for me, with this class?
3 How can I include a series of mini plenaries in the work I am doing with the class?
4 How can I get the class actively involved in the plenary?

Further reading

Brooks, V., Abbott, I. and Bills, L. (2007) *Preparing to Teach in Secondary Schools: A Student Teacher's Guide to Professional Issues in Secondary Education*, 2nd edn. Maidenhead: Open University Press.
Shilvock, K. and Pope, M. (2008) *Successful Teaching Placements in Secondary Schools*. Exeter: Learning Matters.

Policy

There are many aspects of education which have been increasingly politicized over recent years, and education policy is clearly one of these. There are things which have been considered as policy which teachers and parents would find it very difficult, on the face of it, to disagree with. So things like 'raising standards', 'equal opportunities for all', 'every child matters', 'healthy eating', and having fewer young people who are classified as NEET (not in education, employment, or training) are examples. But in among these points of broad agreement there are education policies which do not command such universal acclaim. For example, some policies which have caused division include:

- Free Schools;
- academies;
- Teach First;
- selling off playing fields;
- no need for Qualified Teacher Status to teach in academies or Free Schools;
- reduced initial teacher education in higher education institutions;
- grammar schools;
- introduction of the National Curriculum.

This list includes things which you might be in strong agreement with, but which are still controversial. You might be on a Teach First programme for example, or be doing your initial teacher training on-the-job. Some of these policies come from one political standpoint. Others, for example academies, can have cross-party support but still be controversial. In recent years we have seen increasingly political or ideological policy decisions, with the UK government not being alone internationally in trying to control what goes on in schools to an increasing extent.

Government policies on education are designed, it is safe to say, to try to raise standards. No minister is going to say they are in favour of falling standards, although this is what they will often accuse those who disagree with them of wanting to do! So, if raising standards is seen as a good thing, why is it controversial? The answer to this lies in the route that various governments take to enact and implement their policy decisions. One of the problems with education is that as a social science, there are very few cause and effect relationships which can be established to show what works, and what does not. So, for every example of, say, a Steiner school, where pupils have a degree of latitude in their learning, another school can be found where pupils are taught in ways the Victorians would recognize, yet both seem to achieve good results. The effect of this is that some politicians can become anchored in decisions about what is 'good' in education based on ideology, rather than evidence.

As a teacher, you will be on the receiving end of policy decisions and will often have very little say in them. So, if the government decides that something will be done in schools, it will be up to the school to implement this policy, and for you to carry this out.

Key questions

1 What governmental policies have affected me?
2 How do I feel about the increasing politicization of schools?
3 How do government policies affect the pupils I teach?

Further reading

Benn, M. (2011) *School Wars: The Battle for Britain's Education*. London: Verso Books.

Hatcher, R. and Jones, K. (2011) *No Country for the Young: Education from New Labour to the Coalition*. London: Tufnell Press.

Presentations

Many classrooms now have interactive whiteboards, or projectors and screens, where computers are or can be connected. The reason for this is the use of presentation technology, and suitable software. Among these, it is safe to say that Microsoft's PowerPoint has become ubiquitous in the presentation of information in schools and elsewhere. So common is this that when a colleague has been on a course and is asked how it was, if we hear 'death by PowerPoint' we know exactly what they mean:

> The phrase 'Death by PowerPoint' wasn't born in the offices of Microsoft's competitors; it came from meeting attendees. In fact, Microsoft estimates that at least 30 million PowerPoint presentations are made every day, with many of them looking and feeling exactly the same.

> But the audience isn't the only entity that's dying from presenters' ignorance and/or misplaced zeal in creating PowerPoint presentations. All too often, originality and quality content get buried, too.
>
> (Goldstein 2003: 20)

So, how do you avoid it? Preparing a presentation for use in your teaching has many benefits. These include your being able to:

- research in advance;
- control the sequence in which information is presented;
- use suitable images, videos, audio to emphasize your point;
- use it in more than one lesson;
- share it with colleagues.

But preparing the content of a PowerPoint is only half of the story. As Cherie Kerr observes: 'There are two fundamental areas to consider when creating a PowerPoint show: Content and Delivery. . . . In the end it's hard to say that one is more important than the other' (Kerr 2001: 21). The important factor is that you are presenting a lesson. This involves teaching and learning, where the purpose of the PowerPoint is to present information for this purpose. This means that although you can do whizzy exciting features, animate the text, and use sound effects for slide-turns, you need to ask if this will enhance your educational message. Although keeping the attention of the class is an important factor, entertaining them is a different matter! So, your presentations should be pedagogically sound, and have content which is relevant to the lesson.

There are many significant learning opportunities which presentations offer, so you will want to exploit these. It is also useful to think about the learning you are hoping to develop in the lesson, and your learning objectives should make this clear. The reason for using a presentation is to develop learning, not replace it with activity or entertainment!

Key questions

---

1   What do I want the students to learn?
2   What is the best way to present this?
3   How can I ensure my PowerPoint presentations achieve maximum learning impact?

References

Goldstein, M. (2003) It's alive! The audience, that is, but some presenters don't seem to know it. *Successful Meetings*, 52: 2.
Kerr, C. (2001) *Death by PowerPoint*. Santa Ana, CA: ExecuProv Press.

Further reading

Kerr, C. (2001) *Death by PowerPoint*. Santa Ana, CA: ExecuProv Press.

Profession

There are many arguments concerning the status of teaching as a profession. Some of these are political, in the sense that the way that the government of the day views teachers can affect the way that it makes and enacts legislation; some arguments are ideological, in that there are different views as to what teaching involves; and some arguments are concerned with finance as paying teachers costs money! So why is teaching problematic in the sense of being a profession? And why does it engender arguments and discussions concerning its role? Let us try to unpick some of these issues.

Throughout this book we have made much of the fact that teaching is not just about telling. It is, in our view, not the case that the teacher holds the knowledge, and that teaching is simply the transmission of this knowledge to the learners. We discuss learning theory, and ways of viewing what goes on when people learn, and have taken the position that an informed pedagogy is the best way for teaching and learning to take place.

According to Wise:

> A profession is an occupation that seeks to regulate itself by (a) developing a consensus concerning what its practitioners must know and be able to do and (b) developing an accreditation and licensing system to ensure the transmission of that knowledge and skill. An occupation becomes a profession when organizations such as universities, states, and the public accept that system.
>
> (Wise 2005: 318)

And herein lies the political rub. There is too much at stake for governments to let teachers get on with being a true and fully self-governing group of professionals. Ideological issues surface very rapidly. On the one hand we have views that place teacher trainers as some sort of left-wing guerrilla movement, with comments such as 'the Marxist drivel taught in teacher training colleges' (Heffer 2007), and on the other hand we have statements like this, 'The best education systems in the world draw their teachers from among the top graduates and train them rigorously and effectively, focusing on classroom practice' (Department for Education 2010: 9). So, in between Marxist drivel and high-quality training we have teachers being prepared for working in schools. But teaching is a social science, and unlike hard science there is no simple cause-and-effect procedure equating high-quality training with high-quality teaching.

To be a professional means to be a reflective self-regulatory group. Historically, teachers have done themselves no favours:

> Teachers are atheoretical and inconsistent in their beliefs. Many teachers have neither philosophical moorings nor empirical evidence to guide their practice. They are guided by pragmatic considerations related to student characteristics, availability of curriculum materials, experiential factors, and what is popular.
>
> (Snider and Roehl 2007: 881)

So with standpoints like this it is little wonder that teaching can be reduced to telling.

But we can hope that things are changing, that teaching is becoming recognized as requiring knowledge, skills and, importantly, wisdom. Teaching in the inner-city is not the same as teaching in a fee-paying school in the leafy suburbs, and a true professional recognizes this and acts accordingly. We can but hope that teaching at least retains the status it currently has, and that it will be continued to be recognized that pedagogy is not a simplistic transmission, that good subject knowledge is not in itself sufficient, and that our young people deserve the best people teaching them, not a transient population of here-today-gone-tomorrow opportunists. Surely our country's young people are worth that?

Key questions

1 How do I demonstrate being professional?
2 What teaching and learning skills do I have beyond my subject knowledge?
3 Why do some people denigrate teaching as a profession, and how would I respond to these arguments?
4 What are the ideological drivers behind political arguments for the status of teachers?

References

Department for Education (2010) *The Importance of Teaching*. London: DfE.

Heffer, S. (2007) Thank Marx for our children's low marks, *The Daily Telegraph*, 17 November. http://www.telegraph.co.uk/comment/personal-view/3644070/Thank-Marx-for-our-childrens-low-marks.html (accessed 31 January 2013).

Snider, V.E. and Roehl, R. (2007) Teachers' beliefs about pedagogy and related issues. *Psychology in the Schools*, 44(8): 873–86.

Wise, A.E. (2005) Establishing teaching as a profession: the essential role of professional accreditation. *Journal of Teacher Education*, 56(4): 318–31.

Further reading

Hatcher, R. and Jones, K. (2011) *No Country for the Young: Education from New Labour to the Coalition*. London: Tufnell Press.

Qualifications

Qualifications come in many different shapes and sizes! There are a number of quite complicated frameworks within which individual qualifications (e.g. the General Certificate of Secondary Education (GCSE) or Advanced (A) levels) fit. There are three main frameworks:

1 *National Qualifications Framework (NQF)* This sets out the level at which a qualification can be recognized within the United Kingdom. It ensures that all qualifications are of a suitable quality.
2 *Qualifications and Credit Framework (QCF)* This contains vocational and work-related qualifications available across the United Kingdom.
3 *Framework for Higher Education Qualifications (FHEQ)* This was designed by the higher education sector and covers qualifications you might gain at a university or higher education college.

Table 1 shows how any one individual qualification (e.g. a GCSE) fits within the various frameworks and the common levels (1–8) that span across them.

Table 1

Level	NQF qualifications	QCF qualifications	FHEQ qualifications
Entry	Entry level certificates; English for speakers of other languages (ESOL); Skills for Life; Functional Skills (at entry level including English, maths and ICT)	Awards, certificates and diplomas at entry level; Foundation learning at entry level; Functional skills at entry level	

(Continued)

Table 1 continued

Level	NQF qualifications	QCF qualifications	FHEQ qualifications
1	GCSE grades D–G; BTEC introductory diplomas and certificates; Key skills level 1; Functional skills at level 1	BTEC awards, certificates, and diplomas at level 1; Functional skills at level 1; Foundation learning tier pathways; NVQs at level 1	
2	GCSE grades A*–C; key skills level 2; Skills for life; Functional skills at level 2	BTEC awards, certificates, and diplomas at level 2; Functional skills at level 2; OCR nationals; NVQs at level 2	
3	A levels; GCE in applied subjects; International Baccalaureate; Key Skills level 3	BTEC awards, certificates, and diplomas at level 3; BTEC nationals; OCR nationals; NVQs at level 3	
4	Certificates of higher education	BTEC professional diplomas, certificates and awards; HNCs; NVQs at level 4	Certificates of higher education; Higher national certificates
5	HNCs and HNDs; Other higher diplomas	HNDs; BTEC professional diplomas, certificates and awards	Diplomas of higher education; Foundation degrees; Higher national diplomas
6	National diploma in professional production skills; BTEC advanced professional diplomas, certificates and awards	BTEC advanced professional diplomas, certificates and awards	Bachelors degrees; Bachelors degrees with honours; Graduate certificates and diplomas; Postgraduate certificate in education (can also be at next level)
7	Diploma in translation; BTEC advanced professional diplomas, certificates and awards	BTEC advanced professional diplomas, certificates and awards	Masters degrees; Integrated masters degrees; Postgraduate certificates; Postgraduate diplomas; Postgraduate certificate in education (with 'M' level components)
8	Specialist awards	Award, certificate and diploma in strategic direction	Doctoral degrees, including EdD and PhD qualifications

Within the typical secondary school, teachers will be mainly concerned with qualifications that fall within the entry level and levels 1–3 (e.g. GCSEs). Teachers working with students aged 16 or above will need to be familiar with the structure of qualifications at levels 4–6 in order to give appropriate careers advice for their students as they progress into the next phase of their education.

For teachers, the opportunities to extend your own qualifications will mainly be focused around levels 6–8. At the moment, teaching is a graduate profession. Anyone without a qualification at level 6 would not be able to become a qualified teacher in the traditional sense.

Postgraduate courses of initial teacher education are run at two levels (6 and 7) depending on whether or not they contain an element of Level 7 (Masters or 'M' level) study within their content. If you are considering undertaking study for a PGCE, and become a qualified teacher, you will need to ask the higher education institute to which you are applying whether or not the course they offer has this additional component. If it does, it will mean that if you successfully complete the course, you will get three things: a PGCE, QTS and a number of 'M' level credits (normally 60) that you can use to obtain credit against a Postgraduate Diploma (which requires a total of 120 credits) or a Masters degree (180 credits) at a later date.

Key questions

1 Which 'level' of qualifications will I be mainly concerned with in my teaching?
2 Where can I find out further information about specific qualifications within that level?

Further reading

For further information about the three frameworks and the various qualifications within them, the Directgov website has plenty of helpful advice: http://www.direct.gov.uk/en/EducationAndLearning/index.htm

Quality

How do you define 'quality' in education? In this short discussion about 'quality', we will explore what one leading organization thinks about this and apply their ideas to your work as a teacher in a specific school.

UNICEF believe that every child has a right to a 'quality education'. They define a 'quality education' as including:

1   Learners who are healthy, well-nourished and ready to participate and learn, and are supported in learning by their families and communities;
2   Environments that are healthy, safe, protective and gender-sensitive, and provide adequate resources and facilities;
3   Content that is reflected in relevant curricula and materials for the acquisition of basic skills, especially in the areas of literacy, numeracy and skills for life, and knowledge in such areas as gender, health, nutrition, HIV/AIDS prevention and peace;
4   Processes through which trained teachers use child-centred teaching approaches in well-managed classrooms and schools and skilful assessment to facilitate learning and reduce disparities;
5   Outcomes that encompass knowledge, skills and attitudes, and are linked to national goals for education and positive participation in society.

(UNICEF 2000: 4)

This grand statement about what counts as quality in education may seem a million miles away from your immediate concerns as a teacher. But sometimes it is a good idea to take a step back from your immediate teaching context and consider the bigger questions about what we are doing within our educational system as a whole. So, for example, drawing on the above quote from UNICEF, you could ask yourself some of the following questions:

1   Does our school community have a broad agreement about what constitutes a quality education? Do we have a suitable framework in place to help analyse, monitor and improve our educational provision and help ensure it is a good as possible?
2   How is my school ensuring that our students are in a good physical shape to undertake their schooling? How are we working to support those families that find it difficult to raise heathy and well-nourished children?
3   What steps are we taking to provide an appropriate learning environment within our school? Are our financial priorities suitably focused towards this end?
4   How can our school ensure that every teacher's pedagogy is a quality pedagogy that draws on appropriate teaching strategies

(both general and subject specific) and ensures quality learning outcomes?

5   Are the outcomes of learning that our school facilitates appropriate? Do they relate to the expectations placed on us by our community and wider society? Are we happy with the balance between external and internal measures of quality and how these are represented in public life?

What counts as a 'quality' education is important for everyone in society to consider. However, how 'quality' is interpreted and contextualized can be very different in one school from another. Whilst Ofsted might be concerned about certain aspect of a school's work, it is much more important that the school itself has a robust discussion about quality in education and how they – students, staff and parents – are going to work together to achieve it.

Key questions

1   The above questions relate to the work of the school as a whole. How can I reinterpret these to focus on my classroom teaching?
2   Can I ensure that I am delivering 'quality' teaching? What does this look like?

Reference

UNICEF (2000) *Defining Quality in Education*. New York: United Nations Children's Fund. Also available from http://www.unicef.org/education/files/QualityEducation.pdf (accessed 18 July 2012).

Further reading

UNESCO (2005) *Education for All: The Quality Imperative*. http://www.unesco.org/new/en/education/themes/leading-the-international-agenda/efareport/reports/2005-quality/ (accessed 18 July 2012).

Questioning

Asking good questions is not just a matter of finding out what students know, but is also a way of developing learning and taking it forwards. Questioning is one of the most important student-teacher interactions, and accounts for a great deal of the talk that takes place in classrooms.

Knowing what sorts of questions to ask at what stage in the lesson is something that beginner teachers need to practise, and is also something that experienced teachers can benefit from focusing on. Let us think about this by starting with the most obvious classification of question types: the difference between open questions and closed ones. Closed questions are ones which can be answered with a single or few words, and tend to be of the right/wrong variety:

- What's the capital of France?
- What's 9 divided by 3?
- Where is Brighton?

Some sources decry closed questions, but for short and sharp checking of understanding they have their uses. Problems occur when teachers *only* ask closed questions. This is because for many closed questions you either know the answer, or you do not. There is very little chance of being able to work it out. For example, 'Where is Ulan Bator?' If you know it is the capital of Mongolia you can answer; if you do not know, you can't go through a series of workings to arrive at the right answer. In class, when beginner teachers ask lots of closed questions, they are encouraged when they are answered. They may not realize that it is the same hands, and the same pupils who know. Students who do not know soon tire of this, and their attention wanders. This is 'pub quiz' questioning technique. Another problem with this is that if you know that Paris is the capital of France, and get it right, you have not learned anything in the process. If you did not know, it is likely that the teacher has moved on to another question before you have had a chance to assimilate the information, and so the moment is lost.

Open questions require some working out of the answer, and in more than one word. Often open questions can also have more than one possible answer. 'Why is Paris the capital of France?' is a question that challenges, and will reveal information about the respondent. 'What is ten divided by five?' has one answer, 'Why does ten divided by five equal two?' requires the respondents to explain how they arrived at the answer that they provided.

Many teachers are familiar with Bloom's taxonomy (Bloom 1956) which is a way of classifying questions into a hierarchical form, starting with Knowledge (lower order thinking), and then moving towards higher order thinking (Analysis, Synthesis and Evaluation):

Higher order

1   Evaluation
2   Synthesis
3   Analysis

Lower order

4   Application
5   Comprehension
6   Knowledge

Notice that knowledge, the lowest level of the taxonomy, is the one which features heavily in closed questions.

Using Bloom's taxonomy as a basis for questioning means that questioning is able to move from remembering to learning. Asking a question which requires higher order thinking makes the learners think about their answer and weigh up a number of alternatives. To do this requires some practice to start with, and many teachers find it helpful to have a list of suitable question stems that they can use to formulate appropriate questions when the time occurs.

For student teachers, planning the questions you are going to ask in a lesson in advance may seem lengthy and tedious, but it is a good way of ensuring you do not get stuck in the closed/lower order rut!

Used well, questioning creates knowledge; used badly, prolonged pub quiz questioning simply serves to emphasize differences between students, alienates those who do not know, and provides no new learning for those that do.

Key questions

1   What is a key question?
2   How many questions do I ask which are open/closed?
3   How can I plan to ask more higher order thinking questions?
4   What is higher order thinking in my subject?
5   Can I ask a colleague to observe me and count the number and type of questions I ask?

Reference

Bloom, B.S. (1956) *Taxonomy of Educational Objectives, Handbook I: The Cognitive Domain*. New York: David McKay Co Inc.

Further reading

Capel, S.A., Leask, M. and Turner, T. (2009) *Learning to Teach in the Secondary School: A Companion to School Experience*, 5th edn. London: Routledge.

Fautley, M. and Savage, J. (2008) *Assessment for Learning and Teaching in Secondary Schools*. Exeter: Learning Matters.

R

Reasoning

Reasoning is the mental process by which we absorb, assimilate and rearrange information in order to arrive at a conclusion. The development of reasoning abilities within developing children is one area of research with which Piaget (see **cognition**) was concerned.

There two main types of reasoning: 'Concept formation which relies on abstracting the characteristics of objects or situations in order to form generalizations is known as *inductive* reasoning. Where generalizations are used to describe particular instances, we call the process *deductive* reasoning' (Child 1997: 195). As children develop and mature, their reasoning becomes more complex, until they arrive at the *formal operational* stage, where they are able to think logically.

There are complex discussions in psychology as to whether or not reasoning is a purely verbal activity, which takes place in the mind as non-spoken verbalized thought processes, or through what is known as the *Sapir-Whorf hypothesis* where language determines thought.

We know from the work of Piaget and others that some forms of reasoning and concepts held by students are not always accurate or fully formed. In the pre-operational stage, if a tall and thin glass of lemonade is presented next to a short and fat one, many children will say there is more in the taller glass. If you then pour the drink into the shorter tumbler, the child will now say there is less. Following Piaget, the implications of this are that the child is not yet ready to engage in formal operational thinking, and learning programmes need to take account of this.

But it is not only at the early stages of a student's development that challenges to reasoning can be considered. For example, in maths education the notion of cognitive conflict is quite well established:

> Cognitive conflict can be identified in the classroom whenever learners are heard to exclaim 'Oh!' or 'I didn't expect that!' or 'Hmmm. . .'. The learner, on finding that his existing tools or methods are insufficient to produce a solution, is motivated to resolve the conflict and adapts existing mental models to

accommodate to the new information. Put simply, new learning occurs at the limit of understanding when, provoked by a surprise, contradiction or obstacle, the learner is suddenly 'not sure'.

(Sayce 2009: 4)

Cognitive conflict occurs when previously held beliefs or ideas turn out to be inadequate or incorrect when required to deal with new problems. This does not just occur in maths, cognitive conflict can be introduced into any lessons. Some teachers use challenging starter activities which require students to think through what is going on in certain scenarios, or look at images, and explain their ideas to the class. Developing reasoning is part of the role of the teacher. This can be done by helping students understand why they are wrong, not just being told they are! One way that this has been done is that when students have done a marked task, the teacher tells the students that they have scored 6/10, but has not marked individual elements as right or wrong. The students then need to talk to each other to find out which elements they got wrong and why. Here the talking about the work is part of the learning, not a separate element. As Mercer observes: 'my review leads me to the conclusion that talk between learners has been shown to be valuable for the construction of knowledge. Joint activity provides opportunities for practising and developing ways of reasoning with language, and the same kinds of opportunities do not arise in teacher-led discourse' (Mercer 1995: 98). So, the development of reasoning here uses language, and by facilitating classroom discussion leaners are able to explore and develop in this fascinating area.

Key questions

1 How do I know what the students think?
2 What can I do to challenge their thinking in order to take learning forwards?
3 What is the best way to plan for the development of reasoning skills?

References

Child, D. (1997) *Psychology and the Teacher,* 6th edn. London: Cassell.
Mercer, N. (1995) *The Guided Construction of Knowledge: Talk Amongst Teachers and Learners.* Clevedon: Multilingual Matters.
Sayce, L. (2009) *The Route to Cognitive Conflict.* Reading: National Centre for Excellence in the Teaching of Mathematics.

Further reading

Mercer, N., Wegerif, R. and Dawes, L. (1999) Children's talk and the development of reasoning in the classroom. *British Educational Research Journal*, 25(1): 95–111.

Reflection

Collins Thesaurus (Collins 2002) has the following entry for 'reflection': 'a calm, lengthy, intent consideration'; it follows this with words such as 'musing, rumination, thoughtfulness, contemplation, reflexion, meditation, introspection and speculation'. In the hurly-burly of school life, you might ask yourself whether reflection, whilst desirable, is possible! Many programmes of initial teacher education are built around the idea of the 'reflective practitioner'. But how realistic is an approach to teaching as a reflective practice for every teacher?

We would argue that reflection is an essential type of activity for all teachers to undertake. This is true throughout your whole career, but it could be especially important during moments of transition (e.g. when you are coming into teaching, moving between jobs or taking on a new role).

So, what does it mean to be a reflective teacher? Drawing on the work of Donald Schön (Schön 1983: 332–4), we think it involves the following. The reflective teacher:

- listens to their students and really seeks to understand them as unique individuals, tailoring their instruction, speech and learning resources to respond to their specific requirements;
- thinks beyond their lesson plan in seeking to respond to individual students' needs and requirements;
- uses the curriculum as an inventory of themes to be understood rather than a set of materials to be learnt;
- expands their knowledge of the students to encompass their learning and interests outside of the classroom;
- uses technology in a way to empower students to undertake their own learning rather than to reinforce old-fashioned, teacher-centric pedagogies;
- prioritizes independent, qualitative, narrative accounts of learning over blunt, accountability-driven assessment frameworks that depersonalize the student and their achievements;

- challenges set theories of knowledge and its organization within the school systems of timetables and classrooms, seeking to make links in imaginative ways across and between subject boundaries.

This is quite a challenge! But do not be daunted. Reflective practice can start simply and quietly, in your own mind or in a private teaching journal. It need not be part of a grand scale process of performance management or other accountability mechanisms. In fact, it would be better kept out of these frameworks. We think it too important to be compromised by them.

But, you might argue, the general busyness of school life can compromise any well meaning approach to developing a reflective practice. Clearly, this is a danger. But the writers on reflective practice recognize this and, more importantly, identify the larger structural forces at work in any organization that can compromise an individual's attempt to be reflective. Here, for example, is Schön writing about how the structure of many educational systems works against reflective practice. He asks us to imagine a school whose work is characterized by a range of features (some of which you may recognize). It is:

1   Built around a theory of knowledge which dictates that it is the teachers' job to teach and students to learn. Knowledge is imparted by teachers in 'measurable doses', with students digesting these chunks and teachers planning for students' progressive development.
2   Orderly, in terms of space and time. It has self-contained classrooms and a regular timetable through which knowledge bases (subjects) are partitioned and delivered.
3   Controlled by systems of sanctions and rewards for students, with expectations for individual students set and checked regularly.
4   Controlled by systems of sanctions and rewards for staff, with management structures ensuring standards are maintained.
5   Characterized by objectivity, with quantitative measures of proficiency and progress preferred to qualitative or narrative accounts of learning and teaching.

The bureaucratic model of schooling he outlines imposes significant restraints on the work of the aspiring reflective teacher. However, it need not quash it completely. Part of working through a process of reflective practice is understanding the forces that can mitigate against it.

So, how can you respond as a teacher? You can do the following:

- Make a firm commitment to practise the art of being a reflective teacher.

- Find a short period of time each day, even if it is just a few minutes, to reflect on the teaching you have engaged with during the day. Ask yourself simple questions like:
    - What went well?
    - What did not go so well?
    - How could you improve things?
    - What would you do differently next time?
- Keep a teaching journal, if not all the time at least for a set or specific period (e.g. the introduction of a new unit of work) to help you reflect more deeply on a specific intervention.
- If possible, find a colleague to help share your reflections and act as a 'critical friend'.

Key questions

1 What are broad benefits of developing a reflective approach to my teaching?
2 How can I counteract some of the structural or systematic elements of school life that work against a reflective approach to teaching?

References

Collins (2002) *Thesaurus of the English Language: Complete and Unabridged,* 2nd edn. New York: HarperCollins Publishers.
Schön, D. (1983) *The Reflective Practitioner: How Professionals Think in Action.* New York: Basic Books.

Further reading

Schön, D. (1983) *The Reflective Practitioner: How Professionals Think in Action.* New York: Basic Books.

Relationships

One of the difficulties which new and beginning teachers have in the classroom is in establishing the right level of relationship with students. For younger teachers, where there can be only a few years of age separating the teacher from the older students, the age gap can be much smaller than between, say, the young teacher and the senior leadership team. Knowing how to pitch relationships at the right level might seem an obvious thing to say, but it is not for the students. They will be asking questions, testing boundaries and working out how to place themselves in hierarchical order with the staff.

Smith and Laslett (1993) suggest four simple rules for effective classroom management:

1   get them in;
2   get them out;
3   get on with it;
4   get on with them.

These four rules are based on sound classroom understanding, and it is the final one, 'get on with them', which is of concern to us here. Getting on with the students might seem an obvious thing to say, but we have seen many teachers come unstuck over this issue. There is an old religious saying to the effect of 'punish the sin, care for the sinner'. This is a useful adage for school relationships. As a teacher, it is useful to try to differentiate between what a student has done, and who they are as a person. You will hear experienced pastoral staff say things like 'That was a silly thing to do', rather than 'You are silly'; in the former the action is separated from the person, they can admit it was a silly thing to do; in the latter the only recourses are to either agree they are silly, which can cause loss of face, or argue. Separating out the crime depersonalizes the human relationships involved.

An experienced special school head used to tell his staff to remember that they were not the students' mates. They did not expect Year 9s to be going round to the teacher's house asking if they were coming out to play football! This is the distinction that new teachers find troublesome. You will want to be friendly, but you still want to maintain a professional distance from the students. In the entry on **audience** we discussed the changes in register that you will need to adopt when in and out of the staffroom. Similar things apply with your dealings with students. How you treat a class of thirty Year 7s will be entirely different from how you deal with a small group of upper sixth students.

Relationships with students are very difficult to mend once broken, but it is your responsibility to do so. As one PGCE course leader says to student teachers, 'Remember, you are the adult'. This is important advice; it is the school pupils who are adults with 'L' plates. You are in a position of taking charge of the situation. We often hear beginner teachers and NQTs say things like, 'I hate 9Z, and they hate me'. This can cause a spiral of descent, and it is best addressed before it gets to this stage. This might mean distancing and adopting a more rigid approach, but the situation needs rescuing before it breaks down. Whilst it is to be hoped that the days of the advice given to new teachers of 'don't smile till Christmas' have passed, nonetheless it is important to remember that teaching involves a long series of relationships which will play out over an extended time-scale.

Key questions

1 How do I sound and appear when I talk to classes? Have I watched myself on video?
2 Have I thought about what sort of teacher I am with different age groups?

Reference

Smith, C.J. and Laslett, R. (1993) *Effective Classroom Management: A Teacher's Guide*, 2nd edn. London: Routledge.

Further reading

Brooks, V., Abbott, I. and Bills, L. (2007) *Preparing to Teach in Secondary Schools: A Student Teacher's Guide to Professional Issues in Secondary Education*, 2nd edn. Maidenhead: Open University Press.

Research

'Research is systematic enquiry made public' (Stenhouse 1983: 11). This is not our definition. It comes from the work of Lawrence Stenhouse who probably did more than any other educationalist to establish research as a key component of teachers' work.

In today's educational culture, educational research is often professionalized and marginalized from the work of the majority of teachers. It is seen as an activity that is done by specialist researchers and reported to an academic community with little obvious public interest. However, this model is flawed on many levels. We believe that the time is right to rediscover some of the richness of the Stenhousian tradition for the teacher as researcher.

In our section on **curriculum**, we considered Stenhouse's assertion that there is 'no curriculum development without teacher development'. The process that Stenhouse believed should underpin the development of both the teacher and curriculum was 'action research'.

Action research is defined as:

> the study of a social situation with a view to improving the quality of action within it. It aims to feed practical judgement in concrete situations, and the validity of the 'theories' or hypotheses it generates depends not so much on 'scientific' tests of truth, as on their usefulness in helping people to act more intelligently and skilfully. In action research 'theories' are not validated independently and then applied in practice. They are validated through practice.
>
> (Elliott 1991: 69)

This is one of the classic definitions for action research. It states, unambiguously, that you can study your classroom (a 'social situation') with a view to improving the quality of teaching and learning ('action') within it. It is a practical method through which your ideas are tested out through your practice. Or, to put it another way:

> Action research happens when people are involved in researching their own practice in order to improve it and to come to a better understanding of their practice situations. It is action because they act within the systems that they are trying to improve and understand. It is research because it is systematic, critical inquiry made public.
>
> (Feldman 2007: 239)

Most writers about action research conceptualize it as a spiral of practical and conceptual activities. Perhaps the simplest way of representing it is as a circle with four principal activities (see Figure 1). One of the benefits of this spiral is its simplicity. However, beneath it lies a fair degree of complexity that you would be well advised to read about further before embarking on an action research project of your own. One of the key things you will want to think through is how any structured process of research that you undertake might relate to broader processes of professional development that you are engaging in (whether this be your school's performance management process or an external academic course of study).

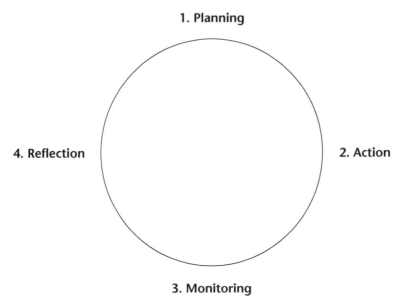

Figure 1

To return, briefly, to the opening definition of 'research' provided by Stenhouse: did you notice the 'made public' bit of it? This is crucial. Whilst you might not have the time or inclination to want to write up and publish a formal account of any piece of research you do, there is a sense in which you can make your work as a teacher more public through various other outlets. The massive explosion in blogs over the last five years or so is one example of self-publishing that can be both therapeutic for the writer and help broaden the knowledge base of our educational community.

Engaging in a strategic action research can be a vital strand in your own professional development and lead to many powerful pieces of curriculum development too. It can help keep your teaching relevant, powerful and a source of enjoyment for you and your students.

Key questions

---

1 Can my time working as a teacher be counted as my time working as a researcher?
2 Are the two roles complementary in practice as well as in theory?

References

Elliott, J. (1991) *Action Research for Educational Change*. Philadelphia, PA:
    Open University Press.
Feldman, A. (2007) Teachers, responsibility and action research. *Educational
    Action Research*, 15(2): 239–52.
Stenhouse, L. (1983) Research is systematic enquiry made public. *British
    Educational Research Journal*, 9(1): 11–20.

Further reading

Elliott, J. (1991) *Action Research for Educational Change*. Philadelphia, PA: Open
    University Press.
McNiff, J. and Whitehead, J. (2005) *Action Research for Teachers: A Practical
    Guide*. London: David Fulton.

Resources

Teaching does not take place in a vacuum! The environment that you create within your classroom has a key impact on the way in which you teach and the way in which your students learn. A key part of your classroom environment are the resources that you choose to use within it.
   Resources can include:

- toys and games;
- books, including exercise books, text books and other reference materials;
- art materials;
- musical instruments;
- computers and other forms of digital technology;
- pieces of software;
- internet resources including music, video or other files;
- and anything else you use in your teaching!

The first rule with resources is to be organized. Make sure that the resources you need for any lesson are collected together and checked prior to the beginning of the lesson. There is nothing worse than the flow of the lesson being disrupted because the teacher is having to find something that they thought they had but that has magically disappeared! In terms of pieces of digital technology such as computers, software, websites, videos or other presentational tools, check, check and check again! Is that video you selected on YouTube to demonstrate an important concept available from the computer in your classroom? If not, have you got a back-up plan? Use your lesson plan to list the resources you need for the lesson. Check that you have them all ready in advance of the start of the lesson.

In terms of your own work, make sure that the resources you are using to explain or model key concepts are well prepared. If you are using text books, make sure you know which page number you want to refer to; if you are using musical or video examples, have these edited to the right portion and/or length to avoid having to fumble through CD or iTunes tracks; if you are using a worksheet have this photocopied clearly and make sure there are enough copies for all the students. These may seem like basic things but you would be amazed how many times we watch lessons where the lack or inappropriate organization of basic resources has a massive negative impact on the students' progress.

If your lesson involves group work, make sure that the resources needed to do that work effectively are placed together, perhaps even within a box for each group. This can help speed up the transition between any explanatory or modelling phase of the lesson and the group work itself. If groups are using common resources that are easily accessible within classroom storage, make sure that there are enough resources for each group.

As both of us were involved in teaching in secondary schools, we marvel at the way in which primary school teachers manage and organize the resources in their classrooms. We would encourage you, if you get the chance, to visit a typical reception-age classroom and look at how the resources of the classroom are managed (including their storage and accessibility). There are many lessons that could be learnt here for all teachers.

Traditionally, certain subjects have additional help in preparing the resources required. As teachers of music, we often bemoaned the extra support our science and design technology staff received! However, it is important to remember the choice and organization of all resources used within a lesson is the teacher's responsibility.

As a final point, why not consider making greater use of the resources that students bring with them to their lessons? The mobile phones that many older students have in their pockets contain significant amounts of processing power that would rival the computers that schools were using even a few years ago. Many schools are beginning to embrace the power of mobile technologies such as phones, iPads and the like. As with any resource, our pedagogy will need to develop in line with the resources. There will be particular challenges that will exercise you and the school as a whole, but there are many positive opportunities too.

Key questions

1 Which resources do I really need to teach effectively? Can I provide a good justification for each resource I use?
2 What practical steps can I take to get my classroom space more organized?

Further reading

Have a look at the following pinboard for some great ideas about getting your resources organized in the classroom: An Organised Teacher is a Happy Teacher. http://pinterest.com/maccuelandry/an-organized-teacher-is-a-happy-teacher/ (accessed 1 July 2012).

S

Safeguarding

Safeguarding covers a wide range of issues appertaining to the emotional, social, physical and personal safety of young people, in schools, colleges and beyond. This includes child protection issues, as well as medical issues, and safeguarding against drug and alcohol misuse.

As the Department for Education note on their website, 'few things are more important than helping and protecting vulnerable children and young people' (DfE 2012). As a teacher you will be responsible for safeguarding children and young people whilst they are in your care. This will involve reporting concerns you have with regard to what is going on in young people's lives in and beyond the school. The guidance published by the DCSF in 2010 states that:

> All organizations that provide services or work with children and young people should:
>
> 1 Have senior managers who are committed to children's and young people's welfare and safety;
> 2 Be clear about people's responsibilities to safeguard and promote children's and young people's welfare;
> 3 Check that there are no known reasons or information available that would prevent staff and volunteers from working with children and young people;
> 4 Have procedures for dealing with allegations of abuse against members of staff and volunteers;
> 5 Make sure staff get training that helps them do their job well;
> 6 Have procedures about how to safeguard and promote the welfare of young people; and
> 7 Have agreements about working with other organizations.
> (DCSF 2010: 9)

It is important for anyone who works in a school to be clear on who the relevant professionals are within that school to whom safeguarding and child protection issues need to be addressed. This is an important part of induction, or of early visits to a school. Indeed, some schools have these details on information sheets, which all visitors to the school need to sign to show they have read. It is important for all adults in schools to be aware of these, and to know who to turn to when needed. If in doubt, all staff in school have a duty of care and so any teacher will treat these matters with the utmost seriousness and tell you what you need to do if you think or suspect that something is amiss. It is crucial this information gets passed on quickly.

Related to this is how you react when talking to young people. If a child asks if they can speak to you in confidence it is important that you allow yourself and the child the condition that if they tell you anything serious you have a legal duty to pass this information on. This means that as you don't know what the child will be telling you, you have not put yourself in the impossible position of not being able to pass on important safeguarding information. You will need to do this carefully, discretely and in a caring fashion; after all we do not want to prevent the child pursuing what might have been a very important conversation. But this gives you the chance to deal with issues appropriately. The student may simply want to tell you that they have split up with their boyfriend, that they are worried about their forthcoming exams, or that they have lost their pencil case. But it may be that they want to tell you something much more serious. Whilst you may well be equipped to deal with any of the issues previously mentioned yourself, for the safeguarding issues you will need to get others involved. But even with some boyfriend/exam worries/lost pencil case issues it is still worth passing this information on to a year head or pastoral care coordinator. Sometimes there can be patterns of behaviour, especially in large secondary schools, which do not become immediately apparent, but only emerge when a number of staff have reported concerns.

The really important messages of this serious section are:

1   You should not keep things to yourself.
2   Do not promise to do so to pupils, but phrase this carefully to them in a way that will not close down the conversation.
3   Refer things immediately to one of the named people in your institution designated to deal with these issues.

Key questions

1   Do I know who the named people for safeguarding and child protection are in the school(s) I am in?
2   Have I considered what my response will be if a child asks to talk to me in confidence?
3   Have I read any school policies on this, before it becomes an issue?

References

DCSF (2010) *A Guide to Inter-agency Working to Safeguard and Promote the Welfare of Children.* London: DCSF.

DfE (2012) Child Protection Reform. http://www.education.gov.uk/childrenandyoungpeople/safeguardingchildren/protection (accessed 12 September 2012).

Further reading

Lindon, J. (2008) *Safeguarding Children and Young People.* London: Hachette Livre UK.

Sequencing

A number of times in this book we talk about planning for teaching and learning in ways that involve sequencing the order in which you present skills and concepts to your classes. This is a key element of educational endeavour, and yet is one which can catch the novice teacher unawares if it has not been factored in.

It is important to begin this entry on sequencing by reiterating the observation that teaching does not equal learning. If it did, things would only need to be taught once, and they would be learned for ever. The implication of this for considerations of sequencing is that planning for teaching things in the most logical order is the task of the teacher. This does not guarantee that it will be learned in this order; you will hear colleagues in the staffroom say things like, 'I don't know why they haven't learned it yet, I've taught it to them a hundred times at least!'. With this in mind, it is worth approaching sequencing as providing the best possible avenue for your students to learn, because you will have decided on the route beforehand.

The types of learning that you are planning for will differ between subject areas, and between topics within subjects, so it useful for you as the teacher to consider what this means for what it is you wish to be teaching. In the entry on **development** we considered the notion of the spiral curriculum. This is one way of sequencing teaching and learning so that topics are revisited.

In thinking about sequencing it is useful to begin with the perspective of learning, and then move to considering the teaching that will enable learning to take place. Lave and Wenger helpfully point out that there are differences between a *learning curriculum* and a *teaching curriculum*. A learning curriculum is one which is 'viewed from the perspective of learners' (Lave and Wenger 1991: 97), whereas a teaching curriculum is 'mediated through an instructor's participation, by an external view of what knowing is about' (Lave and Wenger 1991: 97). From the perspectives of compulsory stages of education, it will be a teaching curriculum which is planned for, as the 'external view of what knowing is about' will be supplied by you and other staff at your school. But this does not mean that you should ignore the learners' perspective; the taught curriculum should benefit from your pedagogic content knowledge (see entry on **judgements**) in terms of sequencing.

So how can you go about this? Diana Burton suggests building up a conceptual hierarchy of ideas within a topic, and drawing a sort of 'mind map' that shows the interlinkages between the ideas (Burton 2009). This is logical, and doing this across a range of topics will give a view as to the ways in which you can sequence learning across a longer timescale (see **planning**). But what is most useful from doing this exercise across a range of topics, working with colleagues, is that it will enable you to see how you can plan for developing knowledge, skills and concepts over time. It will also show where these can usefully be introduced initially, and where reinforcement and development can take place so that skills can be worked at and concepts enhanced.

Key questions

1 What do I want the students to learn?
2 What is the best way for me to present this to them?
3 How I can organize my teaching curriculum based on the sequence of learning I want the students to undertake?

References

Burton, D. (2009) Ways students learn, in S. Capel, M. Leask and T. Turner (eds) *Learning to Teach in the Secondary School: A Companion to School Experience*, 5th edn, pp. 213–49. London: Routledge.

Lave, J. and Wenger, E. (1991) *Situated Learning: Legitimate Peripheral Participation*. Cambridge: Cambridge University Press.

Further reading

Fautley, M. and Savage, J. (2008) *Assessment for Learning and Teaching in Secondary Schools*. Exeter: Learning Matters.

Space

Space refers to the locations within which teaching and learning occur. For many teachers, their classroom provides a dedicated space for their teaching. Many teachers have 'specialist' spaces – e.g. science laboratories, art rooms, playing fields – within which they teach. However, for many teachers classrooms contain many common elements (chairs, tables, classroom displays, interactive whiteboard, etc.). It is worth exploring how the spaces within which we teach affect the processes of teaching and learning.

The organization of the classroom space is an integral part of a teacher's pedagogy. This is because you cannot teach in a vacuum! Everything you do as a teacher takes place in a particular context. The organization of the elements within that context will play a part in shaping what occurs. But, unfortunately, for many teachers the 'environment' that their teaching occurs within is seldom flexible enough, either practically or conceptually, in its design. The Design Council comment that:

> The environment can only make a difference if it is used by creative teachers with an appropriate curriculum and resources. Yet for many teachers their environment is still a blind spot: unchanging, unchangeable and beyond their control – an obstacle that they must work around, rather than a tool to support and enhance their practice.
>
> (Design Council 2005: 18)

Generally, teaching spaces have not changed significantly over the last hundred years. They are still dominated by one type of design, which is:

> tutor-focused, one way facing and presentational, with seating arranged in either a U-shape or in straight rows. Technologies have subsequently been added – interactive or conventional whiteboards mounted on the wall behind the main speaker, ceiling-mounted projectors with cabling to a laptop, a wireless network and/or wired computers – but these have rarely altered the dynamics of the design.
>
> (JISC 2006: 10)

But things can be different. Recent research into the design of alternative spaces for teaching and learning in our schools has suggested a number of key features that need to be included (McGregor 2007: 18):

1   Accommodating the formation and function of small learning groups alongside more traditional approaches to pedagogical

instruction. When groups work they need a degree of separation within a space otherwise they will become distracted; therefore . . .

2   Classroom space needs to be flexible to allow for the easy reorganization of the class into groups; but . . .

3   The space needs to be managed by a single teacher so they need to be positioned appropriately and the space needs to be compact and open.

In light of these suggestions, here are some specific questions related to common resources found in a typical classroom.

1   *Tables and chairs*   How are these organized in your classroom? Are they in rows or lines? Are they easily moved? What would happen if you got rid of them completely? How would that affect the way that you teach? Would it matter if your students did not have anything to write on? What would you do instead?

2   *Blackboard or interactive whiteboard*   Where are these situated? What type of teaching style do these technologies facilitate? How do you use them in a typical lesson? How do they implicate the way in which your class is organized (i.e. where students sit in order to see the board)?

3   *Classroom displays*   What are these used for? What type of information is displayed on them? Do you make any attempts to integrate these within your teaching? Are they there solely to provide information, or celebrate students' achievements, or something else?

4   *Alternative spaces*   If your classroom contains too many fixed elements, are there alternative spaces that you could teach in on occasions? Ask yourself how your teaching would change if you taught in a different space. Are the benefits worth the inevitable upheaval?

Key questions

1   Are there any practical decisions I can take to make my classroom a more flexible space?

2   How can I ensure that the environment that I teach within does not become a 'blind spot' and that I can keep the classroom space and resources within it under regular review to ensure that they facilitate positive approaches to teaching and learning?

References

Design Council (2005) *Learning Environments Campaign Prospectus: From the Inside Looking Out.* London: Design Council.

JISC (2006) Designing Spaces for Effective Learning: A Guide to 21st Century Learning Space Design. http://www.jisc.ac.uk/uploaded_documents/JISClearningspaces.pdf (accessed 5 July 2012).

McGregor, J. (2007) Understanding and Managing Classroom Space. http://www.teachingexpertise.com/resources/cpd-resource-understanding-and-managing-classroom-space-3324 (accessed 4 July 2012).

Further reading

McGregor, J. (2007) Understanding and Managing Classroom Space. http://www.teachingexpertise.com/resources/cpd-resource-understanding-and-managing-classroom-space-3324 (accessed 4 July 2012).

Speaking

Your voice is your most powerful tool as a teacher. How you train your voice and how you look after it are both really important considerations at every stage of your teaching career.

In terms of training your voice, perhaps the most important point to grasp is that you will need several different 'types' of voice in order to teach effectively. Some of these might be similar to your standard speaking voice, but many are going to be significantly different. For this reason, you are going to have to practise speaking in at least the following types of voice:

- *The 'look at me now class' voice*   This voice needs to grab the students' attention, whatever they are doing, and signal your calm, authoritative expectation that students will stop what they are doing, turn around and face you in silence. This one might take a lot of practice but it is worth developing! You will need to use it at the beginning of lessons and also when you need to change the direction of a lesson from one activity to another.
- *The 'general teaching' voice*   This is the normal teaching voice that you will use to deliver instructions, explain or model something, question pupils and generally conduct the day-to-day business of classroom teaching. It will probably be the closest to your usual

speaking voice but you should ensure that this voice projects well into the classroom space so that all students can clearly hear what you are saying.

- *The 'calming' voice* This is quieter than your general teaching voice. It should draw students in to what you are saying and foster a sense of curiosity and engagement. You should use this voice for key moments in a lesson as it can be very powerful when used occasionally at the right moment.
- *The 'praising' voice* This voice should be full of heartfelt praise for what a student has achieved. It must never be patronising (in fact, a patronising tone should be avoided at all costs in the classroom) and should be an authentic response to a student's efforts.
- *The 'frustrated' voice* This is a difficult one. This voice should be reserved for occasions when you want a student or students to realize that you are not happy about a certain aspect of the lesson, e.g. their lack of engagement in a particular task. Please note that we have not called this an 'angry' voice. We do not think that raw displays of anger achieve much in a classroom. Rather, this voice needs to show that you are unhappy, but not weak, and that you expect things to change. In this sense, the 'frustrated' voice can be closely followed by the 'look at me now class' voice in order to turn a potentially negative situation around quickly. We suggest that this voice is reserved for special occasions only!

Clearly, there will be other 'voices' that you can develop within your teaching, but this is a good starting list. It is important to find your own voice. There is no point in trying to copy another teacher. What works for them may not work for you. Our voice is an incredibly individual thing and you must maintain a sense of your own individuality and integrity in how you use your voice. Practise each of the above voices. Find a private space with a mirror, look at yourself and rehearse some common phrases with the various voices. This might feel a bit odd to start with but it is important you get over any initial embarrassment. This will be time well spent. You do not want to try out these voices for the first time in front of a group of students!

All teachers need to look after their voice. As we stated above, it is the most powerful tool you have as a teacher. The following tips come from a range of materials that we have reviewed related to how an actor or singer might train their voice. However, they are just as appropriate for the 'performance' of teaching as they are for any other.

First, make sure you warm your voice up. There are lots of exercises that you can do, including humming, hissing, articulating various consonant sounds (ssssss, shhhhh, etc.) and vocal slides. Tongue twisters help (you will get better at them) and whilst doing all these warm up exercises, remember to breath in deeply and exhale slowly. Breath control is vital for good vocal production.

Second, whilst teaching make sure you stand tall. Keep your shoulder blades sloping down your back and do not sag in the middle! Good posture is vital for effective use of the voice. This has the added benefit of portraying a confident body language, which should help with maintaining discipline. Also, try to avoid shouting over your class. This presents a very weak image and can strain your voice over time. Instead, find another 'cue' for the class to stop what they are doing (i.e. there is a reason why PE teachers have a whistle).

Third, try to minimize drinking caffeinated or fizzy drinks prior to teaching. These dry out your vocal folds. Rather, drink water instead. Also avoid eating too many dairy products. These encourage the production of phlegm which interferes with the natural working of the vocal chords. Try to rest your voice when possible and, if it is feeling under strain, use steam inhalations and gargle with boiled, salty water to help reduce pain and fight infections. Medicated lozenges that kill pain can lead to further problems later on (the pain is there for a reason), so please use these carefully.

From many years of observing trainee teachers, another factor we have noted is the inappropriate use of pitch when talking, or more usually, when raising the voice. This can be unconscious, but it does place more strain on the vocal chords. Each voice has an optimum pitch range, moving beyond which causes problems in the long term and leads to strain and fatigue in the short term. It is worth studying video recordings of your teaching technique to see if this is what you are doing. Surprisingly many teachers find that when they raise their voices in volume, they also unknowingly raise them in pitch too.

And, finally, we deal with sleep in another section, but 'a good night's sleep is an essential factor for appropriate vocal production' (Ferreira et al. 2010: 86).

Remember that although your voice is an important tool it is not the only one you have. Good teachers rest their voices whenever possible and use a range of non-verbal signs to ensure that their students remain focused and engaged. If you are really struggling with your voice, the best solution is to take some time off work and recover fully. Just ploughing on teaching and speaking with a damaged voice risks permanent vocal damage which must be avoided at all costs.

Key questions

1 What steps do I need to take to look after my voice effectively?
2 Which of the above voices do I need to develop further?

Reference

Ferreira, L.P., de Oliveira Latorre, M.R.D., Pinto Giannini, S.P. et al. (2010) Influence of abusive vocal habits, hydration, mastication, and sleep in the occurrence of vocal symptoms in teachers. *Journal of Voice*, 24(1): 86–92.

Further reading

Teaching Expertise (2012) Saving Your Voice. http://www.teachingexpertise. com/articles/saving-your-voice-2029 (accessed 17 July 2012).
Voice Care Network UK (2012) Voice Tips. http://www.voicecare.org.uk/vcn/ voice-tips (accessed 17 July 2012).

Special educational needs (SEN)

'Special educational needs' describes the needs of a child who has a difficulty or disability that makes learning harder for them than it might be for other children of their age. It is a legal term that covers a broad spectrum of difficulties and disabilities. Many children will have special educational needs at some point in their education. As a teacher, it will be your responsibility to work as part of a team to support these children, adopting and implementing specific support to help them engage and learn within your classes.

There are numerous 'types' or 'categories' of special educational needs. It is beyond the scope of this short entry to discuss them all, but some of the most common types or categories of SEN that you may come across in your school include:

- attention deficit hyperactivity disorder (ADHD);
- Asperger's syndrome;
- autism;
- dyslexia;

- emotional and behavioural difficulties (EBD);
- epilepsy
- obsessive compulsive disorder (OCD);
- speech and language disorder;
- Tourette's syndrome.

You can find a comprehensive list and description of many different SEN at http://www.specialeducationalneeds.co.uk/typesofsen-disability.htm

Whatever form of SEN a student has, there are some basic principles that all schools and teachers must be aware of. These include:

- the right of the child to have their SEN meet through a broad, well-balanced and relevant education;
- the right of the child and their parents to have their views listened to, taken into account and acted on if they are in their best interests;
- the incorporation of children with SEN into mainstream schooling whenever and wherever possible, sometimes with the assistance of outside specialists working collaboratively with the school.

Once a child with SEN has been formally identified, schools will normally write an individual education plan (IEP) to help formulate a coherent approach to that child's educational entitlement in the school. This IEP would normally include:

- what special or additional help is going to be given to that particular child;
- who will provide that help and how often it will be delivered;
- what help can the parents give their child at home to support the work being done by you and other teachers within the school;
- the setting of some individual targets for that child's progress during the term or academic year;
- a description of how and when the child's progress will be checked or assessed.

As a classroom teacher, you will have a vital role in supporting children with SEN. This will include helping to identify and diagnose particular issues as soon as possible. It will also include adapting and implementing alternative teaching strategies in light of the individual needs that a particular child or group of children in your class might have. To give some practical examples, children with SEN may need additional help with the following:

- General work within your classes including reading, writing, number work or understanding information. This might require amending or adapting the resources that you are using to assist them in a specific way.

- Expressing themselves or understanding what others are saying. This may result in you having to consider the social groupings in your class and the ways in which students engage with each other in different activities.
- Making friends or relating to adults. Perhaps this is an aspect of support that extends beyond your individual classroom and will affect how these students are integrated into the life of the whole school.

Key questions

1 What are the various types or categories of SEN and disability that I am likely to come across working within my school?
2 What practical approaches will I need to make to my teaching in order to accommodate the specific SEN of the students in my classes?

Further reading

Department for Education: Special Educational Needs. http://www.education. gov.uk/schools/pupilsupport/sen (accessed 31 July 2012).

Frederickson, N. and Cline, T. (2009) *Special Educational Needs, Inclusion and Diversity*. Maidenhead: Open University Press.

Teaching Expertise: Special Educational Needs. http://www.teachingexpertise. com/special-educational-needs (accessed 31 July 2012).

Starters

Starters are the first part of the famous three part lesson (starter, main, plenary) that was popular in schools throughout the first decade of the twenty-first century. Starters exploit those key moments at the beginning of the lesson when your students may be at their most receptive. Effective starters have three main characteristics. They:

1   engage all students;
2   establish the pace of the lesson;
3   provide challenge.

In terms of engagement, the challenge for you is to use the starter to get all students on task quickly. This is not the time for lengthy explanations, detailed feedback on recent assessment items, or anything else that will clutter the opening minutes of the lesson. Your starter is going to be engaging if:

- the task involved in the starter is immediately accessible to all or most students;
- it captures the students' interest, perhaps with an element of novelty, curiosity or mystery;
- the expectations relating to the class are made clear and given a specific timescale;
- it builds on what students already know or understand in their skills, knowledge or understanding within your subject area;
- you use the opportunity to help develop new activities that allow students to practise or apply subject or generic skills in a new way;
- you intervene, when necessary, to help sustain student engagement and ensure that the task does not outlast the concentration span of the students.

The most common failure that we have seen over the years in the student teachers that we have worked with is that starters can last for too long, sometimes taking over half the lesson! This is wrong. Make sure your starters are just that, starters. They are not the main course. We would suggest that no starter activity should last more than 10 per cent of the allocated lesson time.

Second, starters should be delivered at a good pace. This is not the same as rushing through the starter. It means you move the task through purposefully, ensuring that distractions are kept to a minimum. So, with your starters:

- Make sure that the task is not overly complicated and does not require masses of resources to set up. If possible, make sure all the resources for the starter are in place before your lesson commences. Organization is key!
- Ensure you communicate the key learning objective relating to the starter quickly and simply either before the starter begins or, if you would rather, once the students have engaged with the task by way of summing up and moving onto the main teaching activity.

Third, make sure your starters are challenging. There is a fine line here. The relationship between challenge and engagement needs to be monitored.

If a starter activity is too easy, then students will disengage and get bored; if it is too difficult, frustration can impact on their motivation. So, simple starters may require students to engage in a particular process, explore a new idea or revise something learnt in a previous lesson; more challenging starters may require them to apply knowledge in a new way, analyse, synthesize or evaluate information or ideas.

Finally, starters will need careful planning. They are a key part of your lesson and vitally important for setting the right tone and expectation for everything that follows. You really need to make sure that lessons start off in the right way. It is very hard to turn around a lesson that has started badly. So, for these reasons, make sure that you do the following:

- Ensure that your starter has a clear purpose and relate this to your chosen learning objective.
- Ensure that the content of the starter engages and challenges students at an appropriate pace.
- Connect the starter to prior learning, either by building on what has been learnt in previous lessons or by using it to establish or assimilate a new idea or topic.

Key question

How can I build starters into my lessons that are engaging, delivered at the right pace and have an appropriate degree of challenge?

Further reading

Brown, K. (2009) *Classroom Starters and Plenaries: Creative Ideas for Use Across the Curriculum*. London: Continuum.

Streaming and setting

Streaming and setting refer to ways of grouping students by ability. Setting occurs when grouping by ability changes according to the subject involved, so a pupil could be in set 1 for English, and set 3 for maths. Streaming occurs when students stay in the same group for all subjects on the timetable, but they have been organized into class groups based upon some notion of overall ability for this purpose.

Streaming and setting are emotive issues in education, and there is disagreement about whether streaming, setting or mixed ability teaching is the best way of organizing students. One view is that children should be divided by ability, so that all can be taught at an appropriate level. The opposite view is that mixed ability teaching allows children to work cooperatively together, and has positive effects on those students who might otherwise underachieve, with a reduction in worries about status. In terms of educational research into this area, it seems fair to say that there is not a consensus as to whether either of these two views is correct. As Ireson and Hallam observe: 'Although there is considerable disagreement in the literature, the weight of evidence indicates that selection and ability grouping do not have a powerful impact on the overall attainment of students' (2001: 17). However, this did not stop the then Government in 1997 publishing a White Paper, *Excellence in Schools*, which stated that 'Unless a school can demonstrate that it is getting better than expected results through a different approach, we do make the presumption that setting should be the norm in secondary schools' (DfEE 1997: 197).

The arguments against setting and streaming focus on two areas, the academic and the social. As Richard Hatcher observes: 'The most overt mechanisms of social differentiation within the school system arise from processes of selection, both between schools, as a result of parental choice and school admissions procedures, and within schools, as a result of forms of grouping students' (Hatcher 1998: 494). This social argument says societal inequalities are mirrored in streaming and setting. This argument is amplified by Adam Gamoran, who notes that 'minority and disadvantaged students tend to be over-represented in low-level classes' (Gamoran 2002).

Arguments in favour of streaming and/or setting tend to relate to students being able to operate at their own speed, and for teachers to be able to address the needs of individual students. Teachers told Smith and Sutherland (2003: 142):

1   It is easier for teachers to deal with a smaller range of ability.
2   It was a way of separating out students with behavioural problems so that at least some could have a chance to learn.
3   More able students could be challenged more easily.
4   Mixed ability encourages teaching to the middle and therefore is inappropriate for a good number of students in the class.

However, running counter to this it has also been argued that setting and/or streaming can actually lower the results from those students in top sets. There can also be a gender dimension to this, as Boaler et al.

point out: 'Approximately one-third of the students taught in the highest ability groups were disadvantaged by their placement in these groups because of high expectations, fast-paced lessons and pressure to succeed. This particularly affected the most able girls' (Boaler et al. 2000: 633).

As there are conflicting arguments on both sides, it is informative to look into how prevalent streaming and setting are. In 2010 a Freedom of Information request response was published by the DfE in the UK which shows the percentage of streamed and set classes that were known about: 'Of about 18,400 classroom observations conducted by Ofsted inspectors in secondary schools last year (2008/09), roughly only four in ten represented set lessons' (DfE 2010).

This section has tried to present the arguments for and against streaming and setting. Doubtless you will have opinions of your own, and your school may well have a policy which will affect how the classes you teach are organized. This is an area which is politically sensitive as well as pedagogically important, and there will be future reports, statutes and publications which will affect the ways students in schools are organized.

Key questions

1 How are students organized in the classes I teach?
2 What are the reasons for this? What is my opinion on it?
3 How would I organize my classes if I could?

References

Boaler, J., Wiliam, D. and Brown, M. (2000) Students' experiences of ability grouping: disaffection, polarisation and the construction of failure. *British Educational Research Journal*, 26(5): 631–48.

DfEE (Department for Education and Employment) (1997) *Excellence in Schools*. London: Stationery Office.

DfE (Department for Education) (2010) Streamlining within English Comprehensive Schools. http://education.gov.uk/aboutdfe/foi/disclosuresaboutschools/a0068565/streamlining-within-english-comprehensive-schools (accessed 18 September 2012).

Gamoran, A. (2002) *Standards, Inequality and Ability Grouping in Schools*. Edinburgh: Centre for Educational Sociology, University of Edinburgh.

Hatcher, R. (1998) Labour, official school improvement and equality. *Journal of Education Policy*, 13(4): 485–99.

Ireson, J. and Hallam, S. (2001) *Ability Grouping in Education.* London: Paul Chapman.

Smith, C.M.M. and Sutherland, M.J. (2003) Setting or mixed ability? Teachers' views of the organization of students for learning. *Journal of Research in Special Educational Needs*, 3(3): 141–6.

Further reading

Ireson, J. and Hallam, S. (2001) *Ability Grouping in Education.* London: Paul Chapman.

Subjects

In most schools, subjects are the individual building blocks of the curriculum. Whether in primary or secondary contexts, the notion of the individual subject, the key knowledge, skills and understanding that each subject contains, and the development of your skilful pedagogy in introducing students to a particular subject are all self evident and often unquestionable.

The love of a particular subject is one of the key reasons that potential teachers cite for wanting to learn to teach. For many of us, our academic subject was our 'first love' and something that we treasure very dearly. And therein lies a problem. The nature, culture and tradition of 'subjects' can lead to difficulties: 'School subject communities are neither harmonious nor homogeneous and members do not necessarily share particular values, subject definitions and interests' (Jephcote and Davies 2007: 210). As Cooper (1983: 208) states: 'The diverse memberships of school subject communities create conditions conducive to contest, conflict and tension, both within a subject and between it and other subjects where we need to understand the effects of interaction across a series of boundaries between subject subcultures'.

Every subject that is represented within our schools has a particular culture that underpins it. This culture informs the 'identifiable structures which are visibly expressed through classroom organization and pedagogical styles' (Goodson and Mangen 1997: 120). A subject's culture is what makes it unique and, in a simple sense, helps students sense that they are studying a particular subject at a specific moment in the school day. It is important to recognize that a subject's culture goes beyond its knowledge. It also incorporates ways of thinking, acting and being that inform the processes by which teachers teach (your pedagogy) and students learn.

Subject cultures are not homogeneous. A lack of sensitivity to a subject culture can lead to significant problems for a subject and the ways in which teachers seek to educate their students through it. We will illustrate this briefly by considering processes of assessment.

Is it right that all teachers should assess their students in a similar way, regardless of subject culture? Can all teachers be expected to produce a common set of assessment data that represents student attainment in their subject? Our answer to these questions would be 'no'. There are intrinsic subject cultural differences that need to be respected and acknowledged in any meaningful process of assessment. Art teachers will assess their students' work in a different way to that of a geography teacher, or a teacher of mathematics. This is not because individual teachers are being awkward or difficult. It is because well established traditions of thought and the resultant forms of cultural practice have been established over many years. As an individual subject teacher, we may not recognize the historical development of these lines of thinking fully, but they are there at the subject level and we may respond defensively if we feel they are being threatened (even if we do not know why).

Therefore, our subject cultures can lead to fundamental differences of opinion about what should be taught within a particular subject, how it should be taught and assessed. Jephcote and Davies give a flavour of the complexity of the situation through the notion of the 'teacher as actor': someone who has to work within different contexts or levels in order to present the subject as a meaningful 'whole' within the curriculum:

> Changing the curriculum is an outcome of contexts between actors in different arenas and at different levels. Its story needs to be told at a number of levels to reflect the membership and structure of subject communities and to provide a means of illustrating each level and their interconnectedness. At the micro-level accounts have been concerned mainly with teachers, school classrooms and subjects and at macro-level with processes of policy-making and its implementation. At the same time, the meso-level has been taken to comprise of subject associations, local education authorities and sponsored curriculum projects where there are mediating processes which provide means to reinterpret macro-level changes and to assess the range of new choices they present to subject factions.
>
> (Jephcote and Davies 2007: 208)

These ideas remind us that our work as a subject teacher in school extends outwards to the broader notions associated with our subjects in society generally. The imposition of the English Baccalaureate in 2011 caused many difficulties because, at a stroke it seemed, it reordered the traditional balance of the subjects within the Key Stage 4 curriculum. Some subjects were seen to be winners, others losers. These changes did not just affect the structure of the school curriculum. They also had a significant impact on the ways in which certain subjects were perceived by students and their parents. The academic value of non-English Baccalaureate subjects was questioned and some subjects did not recover from the resulting lack of recruitment, loss of resources and staff.

This episode represents a particularly sorry state of affairs for education in the United Kingdom. The reckless imposition of an ill-considered policy has caused much harm throughout our schools. However, it is important not to be downhearted. The role that subject specialists play in our primary and secondary schools is vital in capturing and sustaining our students' engagement with subjects. The love for a particular subject can be one of the most intrinsically rewarding and motivating forces in our lives. Many of us can trace our passion for our subject back to one teacher who inspired us. We should all aim to do the same for the students that we teach today. What will your students say about you in years to come?

Key questions

1 What are the key elements of my subject's culture that I need to understand in order to teach it effectively?
2 How can we respect and maintain the differences between subject cultures in our schools to avoid situations like those created by the careless imposition of the English Baccalaureate?

References

Cooper, B. (1983) On explaining change in school subjects. *British Journal of Sociology of Education*, 4(3): 207–22.

Goodson, I.F. and Mangen, J.M. (1997) Subject cultures and the introduction of classroom computers, in I.F. Goodson et al. (eds) *Subject Knowledge: Readings for the Study of School Subject*, pp. 105–21. London: Falmer Press.

Jephcote, M. and Davies, B. (2007) School subjects, subject communities and curriculum change: the social construction of economics in the school curriculum. *Cambridge Journal of Education*, 37(2): 207–27.

Further reading

Goodson, I., Anstead, C. and Mangan, J. (eds) (2007) *Subject Knowledge: Readings for the Study of School Subjects*. London: Falmer Press.

Synthetic phonics

Synthetic phonics is an approach to learning to read and write in English that has been prioritized, to the exclusion of any other approaches, by the current Government in the United Kingdom. As such, every teacher who teaches early reading is expected to demonstrate a clear understanding of synthetic phonics. This has been legislated for in law within the Teachers' Standards.

The following description of synthetic phonics comes from an unpublished document designed to support those working within initial teacher education programmes to implement a structured approach to training student teachers in synthetic phonics:

> Language is made up of words. Words are made up of sounds (phonemes). When we write, we use written symbols (graphemes) to represent the sounds. These graphemes may be single letters or combinations of letters such as sh, oy and igh. Once we know how these grapheme–phoneme correspondences (GPCs) work we can encode spoken words in writing for others to read, and we can decode words that others have written.
>
> The 'synthetic' part of the term 'synthetic phonics' comes from the part played by synthesising (blending) in reading as outlined below. Children are taught GPCs and how to use this knowledge to work words out from the beginning, starting at the simplest level:
>
> 1   For reading, children are taught to look at the letters from the left to right, convert them into sounds and blend (synthesise) the sounds to work out the spoken forms of the words. For example, if children see the word hat, they need to know what sound to say for each grapheme (/h/ - /a/ - /t/) and then to be able to blend those sounds together into a recognisable word. Once words have been read this way often enough

(and this can vary from child to child), they become known and can then be read without sounding out and blending.

2   For spelling, children are taught to segment spoken words into sounds and write down graphemes for those sounds. For example, if children want to write hat, then they need to be able to split it into the sounds /h/ - /a/ - /t/ and write the appropriate letters.

Learning to read and write in English is particularly difficult because written English uses a complex alphabetic code, which is why it needs to be taught by a systematic approach which goes from the simple to the more complex. Children can thus grasp the basic workings of alphabetic writing before they have to start dealing with the complexities which are unavoidable in English. By clearly defining what should be known at each stage, synthetic phonics programmes allow the early identification of children who are falling behind and of the areas where they need help (e.g. remembering GPCs, blending, segmenting). Prompt help can prevent long-term problems.

Following the Government's adoption of this strategy, a whole host of commissioned teaching materials, funded by Government subsidy, have been produced by various approved publishers. These materials have been made available to schools at subsidized rates.

Many teachers are unhappy about what they see as the imposition of one particular approach to the teaching of early reading and writing within their schools. Whilst it is beyond the scope of this entry to provide a critique of synthetic phonics or alternative methods, the general point about what some perceive as Government 'interference' within a subject's pedagogy is well made. At the time of writing, similar stories about the draft proposals for the mathematics National Curriculum and the teaching of long division have been circulating in the press (Mansell 2011). Three out of four of the DfE's own National Curriculum advisors resigned at what they saw as the political interference of Government ministers in their work.

Leaving these political accusations to one side, teachers with a responsibility for the teaching of early reading, and all teachers who, in various ways, are responsible for developing our students' literacy skills, need to be aware of the methodology of synthetic phonics. There is a strong and rigorous expectation at the current time that this approach to early reading and writing will be used within all schools by all teachers.

Key questions

1 How can an approach to the teaching of synthetic phonics be implemented within my own subject pedagogy?
2 What knowledge or skills relating to synthetic phonics do I need to obtain in order to use this methodology constructively?

Reference

Mansell, W. (2011) England's School Curriculum Review Sparks Debate. http://www.guardian.co.uk/education/2011/oct/03/england-curriculum-review-debate-controversy (accessed 20 December 2011).

Further reading

Green, A. (2012) *A Practical Guide to Teaching English in the Secondary School.* London: Routledge.
Johnston, R. and Watson, J. (2007) *Teaching Synthetic Phonics.* Exeter: Learning Matters.

T

Teachers' Standards

The *Teachers' Standards* is a new document produced by the Department for Education which outlines the values and behaviours expected of all teachers, the specific standards they must obtain in their teaching, professional and personal conduct. This document is freely available online (DfE 2012). It is vital that all teachers, whatever stage they are at in their careers, are familiar with this document.

This is an important document in many respects. First, it sets a benchmark for all students who are undergoing a process of initial teacher education in any context; second, it provides a framework for assessment of a teacher's work at the end of their first year of teaching (their 'induction' year); and for more experienced teachers it presents a set of standards for use within a school's performance management/appraisal framework. However, unlike previous versions of the professional standards for teachers, there is only one set of statements that are applicable in all the above contexts.

The *Teachers' Standards* contains three main sections: a preamble, standards for teaching, and standards for professional and personal context. The preamble describes the key characteristics of any teacher. They:

- make their pupils their first concern;
- aim for the highest possible standards in all their work;
- act with honesty and integrity;
- have strong subject knowledge;
- keep their knowledge and skills up to date;
- are self-critical;
- forge positive professional relationships;
- work collaboratively with parents in the best interests of their pupils.

Part One presents the key features that should characterize a teacher's work. Each of the following 'standards' is exemplified in the document. The standards are that a teacher must:

- set high expectations which inspire, motivate and challenge pupils;
- promote good progress and outcomes by pupils;
- demonstrate good subject and curriculum knowledge;
- plan and teach well structured lessons;
- adapt teaching to respond to the strengths and needs of all pupils;
- make accurate and productive use of assessment;
- manage behaviour effectively to ensure a good and safe learning environment;
- fulfil wider professional responsibilities.

Part Two outlines the Government's expectation in terms of a teacher's professional and personal conduct. There are three main points here, with each point being exemplified further in the document itself. Teachers must:

1   uphold public trust in the profession and maintain high standards of ethics and behaviour, inside and outside school;
2   have proper and professional regard for the ethos, policies and practices of the school and maintain high standards in their own attendance and punctuality;
3   have an understanding of, and always act within, the statutory frameworks which set out their professional duties and responsibilities.

This document is vital reading for anyone involved in teaching, either as a trainee or qualified teacher. It is backed with the force of law and came into effect in September 2012. With the abolition of the General Teaching Council for England, this document is used by the Teaching Agency for any matters relating to cases of serious misconduct. Individual schools should also be adopting this framework for performance management and appraisal processes.

Key question

How can I provide evidence of my work against these standards, either as a trainee teacher seeking QTS or as part of an annual performance management process?

Reference and further reading

DfE (2012) *Teachers' Standards*. London: DfEE. Also available at https://www.education.gov.uk/publications/eOrderingDownload/teachers%20standards.pdf (accessed 5 July 2012).

Theory

In this entry we look at learning theory generally, and we investigate some of the aspects of learning theory that impinge upon the ways in which teaching and learning take place in schools.

We need to start with the observation that even classifications of learning theory are not themselves straightforward. Strauss observed that 'notions of learning and development are neither fixed nor agreed upon' (Strauss 2000: 31). For our purposes we will follow James's (2006) classification system and concentrate here on three theories: behaviourism, constructivism and social constructivism, as these are more commonly discussed and investigated from a UK perspective.

Behaviourism views observable human activity as being at the centre of what is investigated. (It is important to note that behaviourism is *not* about getting pupils to behave well, it is about behaviour in the sense of human or animal activity.) Classical behaviourism downplays the role of the mind. This approach views learning as a trained response to a stimulus, the most famous being the story of Pavlov, who trained his dogs to associate a sound with a food; ultimately they would salivate when the sound alone was presented. The dogs had been *conditioned* to associate the stimulus of the sound with the food, and responded accordingly. *Reinforcement* could take place to reward a correct response, and *punishment* could be used to try to stamp out unwanted behaviour. Behaviourist theories have a place in teaching and learning, especially in their use of rewards and punishments, and, to a certain extent, in the notion of conditioned responses. Some aspects of behaviourism have fallen out of fashion, but this does not negate the view, which forms the backbone of things like training programmes and repeated practice tests.

The work of Piaget is discussed in the entry on **cognition**, and Piaget was one of the early pioneers of the constructivist approach to education. In opposition to the classical behaviourists, constructivists say that mind is involved in learning, and that mental structures develop. Humans construct meaning, and make sense of things through mental models. 'Differences between experts and novices are marked by the way experts organize knowledge in structures that make it more retrievable and useful' (James 2006: 55). This notion of novice–expert progression is of value in education, and in this view is the creation of increasingly elaborate mental structures that is the key to this.

Social constructivism includes Vygotsky's work, which is outlined in the entry on the **zone of proximal development** (**ZPD**). 'Vygotsky believed that mind is transmitted across history by means of successive mental sharings which pass ideas from those more able or advanced to those who are less so' (Roth 1999: 10).

Social constructivism states that knowledge is made socially in a constant interaction between individual and society:

> For Vygotsky, it is cooperation that lies at the basis of learning. It is instruction, formal and informal, performed by more knowledgeable others, such as parents, peers, grandparents or teachers that is the main means of transmission of the knowledge of a particular culture. Knowledge for Vygotsky, as for Piaget, is embodied in actions and interactions with the environment (or culture), but unlike Piaget, Vygotsky stresses the importance of interaction with a living representative of the culture.
>
> (Muijs 2007: 50)

Novice development takes place by interaction with more experienced others, and by participation in societally focused activity. In this view, 'group work is not an optional extra' (James 2006: 57).

From this very rapid overview it is clear that the different theories of learning all have points in their favour. However, 'no one theory has provided all the answers to the kinds of questions of concern to teachers' (Child 1997: 113), and so it is inevitable that teachers adopt a 'pick and mix' approach to theory, taking what is appropriate at the time. For everyday classroom purposes, the way that you as a teacher view learning taking place will have an effect on the way in which you teach a topic. Thus if you think that social constructivism is the way forwards, your classroom will be full of talk, group work and the construction of knowledge. If you adopt a behaviourist approach you will be training the pupils to respond in the correct way when a stimulus is presented.

Key questions

1 How do the various approaches to learning theory outlined here connect to the ways in which I teach certain topics?
2 Are there ways I could teach the same topic differently, depending on which view of learning I take?
3 How does the way I view learning affect the ways in which I undertake assessment?

References

Child, D. (1997) *Psychology and the Teacher*, 6th edn. London: Cassell.

James, M. (2006) Assessment, teaching and theories of learning, in J. Gardner (ed.) *Assessment and Learning*, pp. 47–60. London: Sage.

Muijs, D. (2007) Understanding how pupils learn: theories of learning and intelligence, in V. Brooks, I. Abbott and L. Bills (eds) *Preparing to Teach in Secondary Schools: A Student Teacher's Guide to Professional Issues in Secondary Education*, p. xvii. Maidenhead: Open University Press.

Roth, W.-M. (1999) Authentic school science, in R. McCormick and C. Paechter (eds) *Learning and Knowledge*, pp. 6–20. London: Paul Chapman.

Strauss, S. (2000) Theories of cognitive development and learning and their implications for curriculum development and teaching, in B. Moon, M. Ben-Peretz and S. Brown (eds) *Routledge International Companion to Education*, pp. 28–50. London: Routledge.

Further reading

Muijs, D. (2007) Understanding how pupils learn: theories of learning and intelligence, in V. Brooks, I. Abbott and L. Bills (eds) *Preparing to Teach in Secondary Schools: A Student Teacher's Guide to Professional Issues in Secondary Education*, p. xvii. Maidenhead: Open University Press.

Thinking

Thinking, cognition, learning, brains and knowledge all have separate entries in this book. From this fact alone it should be clear that we view developing students' thinking to be a key feature of the role of the teacher. Indeed, thinking is so central to pedagogy, to teaching and to learning, that you may wonder why we are bothering to describe it at all!

Thinking is often accompanied by the word 'skills' when met in schools, and the development of thinking skills is clearly part of the role of schooling. It would be obviously false to assume that development would not take place without intervention, but what does this mean in practice, and what can you as a teacher do about it?

Thinking skills generically are often taught through programmes designed to help students in this area. For example, Edward de Bono (1985) has developed a programme built around six different coloured 'thinking hats', where students literally or metaphorically don a specific hat to think about approaches to a problem. The six 'hats' identified are:

1   facts and figures (white);
2   emotions and feelings (red);
3   cautious and careful (black);
4   speculative positive (yellow);
5   creative (green);
6   control of thinking (blue).

The use of the hats helps learners undertake different type of thinking, and aids moving from one approach to another with relative ease.

An entirely different approach to thinking is that of Howard Gardner. His book *Frames of Mind* (Gardner 1983) outlines a series of separate 'intelligences', all of which we each possess to differing degrees. These intelligences are:

1   logical-mathematical
2   spatial
3   linguistic
4   bodily-kinaesthetic
5   musical
6   interpersonal
7   intrapersonal
8   naturalistic
9   existential.

The theory of multiple intelligences has been useful in ascribing the importance of differing subject areas in making a positive contribution to the development of a well-rounded individual. More recently Gardner has written about what he describes as 'five minds for the future' (Gardner 2006), where he describes the types of mind-set that he believes will become increasingly important in the future. These are:

1   The Disciplinary Mind: the mastery of major schools of thought, including science, mathematics, and history, and of at least one professional craft;
2   The Synthesizing Mind: the ability to integrate ideas from different disciplines or spheres into a coherent whole and to communicate that integration to others;
3   The Creating Mind: the capacity to uncover and clarify new problems, questions and phenomena;

4   The Respectful Mind: awareness of and appreciation for differences among human beings and human groups;
5   The Ethical Mind: fulfilment of one's responsibilities as a worker and as a citizen.

Aside from these approaches, and probably of equal importance to the everyday work of the teacher in the classroom, are subject- or domain-specific ways of thinking. For example, what does it mean to think like a geographer, an artist, a poet, a physicist? These ways of thinking also need fostering and developing in students.

Key questions

1   What does thinking in different subject areas look like?
2   How can I develop thinking in my classes?
3   Do I give students the opportunity to discuss the ways in which they think?

References

de Bono, E. (1985) *Six Thinking Hats*. Harmondsworth: Viking.
Gardner, H. (1983) *Frames of Mind*. London: Heinemann.
Gardner, H. (2006) *Five Minds for the Future*. Boston, MA: Harvard Business Press.

Further reading

Barnes, J. and Shirley, I. (2007) Strangely familiar: cross-curricular and creative thinking in teacher education. *Improving Schools*, 10(2): 162–79.
Rogoff, B. (1990) *Apprenticeship in Thinking*. Oxford: Oxford University Press.
Sefton-Green, J., Thomson, P., Jones, K. and Bresler, L. (2011) *The Routledge International Handbook of Creative Learning*. London: Routledge.

Tools

There are a variety of ways in which learning is developed by the use of technology, and of tools in general. In this entry, rather than consider specific tools, we are going to consider the place of tools in general.

Learning is complex, and we have said throughout this book that it is a dynamic process, which involves the teacher and learners in activity. The role of tools in learning is well documented; indeed, building on the work of Vygotsky, activity theory (Engeström 1999; Nardi 1996) puts tools firmly into a consideration of learning. In activity theory, tools are considered as 'mediating artefacts', and can include cognitive and conceptual tools.

So, tools can be many things used in thinking, and in teaching and learning. Although there are current concerns with ICT as a tool, it is important to remember that tools can also be 'low-tech', like a pencil! As a starting point, tools for use in schools include:

- visual representation tools: chalkboard, IWB, PowerPoint;
- information storage tools: books, computers, internet, PCs;
- recording tools: video, audio, webcams, streaming video, software;
- measuring tools: rulers, weighing machines;
- viewing tools: microscopes, binoculars, televisions, computer screens.

This is a brief overview, there will be many more. But this plethora of availability should not detract from the fundamental question, which is about *learning*. Tools can come and go (one of the authors recalls spending many hours at school learning to use the slide rule, a now useless skill!), but what should be important is learning the concepts involved, which are facilitated by the use of the tool. Although there is a point to learning about how to use tools, it is useful to remember that tools are a means to an end, not necessarily an end in themselves.

In the subject or subjects you teach there will be a range of tools. In thinking about their use in the classroom a logical starting point in lesson planning is to think about which lessons will be about tool use, which will be about applying the tools, and which will be about using the tools incidentally as a normal part of the learning in the subjects required. For example, in geography there will be a place for learning about the compass. This can start with finding North in and around the classroom, then progress to an understanding of maps. This knowledge can later be put to use in drawing maps of the local area, where the tool use has become embedded through preparation. We would want army recruits to have been through these learning processes before they go on a winter expedition in the Cairngorms, for example.

What this means is that in order to be effective you, the teacher, need to have thought about the ways in which you will introduce your students to tools they will need, but may not have met, or how you can exploit tools they already know how to use, and can now put to more efficacious use. This seems an obvious thing to do, but as we describe elsewhere sequencing learning activities can be really problematic for curriculum planners, and the danger of things 'slipping through' has to be countered by knowing what to do and when, so that the learners not only know, but apply. Bloom's taxonomy places knowledge as a low-level thinking skill, but knowing how to use the necessary tools is essential for learning to develop in other areas. We need to be teaching our students not only how to use tools, but also what the thinking is behind them.

Key questions

1 What do I want the students to learn? What is the best order for them to learn it in?
2 What tools will they need to know how to use? When is the best time to introduce them to this tool use?

References

Engeström, Y. (1999) Activity theory and individual and social transformation, in Y. Engeström, R. Miettenen and R.L. Punamaki (eds) *Perspectives on Activity Theory*, pp. 9–52. Cambridge: Cambridge University Press.
Nardi, B. (1996) Studying context: a comparison of activity theory, situated action models, and distributed cognition, in B. Nardi (ed.) *Context and Consciousness: Activity Theory and Human–Computer Interaction*, pp. 69–102. Cambridge, MA: MIT Press.

Further reading
Daniels, H. (2001) *Vygotsky and Pedagogy*. London: Routledge.

Transition

Transition refers to the movement of students between schools. For the majority of students, the main transition is from primary school to secondary school. However, some students will transfer between schools on more regular occasions, perhaps as a result of their parents moving into a new area.

Secondary schools are very different from primary schools. They organize the teaching and learning differently, with subject specialist teachers working in designated spaces; they are generally bigger than primary schools with less individual personal space for the student; there is a greater amount of homework demanded; and a greater degree of student autonomy is expected, not least in the organization of their workload across the various subjects being studied.

The research that has been done in this area has identified a range of common anxieties among students. For example, common anxieties of students starting secondary school include:

- worrying about how to find their way around a new school, in particular ensuring that they get to their lessons on time;
- meeting new students, many of whom will be significantly older than they are;
- learning to work with an increased number of teachers, many of whom will not have the detailed knowledge of them as an individual (as compared to their primary school teacher);
- learning teachers' names and getting use to the individual teachers' expectations about their work, their classroom environment and style of teaching;
- being increasingly responsible for organizing their workload and ensuring that homework is completed on time;
- managing their social time (e.g. break times and lunchtimes) when there is less adult supervision.

For all these reasons (and many more), the process of transition needs to be handled carefully by parents and schools. Preparation is key. Whilst schools can provide many useful strategies to make their new students feel welcome, there is also much that individual teachers can facilitate within their teaching. This is what we are going to focus on below. In particular, try and ensure that you do the following things in the first few lessons with a new class:

- Make sure they know your name! Basic, but it is amazing how many students do not know their teachers' names after a few weeks. Write it down, get them to copy it down, and repeat it regularly!
- As far as possible, try to learn the students' names as quickly as possible. Use a seating plan and make it your first priority to learn their names. Students really appreciate the fact that teachers know them individually.
- Take an interest in the student as an individual. Try and find out a bit about them, their interests within your subject as well as

any other talents or skills, their family background, etc. Much of this information will have been transferred to your school from their previous school.

- Undertake some form of baseline assessment in your lesson. Although you may have a range of assessment data from their previous school, finding out for yourself what your new students are able to achieve is an important first step in getting to know them and their strengths or weaknesses.
- Provide some time and space in your lessons to let them talk about their experiences of being in a new school environment. Use this time to help reinforce common tasks (e.g. where to put your homework) and school policies (e.g. how to wear their uniform correctly).
- Every teacher should exercise pastoral care for their students. So, although your students have a designated form tutor and Head of Year, do make sure that you are approachable and caring in your disposition towards them too and do not pass the buck onto your colleagues too quickly.
- But having said that, do work as a team with other teachers on these things. Communicate any serious or unresolved issues or concerns you have about an individual student to their form tutor or pastoral supervisor. Never promise a student that what they say will remain confidential between you and that student.

And a note to parents: moving your child to a new school is one of the most disruptive events in your child's education. It should be done as infrequently as possible. No school is perfect and, on balance, it is normally much better to work with and support your child's school than imagine that they might be doing better if they were educated elsewhere.

Key question

What practical steps can I use to support students who are new to my school?

Further reading

Evangelou, M., Taggart, B., Sylva, K. et al. (2008) *What Makes a Successful Transition from Primary to Secondary School?*. London: Institute of Education. Also available at https://www.education.gov.uk/publications/eOrderingDownload/DCSF-RR019.pdf (accessed 7 May 2012).

U

Underachievement

We worry a lot about students underachieving in schools. To underachieve means not to attain one's true potential. Normally this is discussed with reference to examination results and test scores. In order to underachieve there is an understanding that the student in question could have attained higher grades with a little more application, more revision, a better examination strategy, better attendance figures, a more positive attitude, or a host of other things.

So, two key questions need to be asked:

1   Are we sure that estimates of a student's attainment are correct in order for us to know that underachievement is occurring?
2   Whose fault is it?

Hopefully in these days of data driven assessment and robust monitoring systems we are able to be fairly sure about the first. The second gives us concerns. As schools are judged by the performance of their students there is a knee-jerk reaction which says it is the fault of the school, or of the teacher. But let us look into this in a bit more detail.

We know, for example, that boys tend not to achieve as well as girls: 'There is a moral panic over underachieving boys and masses of excellent research which shows that it is white working class boys primarily who are underachieving' (Reay 2006: 302). Here there are two enormous cohorts of underachievers – a) boys, and b) white working class boys. This has significant implications for schools, as boys represent 50 per cent (more or less) of the school population. As Jones and Myhill observe, 'Boys within the classroom have been pictured as cast adrift in an alien environment where the preferred ethos and learning styles, the approved literacy practices, even the testing procedures, all favour female strengths and preferences' (Jones and Myhill 2004: 548). And so we hear talk of feminization of the curriculum. Undoubtedly there are not enough men in primary schools and so, this argument runs, underachievement begins early. White working class boys also make up a substantial proportion of the learners in our schools. However, despite a number of national initiatives, there remain significant problems: 'Addressing the "the social class attainment gap" in education has become a government priority in England. Despite multiple initiatives, however, little has effectively addressed the underachievement of working-class students within the classroom' (Dunne and Gazeley 2008: 451). Another group of children who are identified as underachieving are looked-after children. Back in 2000, Theo Cox made the shocking observation that: 'The educational disadvantage suffered by looked-after children is so extreme that, at present, only the most resilient have any chance of success' (Cox 2000: 77). Looked-after children are now an identified cohort that you will be expected to know about in your classes, and be differentiating materials, or otherwise making provision, to suit.

We have considered some groups of students who are currently known to be underachieving. There are many more groups, including, but not confined to, the underachieving gifted and talented; girls in STEM (science, technology, engineering and maths) subjects; specific groups of ethnic minorities; some cohorts of EAL students; traveller children; and many more besides. But in addition to known cohorts you will also be dealing with individual students who underachieve.

So what can be done about this? Many initiatives are currently addressing these issues, and you will doubtless be asked to play your part. What remains at the heart of good pedagogy at all times is the notion of doing the best for the students you are teaching, of planning, differentiating, scaffolding learning and supporting. Central to addressing underachievement is first of all to identify where it is, or could be taking place; planning to do something about it, and then making sure those plans are enacted in the classroom, with whole-school support initiatives where appropriate. So knowing your students in this, as so many areas, is a good place from which to start!

Key questions

1 Which groups of potential underachievers can be identified in students that I teach?
2 How can I find out?
3 What initiatives are there to help support me doing something about this?
4 How can I differentiate or otherwise address these issues in my classroom?

References

Cox, T. (2000) *Combating Educational Disadvantage: Meeting the Needs of Vulnerable Children.* London: Falmer Press.

Dunne, M. and Gazeley, L. (2008) Teachers, social class and underachievement. *British Journal of Sociology of Education*, 29(5): 451–63.

Jones, S. and Myhill, D. (2004) Troublesome boys and compliant girls: gender identity and perceptions of achievement and underachievement. *British Journal of Sociology of Education*, 25(5): 547–61.

Reay, D. (2006) The zombie stalking English schools: social class and educational inequality. *British Journal of Educational Studies*, 54(3): 288–307.

Further reading

West, A. and Pennell, H. (2003) *Underachievement in Schools*. London: Routledge.

Unit of work

The unit of work is an important middle stage of planning. Whilst lesson plans detail the learning objectives, teaching activities and assessment strategies for the individual lesson, the unit of work provides an overview of a sequence of lessons. Units of work are referred to as 'schemes of work' by some teachers.

A unit of work normally contains the following:

1   A title that is brief, concise and describes the unit of work.
2   A broad description of the unit of work, the key content or themes, and where it sits within the broader long term plan for the Key Stage within which it is placed.
3   A set of learning objectives for the whole unit, from which the learning objectives for individual lessons can be drawn. They can also give an indication of any prior learning that students should have achieved before commencing this particular unit of work.
4   Time: an outline of how much time is available for the unit, including any homework time that might be utilized.
5   Key resources for the unit, including any specific pieces of information and communication technologies (ICT) that the unit might feature.
6   A broad description of any assessment and personalization/ differentiation strategies that will be utilized throughout the unit. These should be general, not specific to individual lessons, and should highlight any innovative approaches or specific assessment requirements (i.e. those related to the National Curriculum or examination specifications if appropriate).
7   A list of the individual lessons within the unit of work, together with one or two sentences describing each one. The unit of work

should present an overview of these lessons (i.e. not detailed content) so that anyone reading the unit of work gets a general feel for the flow of lessons throughout the unit.

8   General statements related to the other curriculum links, e.g. cross-curricular links, extension and enrichment strategies, future learning (i.e. what the unit of work leads into) and key vocabulary.

In a secondary school setting, units of work are often written by heads of department for their curriculum team. Therefore, individual teachers may find themselves delivering a unit of work written by someone else. It is important to remember that these documents are there to serve as a guide to your teaching. There will be many different ways that a unit of work can be delivered. How you plan your individual lessons within a unit of work depends on a range of factors, of which the general coverage provided by the unit of work is just one important factor. So, consider the unit of work as a map of the terrain. How you move the students from point A to point B is still your responsibility!

More generally, all teachers are responsible for creating a sense of direction, purpose and flow between their lessons. The unit of work document can help provide that formal framework for teaching. But pedagogical strategies such as providing summaries of learning through plenaries, highlighting or signposting future learning opportunities, using homework opportunities to establish links between lessons, and much more are equally important. As with the lesson plan, the unit of work planning process is something that you will need to bring to life within your teaching! Otherwise, it just remains a paper exercise that will only serve to frustrate you.

Key questions

1   How can I ensure that all my curriculum planning, whether it be for individual lessons or sequences of lessons, really is brought to life in my teaching?
2   What strategies can I use to ensure that lessons are linked together meaningfully and that students are secure and confident on their learning journey with me?

Further reading

From Good to Outstanding (2012) How to write a scheme of work: 10 tips. http://www.fromgoodtooutstanding.com/2011/07/how-to-write-a-scheme-of-work-10-tips (accessed 3 July 2012).

Virtual learning environments (VLE)

Virtual learning environments are online spaces where teaching and learning can occur. During the first decade of the twenty-first century, the Labour Government passed legislation that required all schools to provide a VLE for their staff and students to use. Various software solutions were provided by companies (e.g. Blackboard, Web CT, etc.) and many of these were successfully implemented. Like any technological innovation, some of the companies involved in providing schools with these early VLEs did not provide a great amount of follow-up support. As with any technology, technical support does not always get followed by pedagogical support. However, this process did mean that all state schools were required to provide and use a basic VLE.

More recently, many schools have moved on from this basic provision and sought a greater degree of complexity within their VLE provision. Open source solutions such as Moodle have provided schools with core functionality and a range of 'add ons' which, whilst free at the point of installation, do require management and support by appropriately trained technical staff. Publishing companies have also begun to produce a range of subject content in electronic formats that can help teachers make use of VLEs in new ways, e.g. the provision of homework tasks online that students can access through the school's VLE.

Pedagogically, there are some important questions about VLEs that you will want to consider. For many teachers, the VLE is 'out there' in a different, but complementary, space to their physical classroom. Perhaps there is a reason why they are called 'virtual' learning environments (in contrast with the 'physical' learning environment of my classroom). It is easy to conceptualize the VLE as a useful tool for the storage of key documents, the easy access of worksheets or other materials, the provision of homework opportunities, communicating the results of assessments with parents, or the sharing of students' work with the wider school community. For many schools this is as far as their use of the VLE has got.

But the functionality of the VLE and what it can provide can also be adopted within the physical environment of the classroom. Interactive features of VLEs (e.g. blogs, polling, conferencing facilities, multimedia resources, quizzes, forums, podcasting, wikis, etc.) can all have a role to play in the classroom. Conceptualizing the VLE as an augmentation to your classroom could have important impacts on the structure of teaching activities within your lessons and help you develop an interactive and dynamic pedagogical style.

As with any technology, this is not going to happen overnight. It will be important to maintain a critical approach and examine the potential benefits against the potential disadvantages. But the key point here is that the VLE should not be viewed as something that students only interact with when they leave your classroom. Try to build a structured approach and engagement with the school VLE into your lessons on occasions. Explore its potential in a constructive way and your teaching will benefit.

Key questions

1 To what extent am I using the opportunities provided by my school's VLE within my own teaching?
2 If appropriate, how can I extend my use of the features it provides within my teaching?

Further reading

Barber, D. and Cooper, L. (2012) *Using New Web Tools in the Primary Classroom: A Practical Guide for Enhancing Teaching and Learning.* London: Routledge.

Gillespie, H., Boulton, H., Hramiak, A. and Williamson, R. (2007) *Learning and Teaching with Virtual Learning Environments (Achieving QTS Practical Handbooks).* Exeter: Learning Matters.

Visual learning

The importance of the visual component in learning is significant. We know that learning is complex, and that students learn things in different ways. There are clearly areas of teaching and learning where the visual component of learning assumes a dominance in pedagogic situations, art lessons being an obvious example. We are also aware that the visual quality of the classroom environment makes an impact on the quality of schooling. In this entry we consider the notion of treating learning through visual means separately from other components.

One of the arenas in which the notion of visual learning is met is *learning styles*. These most often correspond to the acronym V-A-K, where V=visual, A=Auditory, and K=kinaesthetic. The hypothesis is that these learning styles correspond to individual preferences for learning in a particular fashion. It is claimed that significant gains can be noted when an individual is taught with methods that match their preferred learning style; 'significantly higher standardized achievement test scores resulted among previously failing students when they were taught with strategies that complemented their learning-style preferences' (Dunn et al. 1995: 353). This, and similar claims, have been taken up readily by a number of teachers and advisors: 'Many local authority advisors and head teachers have been busy promoting VAK in primary schools and many primary teachers, in turn, have been busy administering VAK learning styles questionnaires to children and labelling them as visual, auditory or kinaesthetic learners' (Sharp et al. 2008: 293). We know that in some schools these learning styles are taken very seriously. We have heard of instances where pupils have to wear little badges with 'V', 'A', or 'K' upon them, and others where the pupils are grouped around tables based upon their learning styles. Indeed, in one school when a pupil was being spoken to by a teacher, the pupil raised their hand, palm towards the teacher, and said 'It's not good talking to me, I don't do auditory!' This is clearly nonsense.

All of this is very sad, as:

> The research evidence for these styles is highly variable, and for many the scientific evidence base is very slender indeed, since the measures are of doubtful reliability and validity. The authors are not by any means always frank about the evidence for their work, and secondary sources – often the ones that teachers are most likely to encounter – may ignore the question of evidence altogether, leaving the impression that there is no problem here . . . there is usually even less evidence that, when applied in classrooms, these schemes really do help to enhance the character of teaching so that learning is improved.
>
> (Hargreaves et al. 2004: 11)

In which case labelling pupils on the basis of very tenuous evidence is clearly problematic at best, or as Hattie calls it, a 'fruitless pursuit' (2012: 79). Even more scathing are Sharp et al: 'The labelling of children in schools as visual, auditory or kinaesthetic learners is not only unforgivable, it is potentially damaging' (Sharp et al. 2008: 311).

But what we can take from the VAK debacle is the notion of good teaching. Too much talk without visual input is as unhelpful as no talk at all. Varying the teaching and learning diet of classroom interaction is just good practice. This is, after all, what teachers in classrooms should be aiming for.

Key questions

1 Does my school pay heed to VAK? If so, has it been questioned?
2 What can I take from VAK learning that is of any use though?
3 How can I best address different pupils' needs?

References

Dunn, R., Griggs, S.A., Olson, J., Beasley, M. and Gorman, B.S. (1995) A meta-analytic validation of the Dunn and Dunn model of learning-style preferences. *The Journal of Educational Research*, 88(6): 353–62.

Hargreaves, D., Beere, J., Swindells, M. et al. (2004) *About Learning: Report of the Learning Working Group*. London: Demos, http://www.demos.co.uk

Hattie, J. (2012) *Visible Learning for Teachers: Maximizing Impact on Learning*. Abingdon: Routledge.

Sharp, J., Bowker, R. and Byrne, J. (2008) VAK or VAK-uous? Towards the trivialisation of learning and the death of scholarship. *Research Papers in Education*, 23(3): 293–314.

Further reading

Coffield, F., Moseley, D., Hall, E. and Ecclestone, K. (2004) *Learning Styles and Pedagogy in Post-16 Learning: A Systematic and Critical Review*. London: Learning and Skills Research Centre.

Web

The web is an amazingly powerful tool. It has transformed many of the basic tasks that we do, and take for granted, every day. From booking cinema tickets to scheduling meetings, updating personal profiles on Facebook and sharing key thoughts on Twitter, for many of us it is hard to imagine life off-line. Our students are growing up today in a world that is augmented by various online technologies that powerfully shape the formation of their identity and sense of well-being. Many experienced researchers and writers are very troubled by some of these issues (Keen 2012; Turkle 2011).

There are many potential benefits from using the internet as a learning tool. Research shows that many cognitive skills are substantially strengthened through its use. These include:

- The strengthening of brain functions related to fast-paced problem solving, recognizing patterns in a range of data and analysing their important characteristics, and making judgements about the quality of information contained within a particular source (Sillence et al. 2007).
- Benefits in terms of small increases in our working memory. These increases allow us to become more skilful in juggling ideas, focus our attention on competing ideas and analyse, almost instantaneously, their relative value. Small and Vorgan (2008: 21) report that for many of us this has led to our 'developing neural circuitry that is customized for rapid and incisive spurts of direction attention'.
- Increased hand–eye coordination (through various gaming environments), reflex response and the processing of visual cues (Green and Bavelier 2003).

Developmental psychologists have also explored the effects of different types of media on people's intelligence and learning abilities. The conclusion of Greenfield's recent work (Greenfield 2009) starts with the obvious thought that each medium, each technology, develops a particular aspect of cognitive skill at the expense of others.

In terms of the internet, her research indicates that its growing use within schools has led to a 'widespread and sophisticated development of visual-spatial skills'. But there is a trade off. New strengths in visual-spatial intelligence go 'hand in hand with a weakening of our capacities for the kind of "deep processing" that underpins mindful knowledge acquisition, inductive analysis, critical thinking, imagination and reflection' (Greenfield 2009: 52).

Given findings such as these, writers like Nicholas Carr have argued that whilst:

> the Net grants us instant access to a library of information unprecedented in its size and scope, and it makes it easy for us to sort through that library . . . what the Net diminishes is [a] primary kind of knowledge: the ability to know, in depth, a subject for ourselves, to construct within our own minds the rich and idiosyncratic set of connections that give rise to a singular intelligence.
>
> (Carr 2010: 143)

For teachers, the argument will not be about whether or not the internet has a role to play in education. Clearly it does. How teachers and students use the internet in a constructive way and with a full awareness of the benefits and disadvantages (both in the long and short term) is a much more interesting question that needs further study.

Key questions

1 Why do I ask my students to use the internet in my classes? What are the benefits of using the internet? What are the disadvantages – educationally, psychologically, socially?
2 What difference would it have made if I had given the information to the pupils in a different way, e.g. in a textbook or worksheet?
3 What were my specific reasons for choosing to use the internet at that particular moment rather than any alternative tool?

References

Carr, N.G. (2010) *The Shallows: What the Internet is Doing to our Brains.* New York: W.W. Norton.

Green, C.S. and Bavelier, D. (2003) Action video game modifies visual selective attention. *Nature*, 423: 534–7.

Greenfield, P.M. (2009) Technology and informal education: what is taught, what is learned. *Science*, 323: 69–71.

Keen, A. (2012) *Digital Vertigo: How Today's Online Social Revolution is Dividing, Diminishing and Disorienting Us*. London: Constable & Robinson.

Sillence, E., Briggs, P., Harris, P.R. and Fishwick, L. (2007) How do patients evaluate and make use of online health information? *Social Science and Medicine*, 64: 1853–62.

Small, G.W. and Vorgan, G. (2008) i*brain: Surviving the Technological Alteration of the Modern Mind*. New York: Collins Living.

Turkle, S. (2011) *Alone Together: Why We Expect More from Technology and Less from Each Other*. New York: Basic Books.

Further reading

Carr, N.G. (2010) *The Shallows: What the Internet is Doing to Our Brains*. New York: W.W. Norton.

Keen, A. (2012) *Digital Vertigo: How Today's Online Social Revolution is Dividing, Diminishing and Disorienting Us*. London: Constable & Robinson.

Whole school policy

The notion of something taking place across the whole of a school is an important one, and one which head teachers and senior leadership teams try very hard to inculcate. We hear, for example, of whole school policies on behaviour, learning, assessment, child protection, healthy eating, and many other things too. Policies are one thing; putting those policies into action across the whole school is another matter. To be done effectively, a whole school policy needs to impact on everyone: dinner ladies, the caretaker, teaching staff, teaching assistants, and hopefully, the students and their parents too. Where this is a consensual matter there is unlikely to be much dissent, so whole school policies on child protection or health and safety are likely to receive widespread support. But we hear many times of other policies not being so widely established. For example, 'There is a whole school policy on assessment, but we don't use it in our subject', or, 'There is a uniform policy, but here in the Arts block we don't worry about such things'. It is from these little resistances that cracks appear, and whole school policies start to be shown to have rather shaky foundations. So what are whole school issues, and what should they entail?

One of the first things to investigate here is the purpose of a whole school policy. In some cases, as with child protection, there is likely to be little argument. A school needs to have a coherent and understood approach, lines of communication should be clear, and staff should be in place to deal with instances rapidly. But what of, say, behaviour? A whole school behaviour policy should be designed to ensure that approaches by individual staff are consistent across the school. This means that such a policy needs to be workable, understood by staff and students, and, most important of all, both consistent and consistently applied.

In schools that have a whole school behaviour management policy that is effective, one common thread is to have an escalating series of consequences which are always dealt in the same way. This means that a 'stage one' infringement is understood by all parties to be likely to involve certain sorts of disruption, and which carries with it certain sorts of consequence. Escalation of behaviour infringement carries with it proportional consequences, and these are evenly applied. What is important here is that such systems need everyone on the staff to concur. The death-knell of behaviour policies is when an (often established teacher) says such things as, 'I don't know why you find 9Z a problem, they are fine for me'. This makes the (often less experienced) teacher concerned feel that they are personally inadequate. This is *not* the case. Behaviour management involves everyone on the staff, and pockets of resistance where groups of isolationist teachers are in denial do not help. As Bill Rogers puts it, whole school behaviour policies work when there is a 'move from sectional self-interest to concern for the welfare of colleagues as a group, as a team with their local school' (Rogers 2007: 5). Likewise the Elton report talks about 'encouraging collective responsibility' (Elton 1989: 91) for behaviour management, and this is key to its success.

As with behaviour then, so with other whole school policies; the essential features of these being the following:

- They should be clear.
- Everyone should feel ownership for them.
- They should be simple to put into practice.
- They should be applied consistently.

Finding out about whole school policies is an important early task for teachers in a new school. These should be studied so that when they are needed it is not a matter of finding out what actions to take, but that known chains of events can be put into play. The students will want and expect consistency, so knowing what to do and when is critical for fitting into the working patterns of the school.

> **Key questions**
>
> 1 What whole school policies are in place in my school?
> 2 Am I entirely clear on what my role is in implementing them?
> 3 If I need help, to whom do I turn?
> 4 If someone else needs help, what is my role?

References

Elton, R.E. (1989) *Discipline in Schools: Report of the Committee of Enquiry chaired by Lord Elton.* London: HM Stationery Office.
Rogers, B. (2007) *Behaviour Management: A Whole-School Approach,* 2nd edn. London: Paul Chapman.

Further reading

Hallam, S. and Rogers, L. (2008) *Improving Behaviour and Attendance at School.* Maidenhead: Open University Press.

Work/life balance

Teaching is a never-ending job! How do you know when that lesson plan is perfect? How much feedback is enough feedback on a student's essay? Would that PowerPoint presentation be slightly better with fewer words in it? Or more words, perhaps? Maybe a picture or two? And if you are not writing lesson plans, marking work or preparing presentations and activities, the mental activity of teaching – the questions, explanations, feedback and encouragement you might give to that student tomorrow – can all carry on inside your head for hours after the computer has been switched off and the stack of exercise books placed to one side.

For all these reasons, and hundreds more, it is vital that you think carefully about your work/life balance. 'We work to live, we don't live to work' is, perhaps, a tired saying but there is some truth in it. We do hope that there is something, or someone, in your life that is more important than teaching.

Clearly, it is not our job to prescribe a work/life balance for you, the reader. You will need to work this one out for yourself. All we can really do is warn you about the many teachers each year who take time off work for stress, illness, or in the most extreme cases, perhaps even take early retirement because teaching, as they have conceived it, has dominated their lives to the point of breakdown. We do not want you to go down that path.

So, what can we give in terms of practical advice?

First, work hard and play hard. When you are at work, do it to the best of your abilities. Give it one hundred per cent. Teaching is physically and intellectually demanding. If you are a young teacher, the step up from your training year to a full time job is one of the biggest hurdles you will face. Teaching will get easier. But it will constantly drain you. There are always new challenges and new opportunities.

So, when you are not working hard – play hard. Ensure you make time for your leisure activities. Plan your days so that you have a definite cut-off time. After that, work is put to one side and you focus on other things.

Second, do not be a perfectionist. They do not make good teachers. Perhaps you consider this strange advice. After all, should we not strive for perfection in all we do? Well, yes, to a point. However, perfectionism is a very hard task master. One of the most important things to be able to do as a teacher is realize when something is good enough. It might not be perfect, but it will do. This applies to all your work.

Third, learn to say 'no' and mean it. New teachers are easy prey for others to dump work on. Learn to prioritize and do not take on additional work that falls outside the key priorities of teaching your classes to the best of your ability. Whilst it might be nice to spend a free weekend supporting a geography field trip, or to drive the school minibus to the theatre one evening, or volunteer your time for an after-school club, all these additional pressures will mount up over time and take their toll. Learn to say 'no'.

Fourth, one of the problems with modern technology is that it is pervasive, addictive and hard to turn off. The smartphone or iPad is constantly craving our attention; Twitter feeds, Facebook updates and the like are all making demands on us in different ways. The clear demarcation between work and life is perhaps more blurred than ever. Take a digital sabbatical occasionally. Turn your devices off. Devote time to other things. And get enough sleep!

Finally, do not define yourself as a teacher. This is just one small part of your life. Treasure your privacy at all costs. It will make you a better teacher and result in you enjoying a long and prosperous career.

Please accept our apologies if this section sounds a little patronizing. However, we have both seen enough young teachers burn out early. Our advice is offered humbly and with a recognition that we both need to practise more what we have preached here.

Key questions

1 What practical steps can I take to achieve a sensible work/life balance?
2 How will I know when something is 'good enough' and I can move on?

Further reading

Reid, S. (2011) Can Teachers Even Have a Work/Live Balance? http://www.guardian.co.uk/teacher-network/2011/dec/07/teachers-work-life-balance (accessed 11 June 2012).

Smith, J. (2010) *The Lazy Teacher's Handbook: How Your Students Learn More When You Teach Less*. Carmarthen: Crown House Publishing.

Working with other adults

There are many other adults, apart from teachers, who are to be found working in classrooms today: parents who help listen to children read, parents who help with sports activities, parents who play the piano, parents who help with extra-curricular activities, classroom assistants, EAL (English as an additional language) workers, classroom support staff, special needs assistants, and a whole range of other roles and positions.

For the classroom teacher, managing interactions between all of these people, whilst still managing the class, planning for learning and dealing with behaviour management can seem a real issue. For the other adults in the classroom not knowing what is required of them can be a source of great frustration, as they will want to be involved so as to be as supportive as possible. The issue for both teacher and other adults tends to be planning time. If the teacher is fortunate to have an allocated and clearly delineated series of other adults to work with, then planning and work schedules can be realized over time, and routines established which enable a good working relationship to develop over time. If, on the other hand, you have other adults who only come to one of your lessons each week, and who have fifteen or more teachers to liaise with, then some of this planning needs to be done 'on the hoof', so that maximization of their talents can be worked towards.

The key issues, then, in working with other adults often tend to revolve around planning. Some useful questions for the teacher to ask include:

- What do I want the other adult(s) *specifically* to do?
- How can I convey this information to them simply and rapidly?
- Do I want them to work with a pupil, a group of pupils, or to work with a range of learners?
- Where do I want them to be at different times in the lesson?
- Do I need to prepare any specific materials for them?

Best practice in the engagement of other adults in the classroom is to have regular planning sessions. But in the reality of everyday classroom and busy school life this can feel like a luxury! So knowing in advance how your – and their – time can best be put to good use is the key to the way forwards in this regard.

For you as the teacher, the use of another adult to do some of the things that you feel you would normally do yourself can prove powerful in both engaging the class and allowing both of you to maximize learning. For example, in one school, another adult was asked by the teacher if they would write on the whiteboard whilst the teacher talked with the class. The immediate benefit of this was that the teacher did not have to turn their back on the class, and could instead talk from the back of the classroom looking forwards. Another benefit was that the teacher needed to be clear about what she wanted written on the board; this both modelled her thinking and provided a way for the pupils to see what was required. It involved the other adult in a real hands-on fashion and enabled a higher quality of classroom interaction to develop.

A variation on this idea was used in another school, where the teacher asked the other adult to summarize pupil answers to questions in writing on the board. Here the teacher, adult and pupils were involved in a three-way dialogue which meant that pupil understandings were being checked upon, ways of representing answers in written format were modelled, and the pupils were shown how to engage with the process of moving from thought to written word.

It is important to remember that learning is the key activity you are trying to foster in your classroom, and the use of other adults to do this can be an important tool at your disposal to take learning forwards. It does not take hours of planning meetings or preparation of one-off materials, but it is worth spending a few minutes before, during or after a lesson to discuss the best and most appropriate ways of working together. After all, you both have the same ends in view!

Key questions

1 What learning is best facilitated by the use of other adults?
2 Are there ways (see writing examples) in which other adults can be used so as to free me up for pupil engagement?
3 Can I use the other adult(s) as part of modelling aspects of learning?

Further reading

DfES (2005) *Maximising Progress: Ensuring the Attainment of Pupils with SEN. Unit 2: Making Best Use of Additional Support Within the Classroom.* Norwich: HMSO.

X – positive approaches to marking

All assessment carries with it an emotional component. We see this in the tears of joy and sadness on results day, when national papers carry pictures of students opening envelopes and discovering their grades. We see this too in classes when giving grades to students. Imagine being the pupil who has tried hard, yet for weeks has scored no better than an E grade. How do they feel? They need feedback on their work, but is an E grade alone sufficient information for them? They need to know what to do to improve, and specific information about how to do this. The Assessment Reform Group (ARG) pointed this out:

> Learners need information and guidance in order to plan the next steps in their learning. Teachers should: pinpoint the learner's strengths and advise on how to develop them; be clear and constructive about any weaknesses and how they might be addressed; provide opportunities for learners to improve upon their work.
>
> (Assessment Reform Group 2002)

In order to address this a number of schools have introduced the notion of *comment only marking*. This is where a grade is not given to a piece of work, only comments. We know that when both comments and grades are given, the grade assumes primacy. Comment only marking discusses specifically the points appertaining to that piece of work and suggestions as to how to improve. In some schools comment only marking is then followed by an opportunity to resubmit the work for a final marking. This is logical, as there seems little point in telling a pupil what to do to improve, and then not giving them the opportunity so to do. How far do you agree with Pirsig, who, as long ago as 1974, observed the following?

> Grades really cover up failure to teach. A bad instructor can go through an entire quarter leaving absolutely nothing memorable in the minds of his class, curve out the scores on an irrelevant test, and leave the impression that some have learned and some

have not. But if the grades are removed the class is forced to wonder each day what it's really learning. The questions, What's being taught? What's the goal? How do the lectures and assignments accomplish the goal? become ominous. The removal of grades exposes a huge and frightening vacuum.

(Pirsig 1974: 204)

This takes us to the area of feedback. What is good feedback, and how can you convey it? We know that being negative has an emotional impact, so how can you turn negative comments into positive ones? Indeed, should you? Knowing what a student has done incorrectly, or not well enough, is important, but the effects of this do need thinking about. Consider this example:

Hannah [pupil]: I'm really scared about the SATs [standard assessment tasks]. Mrs O'Brien [a teacher at the school] came and talked to us about our spelling and I'm no good at spelling and David [the class teacher] is giving us times tables tests every morning and I'm hopeless at times tables so I'm frightened I'll do the SATs and I'll be a nothing.

Diane [researcher]: I don't understand Hannah. You can't be a nothing.

Hannah: Yes, you can 'cause you have to get a level like a level 4 or a level 5 and if you're no good at spellings and times tables you don't get those levels and so you're a nothing.

Diane: I'm sure that's not right.

Hannah: Yes it is 'cause that's what Mrs O'Brien was saying.

(Reay and Wiliam 1999: 345)

The impact of assessment has led Hannah to think, 'I'll be a nothing'. This is a state of affairs in which some of your students may find themselves. The effects of high-stakes assessment do filter down into the classroom. As Warwick Mansell observes, 'Throughout England, schools are spending months preparing students for tests which, despite ministers' attempts to argue to the contrary, are not, in themselves, important to the children's futures. Schools have to do this, because they can be punished if results fall' (Mansell 2007: 30).

Should you mitigate the effects of this pressure on your students? This is the purpose of adopting positive marking techniques. Disenfranchised learners will not succeed in tests and examinations. Although students will have to face external testing regimes at key points in their schooling, they need to be prepared for them. Driving instructors do not start every lesson with a driving test where the learner fails, then spend the lesson dealing with why, only to start the process again in the next lesson. The same should be true of marking in the classroom.

See also the entry on **grading**.

Key questions

---

1 How do I give feedback, both written and spoken?
2 What is the impact of my feedback?
3 Have I tried comment only marking?
4 Am I under pressure for my students to succeed? If so, do I convey this to the learners?

References

Assessment Reform Group (2002) Assessment for Learning: 10 Principles, ARG. http://k1.ioe.ac.uk/tlrp/arg/publications.html (accessed 18 September 2012).

Mansell, W. (2007) *Education by Numbers: The Tyranny of Testing*. London: Politico's Publishing.

Pirsig, R. (1974) *Zen and the Art of Motorcycle Maintenance*. London: Vintage.

Reay, D. and Wiliam, D. (1999) 'I'll be a nothing': Structure, agency and the construction of identity through assessment. *British Educational Research Journal*, 25(3): 343–54.

Further reading

Gardner, J. (ed.) (2012) *Assessment and Learning*, 2nd edn. London: Sage.

James, M. (1998) *Using Assessment for School Improvement*. Oxford: Heinemann Educational.

Year groups

Year groups are the most common structure utilized by schools through which students are separated in manageable numbers. 'Year' groups normally refer to academic years which, for historical reasons, normally begin around the beginning of September. So, all pupils whose birthday falls between the 1 September of one year and the the 31 August of the following year become a 'year group'.

Despite year groups being the most common structure within our schools, this system is not without its problems. Research done by the Institute for Fiscal Studies and the Nuffield Foundation in 2011 (Crawford et al. 2011) revealed that not only did babies born in the autumn term do better in their education (by way of examination results) than those babies born in the summer term, but also that the month of a child's birth has a major affect on their cognitive and non-cognitive skill development. Their key findings state that:

> In line with previous literature, we find evidence of large and significant differences between August- and September-born children in terms of their cognitive skills, whether measured using national achievement tests or alternative indicators such as the British Ability Scales. These gaps are particularly pronounced when considering teacher reports of their performance; moreover, they are also present when considering differences in socio-emotional development and engagement in a range of risky behaviours.The absolute magnitude of these differences decreases as children get older, suggesting that Augustborns are 'catching up' with their September-born peers in a variety of ways as the difference in relative age becomes smaller over time.
>
> (Crawford et al. 2011: 2)

Given the clear research in this area, it is curious that the system of dividing year groups by student age has not been challenged more rigorously. Whilst schools enjoy a greater degree of autonomy now than ever before, there are few schools that are re-engineering the year group approach and managing their groups of students in different ways.

The effects of this are particularly acute in the primary school, where age-related differences between students are generally felt to be most significant.

Research done by Cambridge Associates clearly indicates this, stating that:

> The birthdate effect is most pronounced during infant and primary school but the magnitude of the effect gradually and continually decreases through Key Stage 3, 4, and A level. This pattern is particularly evident in research by the Institute of Fiscal Studies. The disadvantage for August-born children over September-born children in expected attainment dropped from an average of 25% at KS 1 to 12% at KS 2, to 9% at KS 3, to 6% at KS 4 and to 1% at A level. Despite this decrease, the effect remains significant at GCSE, A level and in respect of entry into higher education.
>
> (Skyes et al. 2009: 3)

This research has important implications for the organization of schools. Whilst some might argue that the creation of mixed-ability streams of students which cross age-related boundaries might be a way forward, there is also clear research by the OECD that this is ineffective (Field et al. 2007: 78).

Perhaps the constructive work can be done by parents and teachers. It is clear that parents worry about their children born later in the academic year and try to compensate for this in various ways. However, it is you, as a teacher, who has the most influence. Know when your students' birthdays are; they are a major indicator of academic and other performance. Whilst not every child born in August is going to suffer educationally (just like every child born in September is not going to succeed), be aware of these issues and watch out for those younger students in your classes who need additional, targeted support.

Key questions

---

1   Are the birthdays of my students common knowledge? If not, why not?
2   What practical steps can I take in my teaching to ensure that younger students are not disadvantaged by the year group structure that most schools implement?

References

Crawford, C., Dearden, L. and Greaves, E. (2011) Does When You are Born Matter? The Impact of Month of Birth on Children's Cognitive and Non-cognitive Skills in England. http://www.ifs.org.uk/bns/bn122.pdf (accessed 4 July 2012).

Field, S., Kuczera, M. and Pont, B. (2007) *No More Failures: Ten Steps to Equity in Education.* Paris: OECD. Also available from http://www.oecd.org/dataoecd/49/16/49623744.pdf (accessed 5 July 2012).

Skyes, E., Bell, J. and Rodeiro, C. (2009) Birthdate Effects: A Review of the Literature from 1990-on. http://www.cambridgeassessment.org.uk/ca/digitalAssets/169664_Cambridge_Lit_Review_Birthdate_d3.pdf (accessed 5 July 2012).

Further reading

Crawford, C., Dearden, L. and Greaves, E. (2011) Does When You are Born Matter? The Impact of Month of Birth on Children's Cognitive and Non-cognitive Skills in England. http://www.ifs.org.uk/bns/bn122.pdf (accessed 4 July 2012).

Z

Zone of proximal development (ZPD)

We have already mentioned Vygotsky in the **cognition** entry. Possibly his most significant contribution to the educational field is his notion of the *zone of proximal development*, or *ZPD*.

Vygotsky defined the ZPD as being: 'The distance between the actual development level as determined by independent problem solving and the level of potential development as determined through problem solving under adult guidance or in collaboration with more capable peers' (Vygotsky 1978: 86). What this means is that developing learners are capable of attainment at a certain level when they are operating by themselves, and at a higher, more advanced level, when they are working with adults, or with those of their peers who are more capable in this area than they are. As Vygotsky noted, 'We said that in collaboration the child can always do more than he can independently' (Vygotsky 1987: 209).

The implications of the ZPD for groupwork, for example, are clearly significant. Working with other students, an individual is able to attain at a higher level, and then go on to do this by themselves. This means that the cultural and social functions of groupwork act as a precursor to the individual personal response:

> Every function in the child's cultural development appears twice: first, on the social level, and later, on the individual level; first, between people (interpsychological) and then inside the child (intrapsychological). This applies equally to voluntary attention, to logical memory, and to the formation of concepts. All the higher functions originate as actual relationships between individuals.
>
> (Vygotsky 1978: 57)

This has ramifications for the ways in which learning is structured in classrooms. It places groupwork as a central feature of learning for the developing child, and does so in a way which also facilitates individual development. Viewed from this stance, the purpose of working socially in groups of learners is to enable operations in the ZPD, leading to their being subsequently developed in the individual learner as a result. Using the ZPD as a justification for groupwork then, is a factor in why it can be thought of to aid individuals, as well as being a sound pedagogic strategy in its own right (see entry on **grouping**).

As well as being concerned with developmental matters, 'Vygotsky discussed the ZPD in terms of assessment and instruction. Within both frames of reference he discussed the relationship between an individual learner and a supportive other or others' (Daniels 2001: 59). In assessment, it needs to be made clear that working with others allows for higher attainment, and for this to be recognized assessment for groupwork needs to be clear with regard to the contributions of the various individuals within it.

Key questions

1 How can I best foster ZPD learning in my classes?
2 How can I best group students so that this happens?
3 How does social learning impact on the ways in which the school (and society?) views attainment?

References

Daniels, H. (2001) *Vygotsky and Pedagogy*. London: Routledge.
Vygotsky, L. (1978) *Mind in Society*. Cambridge, MA: Harvard University Press.
Vygotsky, L. (1987) *The Collected Works, Vol. 1*. New York: Plenum.

Further reading

Chaiklin, S. (2003) The zone of proximal development in Vygotsky's analysis of learning and instruction, in A. Kozulin, B. Gindis, V.S. Ageyev and S.M. Miller (eds) *Vygotsky's Educational Theory in Cultural Context*, pp. 39–64. Cambridge: Cambridge University Press.
Daniels, H. (2005) *An introduction to Vygotsky*. Hove: Routledge.

Zzzzzz.... teachers and sleep

We know that the sleep habits of young people can come into conflict with the times that school operates: 'Early morning school schedules are in the opposite direction to the sleep–wake cycle in adolescence and early adulthood. This conflict leads to sleep deprivation and irregular patterns' (Azevedo et al. 2008: 34). This offers a biological explanation as to why some of your students may not seem at their best first thing in the morning. But what about teachers and sleep? In this entry we consider the place of sleep in the teacher's schedule.

Teaching is a high-stress occupation:

> HSE [Health and Safety Executive] research in 2000 found teaching to be the most stressful profession in the UK, with 41.5% of teachers reporting themselves as 'highly stressed'. For comparison, the incidence of any kind of stress across the working population is believed to be less than 20 per cent.

> From 2003 to 2006 statistics show that the highest reported rates of occupational stress, depression or anxiety were to be found in the teaching and research professions – indeed the levels of stress amongst teachers were twice that for 'all occupations'.
>
> (NUT 2008)

We also know that 'levels of stress among teachers in the UK compare unfavourably with their European peers' (NASUWT 2012). This means that teaching in the UK is a high-risk occupation in terms of stress.

Dealing with stress is only one aspect of the job though. Simply being in front of a class is tiring, and as good teachers spend very little of their time sitting down whilst teaching, there are physical as well as mental demands. We know from anecdotal accounts that one of the first things that many teachers do when arriving home is to have a short sleep. Research has shown that this is actually beneficial: 'Short daytime naps of less than 30 minutes have been shown to have positive effects on daytime alertness' (Hayashi et al. 2005: 829). This is good news for all those people who have been feeling guilty about dozing off before beginning an evening's marking!

We also know from PGCE and other teacher training routes that students find their time in school one of the most demanding things they have done, and that it has a serious effect on their sleep patterns. Those at university find that this has an effect upon their lifestyles, and that teacher training students prefer to flat-share together, so that their colleagues, even if at different stages in their courses, fully appreciate that those on placement will need early nights, and will not appreciate late-night parties!

Trying to teach when tired is difficult, and full alertness is needed, so sleep really is an important factor for teachers to consider. And if nagged by non-teacher friends to go out, it can be helpful to say that your job is more stressful than theirs, and there are statistics to prove it!

This is the final entry in our book. So, before the key questions, references and further reading, can we say 'thank you' for getting to the end of the final entry. You deserve to go and have a nap for a few minutes! Good luck in your teaching career. We trust that you have found at least a few useful things in this book that will help guide you on your way.

Key questions

1 How much sleep do I need?
2 Is my work–sleep balance causing problems?
3 Would I benefit from a power nap?
4 What's the optimum time for me to get up?

References

Azevedo, C.V.M., Sousa, I., Paul, K. et al. (2008) Teaching chronobiology and sleep habits in school and university. *Mind, Brain, and Education,* 2(1): 34–47.

Hayashi, M., Motoyoshi, N. and Hori, T. (2005) Recuperative power of a short daytime nap with or without stage 2 sleep. *Sleep,* 28(7): 829–36.

NUT (2008) Tackling teacher stress. http://www.teachers.org.uk/stress (accessed 18 September 2012).

NASUWT (2012) European survey reveals UK teachers suffer more stress than European counterparts. http://www.nasuwt.org.uk/MemberSupport/MemberGroups/Bulletins/ETUCSurvey/NASUWT_009159 (accessed 18 September 2012).

Further reading

Maas, J. (1999) *Power Sleep.* New York: HarperCollins.

Index